A BLACK THEOLOGY OF LIBERATION

Twentieth Anniversary Edition

James H. Cone

ORBIS BOOKS

Maryknoll, New York 10545

To my Mother
and
in memory of my Father

Fourth Printing, October 1993

The Catholic Foreign Mission Society of America (Maryknoll) recruits and trains people for overseas missionary service. Through Orbis Books, Maryknoll aims to foster the international dialogue that is essential to mission. The books published, however, reflect the opinions of their authors and are not meant to represent the official position of the society.

Original edition published by J. B. Lippincott Company, copyright © 1970 by James H. Cone, as part of the C. Eric Lincoln Series in Black Religion

Library of Congress Cataloging-in-Publication Data

Cone, James H.
    A Black theology of liberation / James H. Cone. — 20th
anniversary ed.
        p.   cm.
    Includes bibliographical references and index.
    Includes: After twenty years : critical reflections / by G.
Wilmore, et al.
    ISBN 0-88344-685-5
    1. Black theology.   I. Title.
BT82.7.C666   1990
230'.08996—dc20   90-43041
                                                    CIP

Contents

Preface to the 1970 Edition

The reader is entitled to know what to expect in this book. It is my contention that Christianity is essentially a religion of liberation. The function of theology is that of analyzing the meaning of that liberation for the oppressed so they can know that their struggle for political, social, and economic justice is consistent with the gospel of Jesus Christ. Any message that is not related to the liberation of the poor in a society is not Christ's message. Any theology that is indifferent to the theme of liberation is not Christian theology.

In a society where persons are oppressed because they are *black,* Christian theology must become *black theology*, a theology that is unreservedly identified with the goals of the oppressed and seeks to interpret the divine character of their struggle for liberation. "Black theology" is a phrase that is particularly appropriate for contemporary America because of its symbolic power to convey both what whites mean by oppression and what blacks mean by liberation. However, I am convinced that the patterns of meaning centered in the idea of black theology are by no means restricted to the American scene, for blackness symbolizes oppression and liberation in any society.

It will be evident, therefore, that this book is written primarily for the black community, not for whites. Whites may read it and to some degree render an intellectual analysis of it, but an authentic understanding is dependent on the blackness of their existence in the world. There will be no peace in America until whites begin to hate their whiteness, asking from the depths of their being: "How can we become black?" I hope that if enough whites begin to ask this question, this country will no longer be divided on the basis of color. But until then, it is the task of the Christian theologian to do theology in the light of the concreteness of human oppression as expressed in color, and to interpret for the oppressed the meaning of God's liberation in their community.

This book is the result of the encouragement of many persons, and it would be impossible to name them all here. I am especially grateful to the many blacks who responded so positively to my first work, *Black Theology and Black Power* (Seabury Press). Without their encouragement, the present work would be unthinkable.

Many persons read this work in manuscript and offered helpful criticisms. The list is much too long to mention everyone. Also, most of this material was given as lectures at several colleges and universities where insightful dialogue with students and faculty took place.

However, a special word of thanks is due to my friend William Hordern, president of the Lutheran Theological Seminary. His critical reading of the manuscript improved it considerably. After his comments, several parts of this work, especially chapter 7, were rewritten.

I am particularly indebted to Lester Scherer of Eastern Michigan University, my former colleague at Adrian College. His editorial expertise improved the manuscript immensely. Much more important is his friendship, which dates back to our seminary experience at Garrett. We both matured as we faced the reality of the black revolution in America and its meaning for our existence in the world.

I am grateful to C. Eric Lincoln, my colleague at Union, for the invitation to write this work for the C. Eric Lincoln Series in Black Religion. His confidence and encouragement have been invaluable to me.

The members of my family cooperated in the bringing of this work into existence. Without their understanding patience, I could not have written this work.

Foreword to the 1986 Edition

There are some books that so challenge and fascinate us that we cannot put them down until we reach the very last word. *A Black Theology of Liberation* is one of those books.

In 1970, when it had just been published in the United States, I received a copy while in Geneva. Cone was not unknown to me. I had read his first book, *Black Theology and Black Power,* and even though it lacked the formal qualities he later developed, it clearly distinguished him. That was the feeling I had had in 1969. This book, I said to myself, promises something more rigorous to come.

I looked forward to *A Black Theology of Liberation* with ready expectations. Cone's clarity, his seriousness of analysis, and his commitment to the oppressed were no surprise to me—only confirmation of what I had come to expect.

I remember perfectly that I received my copy the day before a trip to Rome. At home that night after dinner, I began reading the book, carefully. I was spellbound page after page, not putting it down until the early morning and finishing it some hours later, en route from Geneva to Rome. When I returned to Geneva, I read it for a second time and then wrote to Cone, giving him my impressions and stressing the importance of its immediate publication in Latin America, because black theology, of which Cone was the foremost proponent in the United States, is unquestionably linked with the theology of liberation flourishing today in Latin America.

Adapted from chap. 11 of Paulo Freire's *The Politics of Education*, South Hadley, Mass., Bergin & Garvey, 1985.

The prophetic nature of both these theologies lies not merely in their speaking for those who are forbidden to speak, but, most importantly, in their side-by-side struggle with the silenced—so that the silenced can effectively speak the word that will revolutionize and transform the society that reduces them to silence. "To speak the word," then, is not to say "good morning" or to follow the prescriptions of the powerful who command and exploit. "To speak the word" is to make and remake history. The dominated and silenced classes can speak the word only when they take history into their own hands and dismantle the oppressive system that crushes them. Through revolutionary praxis, with critical and vigilant leadership, the dominated classes learn to "proclaim" their world, thus discovering the real reasons for their past silence. Hence, the eminently political nature of black theology in the United States and of the theology of liberation in Latin America.

Both these theologies tend increasingly to promote political action, but this does not mean that they are aberrations from theological "purity" or "neutral" theology.

A white theology can be just as political as a black theology or a theology of liberation in Latin America. Although it is easily seen through, political concern seeks to hide the orientation of a white theology toward defending dominant class interests. This is why, though simulating neutrality, white theology is preoccupied with the conciliation of things that cannot be conciliated, why it denies so insistently the differences among social classes and their struggles, and why in its efforts for social good it does not go beyond the kind of modernizing reformisms that only shore up the status quo.

Thinking from the viewpoint of the dominant classes, theologians of this impossible neutrality employ mystifying language. They consistently attempt to soften the harsh, oppressive real world and exhort dominated classes to face their sacrifice with resignation. The pain and degrading discrimination they suffer— their very existence is a form of death—should be accepted by the dominated as purification for their sins. In short, the oppressed should thank their oppressors for the opportunities offered them to save themselves.

The dominated classes need to transform their suffering, not submit to it. Submission to suffering is a form of annihilation, but transformation of suffering rekindles a faith that gives life. Only the faith that is born today, in the "today" of the struggle, can give meaning to the future—not an alienative or vague or predetermined meaning, but the meaning involved in the task of construction, a "deed of liberty."

Some who promote white theology propose an even greater passivity for the oppressed classes by disregarding the link between reconciliation and liberation. For them, reconciliation is nothing more than the capitulation of the dominated to the will of the dominant. Reconciliation becomes a kind of pact between dominant and dominated, rich and poor: a pact that accepts the continuation of the oppression but promises the dominated efficient and modernized social assistance.

Such an elitist concept of reconciliation will find no acceptance in the theology of liberation in Latin America or in the black theology of liberation, of which James Cone is one of the most eloquent representatives. Any reconciliation between oppressors and oppressed, as social classes, presupposes the liberation of the oppressed, a liberation forged by themselves through their own revolutionary praxis.

What is important here, though, is for the reader to begin a convivial relationship with the thinking of James Cone. So, to conclude this Foreword, I only add that in emerging from an incredible reality, the "diabolic" real world of racism in the United States, his thinking gains a singular force. In his theological reflections on this reality, he does not present blacks as strangers from another world, unknown foreigners. James Cone is a committed man, "saturated" in the real world, which he analyzes with the authority of one who has experienced it.

A Black Theology of Liberation is for this reason a passionate book, passionately written. In reading it, some will be chilled by their anger, others will tremble with fear. Many readers, though, will find a stimulus here for their own struggles. This is what James Cone envisages.

PAULO FREIRE

Preface to the 1986 Edition

Theology is not universal language about God. Rather, it is human speech informed by historical and theological traditions, and written for particular times and places. Theology is *contextual* language—that is, defined by the human situation that gives birth to it. No one can write theology for all times, places, and persons. Therefore, when one reads a theological textbook, it is important to note the year of its publication, the audience for whom it was written, and the issues the author felt compelled to address.

A Black Theology of Liberation was first published in 1970, and it was written for and to black Christians (and also to whites who had the courage to listen) in an attempt to answer the question that I and others could not ignore, namely, "what has the gospel of Jesus Christ to do with the black struggle for justice in the United States?" This book cannot be understood without a keen knowledge of the civil rights and black power movements of the 1960s and a general comprehension of nearly four hundred years of slavery and segregation in North America, both of which were enacted into law by government and openly defended as ordained of God by most white churches and their theologians.

I can remember clearly when I first sat down to write this text. It was immediately following the publication of my first book, *Black Theology and Black Power* (1969). Although *Black Theology and Black Power* appealed to many black and white radicals who were interested in the theological implications of black power, I knew that most Christians, black and white, especially theologians and preachers, would need a deeper analysis of Christian doctrine, using traditional theological concepts, before taking black theology seriously. When I began to write *A Black Theology of Liberation*, I was deeply involved in the black struggle for justice and was *still* searching for a perspective on Christian theology that would help African-Americans recognize that the gospel of Jesus is not only consistent with their fight for liberation but is its central meaning for twentieth-century America.

I was completely unaware of the beginnings of liberation theology in the Third World, especially in Latin America. Neither did I know much about the theme of liberation in African-American history and culture. Unfortunately, my formal theological and historical knowledge was primarily limited to the dominant perspectives of North America and Europe. But, despite these limitations, I was determined to speak a liberating word for and to African-American Christians, using the theological resources at my disposal. I did not have time to do the theological and historical research needed to present a "balanced" perspective on the problem of racism in America. Black men, women, and children were being shot and imprisoned for asserting their right to a dignified existence. Others were wasting away in ghettoes, dying from filth, rats, and dope, as white and black ministers preached about a blond, blue-eyed Jesus who came to make us all just like him. I *had* to speak a different word, not just as a black person but primarily as a *theologian*. I felt then, as I still do, that if theology had nothing to say about black suffering and resistance, I could not be a theologian. I remembered what Malcom X had said: "I believe in a religion that believes in freedom. Any time I have to accept a religion that won't let me fight a battle for my people, I say to hell with that religion."[1]

The passion with which I wrote alienated most whites (and some blacks too). But I felt that I had no other alternative if I was to speak forcefully and truthfully about the reality of black suffering and of God's empowerment of blacks to resist it. It was not my task to interpret the gospel in a form acceptable to white racists and their sympathizers. Theology is not only rational discourse about ultimate reality; it is also a prophetic word about the righteousness of God that must be spoken in clear, strong, and uncompromising language. Oppressors never like to hear the truth in a socio-political context defined by their lies. That was why *A Black Theology of Liberation* was often rejected as racism in reverse by many whites, particularly theologians. For example, Father Andrew M. Greeley referred to my perspective on black theology as a "Nazi mentality," "a theology filled with hatred for white people and the assumption of a moral superiority of black over white."[2] White reactions to black theology never disturbed me too much, because Malcolm X had prepared me for them. "With skillful manipulating of the press," said Malcolm, "they're able to make the victim look like the criminal and the criminal look like the victim."[3]

White theologians wanted me to debate with them about the question of whether "black theology" was real theology, using their criteria to decide the issue. With clever theological sophistication, white theologians defined the discipline of theology in the light of the problem of the unbeliever (i.e., the question of the relationship of faith and reason) and thus unrelated to the problem of slavery and racism. Using a white definition of theology, I knew there was no way I could win the debate. And even if I had managed to give a "good" account of myself, what difference would that have made for the liberation of poor blacks?

The task of explicating the gospel as God's liberating presence with oppressed blacks was too urgent to be sidetracked into an academic debate with white scholars about the nature of theology. It was clear to me that what was needed was a *fresh start* in theology, a new way of doing it that would arise out of the black struggle for justice and in no way would be dependent upon be approval of white academics in religion. Again I thought of Malcolm: "Don't let anybody who is oppressing us ever lay the ground rules. Don't go by their games, don't play the game by their rules. Let them know now that this is a new game, and we've got some new rules. . . ."[4]

I knew that racism was a heresy, and I did not need to have white theologians tell me so. Indeed, the exploitation of persons of color was the central theological problem of our time. "The problem of the twentieth century," wrote W. E. B. DuBois in 1906, "is the problem of the colorline,—the relation of the darker to the lighter races of [persons] in Asia and Africa, in America and the islands of the sea."[5] Just as whites had not listened to DuBois, I did not expect white theologians to take black theology seriously. Racism is a disease that perverts one's moral sensitivity and distorts the intellect. It is found not only in American society and its churches but particularly in the discipline of theology, affecting its nature and purpose. White *racist* theologians are in charge of defining the nature of the gospel and of the discipline responsible for explicating it! How strange! They who are responsible for the evil of racism also want to tell its victims whether bigotry is a legitimate subject matter of systematic theology.

I had no patience with persons (white or black) who expected me to remain "cool" and "calm" as whites played their racist theological games. I felt deeply that the time had come to expose white theology for what it was: a racist, theological justification of the status quo. To understand the content and style of *A Black Theology of Liberation*, one must have empathy for the depth of my anger regarding the presence of racism in theology, with white theologians trying first to deny it and then to justify it. I could barely contain my rage whenever I read their books or found myself in their presence. They were so condescending and arrogant in the way they talked about black theology, always communicating the impression that it was not genuine theology, because it was too emotional and anti-intellectual. Furthermore, it did not deal with the "proper" subject matter of theology—namely, the rational justification of religious belief in a scientific and technological world that has no use for God. I refused to let them intimidate me with their intellectual arrogance, quoting persons and documents of the Western theological tradition—as if knowledge of them were a prerequisite for even calling oneself a theologian. I kept thinking about my mother and father (and all the poor blacks they symbolized in African-American history and culture) in order to keep my theological vocation clearly focused and my immediate purpose sharply defined. God did not call me into the ministry (as a theologian of the Christian church) for the purpose of making the gospel intelligible to privileged white intellectuals. Why then should I spend my intellectual energy answering their questions, as if their experience were the only source from which theology derives its questions?

Some of my discussions with white theologians degenerated into shouting matches, because they did not like my "cool" indifference toward the Western theological tradition and my insistence that they must learn something about the black religious tradition in order to be genuine *American* theologians. I must admit that I was often as arrogant toward white theologians as they were toward me. My style of doing theology was influenced more by Malcolm X than by Martin Luther King, Jr. And I am sure that my intemperate behavior prevented some whites, whose intentions were more honorable than my responses suggested, from dialoguing with me. My critical evaluation (deleted from the 1986 edition) of Joseph Hough's *Black Power and White Protestants* (1968) and of C. Freeman Sleeper's *Black Power and Christian Responsibility* (1969) is a case in point. But when I thought about the long history of black suffering and the long silence of white theologians in its regard, I could not always control my pen or my tongue. I did not feel that I should in any way be accountable to white theologians or their cultural etiquette. It was not a time to be polite but rather a time to speak the truth with love, courage, and care for the masses of blacks. Again Malcolm expressed what I felt deep within my being:

> The time that we're living in . . . now is not an era where one who is oppressed is looking toward the oppressor to give him some system or form of logic or reason. What is logical to the oppressor isn't logical to the oppressed. And what is reason to the oppressor isn't reason to the oppressed. The black people in this country are beginning to realize that what sounds reasonable to those who exploit us doesn't sound reasonable to us. There just has to be a new system of reason and logic devised by us who are at the bottom, if we want to get some results in this struggle that is called "the Negro revolution."[6]

Although my view of white theology is generally the same today as it was in 1970, there are several significant shifts in my theological perspective since the publication of this text. Inasmuch as I have given a full account of my theological development in *My Soul Looks Back* (1982) and *For My People* (1984), it is not necessary for me to repeat it here. However, I do want to mention four themes particularly pertinent for readers of this text: sexism, the exploitation of the Third World, classism, and an inordinate methodological dependence upon the neo-orthodox theology of Karl Barth and other European theologians.

The most glaring limitation of *A Black Theology of Liberation* was my failure to be receptive to the problem of sexism in the black community and society as a whole. I have become so embarrassed by that failure that I could not reissue this volume without making a note of it and without changing the exclusive language of the 1970 edition to inclusive language. I know that this is hardly enough to rectify my failure, because sexism cannot be eliminated (anymore than can racism) simply by changing words. But it is an important symbol of what we must do, because our language is a reflection of the reality we create. Sexism dehumanizes and kills, and it must be fought on every front.

Contrary to what many black men say (especially preachers), sexism is not merely a problem for white women. Rather it is a problem of the human condition. It destroys the family and society, and makes it impossible for persons to create a society defined according to God's intention for humanity. Any black male theologian or preacher who ignores sexism as a central problem in our society and church (as important as racism, because they are interconnected), is just as guilty of distorting the gospel as is a white theologian who does the same with racism. If we black male theologians do not take seriously the need to incorporate into our theology a critique of our sexist practices in the black community, then we have no right to complain when white theologians snub black theology.

Another serious limitation was my failure to incorporate a global analysis of oppression into *A Black Theology of Liberation*. Unlike my moral blindness in relation to sexism, the absence of Third World issues in my perspective was due more to my lack of knowledge and personal exposure. Being so concerned about the problem of racism in the United States and being strongly influenced by the analysis of it made by the civil rights and black power movements, it was easy for me to overlook Third World problems. I vehemently rejected any suggestion from whites about this weakness, because I did not trust them. How could they be genuinely concerned about the poor of the Third World when they showed little or no concern for poor blacks at home? I quoted one of their philosophers to them: "The only way of helping the enslaved out there is to take sides with those who are here" (Sartre).

At the time of the writing of *A Black Theology of Liberation*, I had not traveled to Asia, Africa, Latin America, or even the Caribbean; and unfortunately I had done little reading about the problems of poverty, colonialism, human rights, and monopoly capitalism. Largely due to my involvement in the Ecumenical

Association of Third World Theologians (EATWOT), I have now visited many Third World countries, meeting many Third World persons and seeing for myself enormous gaps between rich and poor nations. I am convinced that no one should claim to be doing Christian theology today without making the liberation of the Third World from the exploitation of the First World and the Second World a central aspect of its purpose. There is an interconnectedness of all humanity that makes the freedom of one people dependent upon the liberation of all. No one can be free until all are set free. Martin Luther King, Jr., expressed this point persuasively:

> We are caught in an inescapable network of mutuality, tied to a single garment of destiny. What affects one directly, affects all indirectly. As long as there is poverty in this world, [no one] can be totally healthy. . . . Strangely enough, I can never be what I ought to be until you are what you ought to be. You can never be what you ought to be until I am what I ought to be.[7]

The third weakness of *A Black Theology of Liberation* was the absence of a clearly focused economic, class analysis of oppression. This limitation is unquestionably the result of my strong identification with the common tendency in the black community of defining racism as a domestic problem, largely associated with the exclusion of blacks from the benefits of American capitalism. Racism was primarily identified as social exclusion with disastrous political and economic consequences. I assumed that if blacks were creatively integrated into all aspects of American society, the issue of racism would be essentially solved. This was faulty analysis, because I failed to see that the problem of the human condition involved much more than simply the issue of racism. Anyone who claims to be fighting against the problem of oppression and does not analyze the exploitive role of capitalism is either naive or an agent of the enemies of freedom. I was naive and did not have at my disposal sufficient tools for analyzing the complexity of human oppression. My strong negative reaction to the racism of many white socialists in the United States distorted my vision and prevented me from analyzing racism in relation to capitalism.

An exclusive focus on racial injustice without a comprehensive analysis of its links with corporate capitalism greatly distorts the multidimensional character of oppression and also camouflages the true nature of modern racism. There are black as well as white thieves, and the color of a person's skin does not make wrong right. We are all—blacks and whites, men and women, young and old—sinners, and thus capable of exploiting the poor in order to promote our economic and political interests. No event has demonstrated this truth more clearly than the tragic bombing in Philadelphia (May 1985). It made no difference whether Frank Rizzo (white) or Wilson Goode (black) was the mayor, the dignity and well-being of poor blacks was considered expendable in the killing of eleven persons, including four children. The color of the mayor's skin did not change the immoral character of the act or justify the general silence of civil rights groups about it. The act was murder and ought to be prosecuted as such. We must not allow racial solidarity to distort the truth. Without class analysis, a global understanding of oppression will be distorted and its domestic manifestations seriously misrepresented. There are very few differences between black and white capitalists when viewed in the light of the consequences of their behavior for the poor. When profits are more important than persons, disastrous results follow for the poor of all colors. It does not matter whether blacks or whites do it. This madness must be opposed.

The fourth and last weakness that I wish to comment on was my inordinate methodological dependence upon the neo-orthodox theology of Karl Barth. Many of my critics (black and white) have emphasized this point. It is a legitimate criticism, and I can offer no explanation except to say that neo-orthodoxy was to me what liberal theology was to Martin Luther King, Jr.—the only theological system with which I was intellectually comfortable and which seemed compatible with the centrality of Jesus Christ in the black church community. I knew then as I know now that neo-orthodoxy was inadequate for my purposes, and that most American theologians who claimed that theological identity would vehemently reject my use of Karl Barth to interpret black theology. However, I did not have the time to develop a completely new perspective in doing theology. I had to use what I regarded as the best of my graduate education.

If I were to be writing *A Black Theology of Liberation* today, I would not follow the theological structuring that begins with a methodology based on divine revelation, and then proceeds to explicate the doctrines of God, humanity, Christ, church, world, and eschatology. There is no "abstract" revelation, independent of human experiences, to which theologians can appeal for evidence of what they say about the gospel. God meets us in the human situation, not as an idea or concept that is self-evidently true. God encounters us in the human condition as the liberator of the poor and the weak, empowering them to fight for freedom because they were made for it. Revelation as the word of God, witnessed in scripture and defined by the creeds and dogmas of Western Christianity, is too limiting to serve as an adequate way of doing theology today. Theology, as Latin American liberation theologians have stressed, is the second step, a reflective action taken in response to the first act of a practical commitment in behalf of the poor.

Despite the limitations of *A Black Theology of Liberation*, I decided to publish the 1986 edition without any changes except those related to the elimination of exclusive language and a few adjustments in style. The chief reason for reissuing this text as it appeared in 1970 is its central theme: *liberation*. More than any other text I have written, *A Black Theology of Liberation* represents the new start I tried to make in theology. Alone in Adrian, Michigan, searching for a constructive way in theology that would empower oppressed blacks, the motif of liberation came to me as I was rereading the scripture in the light of African-American history and culture. I had already had glimpses of this theme as a motif for theological construction when writing *Black Theology and Black Power*. However, in that book I was more concerned with problems in society than with developing a new way of doing theology. *A Black Theology of Liberation* represents my initial attempt to construct a new perspective for the discipline of theology, using the Bible and the black struggle for freedom as its chief sources. Liberation emerged as the organizing principle and has remained the central motif of my perspective on the gospel.

I repeat: Theology is always done for particular times and places and addressed to a specific audience. This is true whether theologians acknowledge it or not. Although God is the intended subject of theology, God does not do theology. *Human beings do theology*.

The importance of this point cannot be emphasized too strongly, because there are white theologians (as well as others greatly influenced by their definitions of theology) who *still* claim an objectivity regarding their theologial discourse, which they consider vastly superior to the subjective, interest-laden procedures of black and other liberation theologians. That there are theologians who make such claims today (even after the successful critiques made by black, feminist, and Third World liberation theologians) continues to baffle me. It is like President Ronald Reagan claiming objectivity in his development of a Third World policy of freedom and democracy in South Africa and Central America. He *cannot* be serious! But he is, and so are white theologians regarding the objective character of their way of doing theology. In *A Black Theology of Liberation*, I tried to uncover the wrongheadedness of the white way of doing theology and then attempted to set Christian theology on the right path of liberation. I believe that it was a message worth saying in 1970 and still an important word to say today.

PART I

A BLACK THEOLOGY
OF LIBERATION

1

The Content of Theology

Liberation as the Content of Theology

Christian theology is a theology of liberation. It is *a rational study of the being of God in the world in light of the existential situation of an oppressed community, relating the forces of liberation to the essence of the gospel, which is Jesus Christ.* This means that its sole reason for existence is to put into ordered speech the meaning of God's activity in the world, so that the community of the oppressed will recognize that its inner thrust for liberation is not only *consistent with* the gospel but *is* the gospel of Jesus Christ. There can be no Christian theology that is not identified unreservedly with those who are humiliated and abused. In fact, theology ceases to be a theology of the gospel when it fails to arise out of the community of the oppressed. For it is impossible to speak of the God of Israelite history, who is the God revealed in Jesus Christ, without recognizing that God is the God *of* and *for* those who labor and are over laden.

The perspective and direction of this study are already made clear. The reader is entitled to know at the outset what is considered to be important. My definition of theology and the assumptions on which it is based are to be tested by the working out of a theology which can then be judged in terms of its consistency with a communitarian view of the ultimate. We begin now by exploring some preliminary considerations in my definition.

The definition of theology as the discipline that seeks to analyze

1

the nature of the Christian faith in the light of the oppressed arises chiefly from biblical tradition itself.

(1) Though it may not be entirely clear why God elected Israel to be God's people, one point is evident. The election is inseparable from the event of the exodus:

> You have seen what I did to the Egyptians, and how I bore you on eagles' wings and brought you to myself. Now therefore, if you will obey my voice and keep my covenant, you shall be my own possession among all peoples . . . [Exodus 19:4–5a].

Certainly this means, among other things, that God's call of this people is related to its oppressed condition and to God's own liberating activity already seen in the exodus. *You have seen what I did!* By delivering this people from Egyptian bondage and inaugurating the covenant on the basis of that historical event, God is revealed as the God of the oppressed, involved in their history, liberating them from human bondage.

(2) Later stages of Israelite history also show that God is particularly concerned about the oppressed within the community of Israel. The rise of Old Testament prophecy is due primarily to the lack of justice within that community. The prophets of Israel are prophets of social justice, reminding the people that Yahweh is the author of justice. It is important to note in this connection that the righteousness of God is not an abstract quality in the being of God, as with Greek philosophy. It is rather God's active involvement in history, making right what human beings have made wrong. The consistent theme in Israelite prophecy is Yahweh's concern for the lack of social, economic, and political justice for those who are poor and unwanted in society. Yahweh, according to Hebrew prophecy, will not tolerate injustice against the poor; God will vindicate the poor. Again, God is revealed as the God of liberation for the oppressed.

(3) In the New Testament, the theme of liberation is reaffirmed by Jesus himself. The conflict with Satan and the powers of this world, the condemnation of the rich, the insistence that the kingdom of God is for the poor, and the locating of his ministry among the poor—these and other features of the career of Jesus show that

his work was directed to the oppressed for the purpose of their liberation. To suggest that he was speaking of a "spiritual" liberation fails to take seriously Jesus' thoroughly Hebrew view of human nature. Entering into the kingdom of God means that Jesus himself becomes the ultimate loyalty of humankind, for *he is the kingdom*. This view of existence in the world has far-reaching implications for economic, political, and social institutions. They can no longer have ultimate claim on human life; human beings are liberated and thus free to rebel against all powers that threaten human life. That is what Jesus had in mind when he said:

> The Spirit of the Lord is upon me, because he has anointed me to preach good news to the poor. He has sent me to proclaim release to the captives and recovering of sight to the blind, to set at liberty those who are oppressed, to proclaim the acceptable year of the Lord [Luke 4:18–19].

In view of the biblical emphasis on liberation, it seems not only appropriate but necessary to define the Christian community as the community of the oppressed which joins Jesus Christ in his fight for the liberation of humankind. The task of theology, then, is to explicate the meaning of God's liberating activity so that those who labor under enslaving powers will see that the forces of liberation are the very activity of God. Christian theology is never just a rational study of the being of God. Rather it is a study of God's liberating activity in the world, God's activity in behalf of the oppressed.

If the history of Israel and the New Testament description of the historical Jesus reveal that God is a God who is identified with Israel because it is an oppressed community, the resurrection of Jesus means that all oppressed peoples become his people. Herein lies the universal note implied in the gospel message of Jesus. The resurrection-event means that God's liberating work is not only for the house of Israel but for all who are enslaved by principalities and powers. The resurrection conveys hope in God. Nor is this the "hope" that promises a reward in heaven in order to ease the pain of injustice on earth. Rather it is hope which focuses on the future in order to make us refuse to tolerate present inequities. To see the future of God, as revealed in the resurrection of Jesus, is to see also the contradiction of any earthly injustice with existence in Jesus Christ. That is why Camilo Torres was right when he described revolutionary action as "a Christian, a priestly struggle."[1]

The task of Christian theology, then, is to analyze the meaning of hope in God in such a way that the oppressed community of a given society will risk all for earthly freedom, a freedom made possible in the resurrection of Jesus. The language of theology challenges societal structures because it is inseparable from the suffering community.

Theology can never be neutral or fail to take sides on issues related to the plight of the oppressed. For this reason it can never engage in conversation about the nature of God without confronting those elements of human existence which threaten anyone's existence as a person. Whatever theology says about God and the world must arise out of its sole reason for existence as a discipline: to assist the oppressed in their liberation. Its language is always language about human liberation, proclaiming the end of bondage and interpreting the religious dimensions of revolutionary struggle.

Liberation and Black Theology

Unfortunately, American white theology has not been involved in the struggle for black liberation. It has been basically a theology of the white oppressor, giving religious sanction to the genocide of Amerindians and the enslavement of Africans. From the very beginning to the present day, American white theological thought has been "patriotic," either by defining the theological task independently of black suffering (the liberal northern approach) or by defining Christianity as compatible with white racism (the conservative southern approach). In both cases theology becomes a servant of the state, and that can only mean death to blacks. It is little wonder that an increasing number of black religionists are finding it difficult to be black *and* be identified with traditional theological thought forms.

The appearance of black theology[2] on the American scene then is due primarily to the failure of white religionists to relate the gospel of Jesus to the pain of being black in a white racist society. It arises from the need of blacks to liberate themselves from white oppressors. Black theology is a theology of liberation because it is a theology which arises from an identification with the oppressed blacks of America, seeking to interpret the gospel of Jesus in the light of the black condition. It believes that the liberation of the black community *is* God's liberation.

The task of black theology, then, is to analyze the nature of the gospel of Jesus Christ in the light of oppressed blacks so they will see the gospel as inseparable from their humiliated condition, and as bestowing on them the necessary power to break the chains of oppression. This means that it is a theology of and for the black community, seeking to interpret the religious dimensions of the forces of liberation in that community.

There are two reasons why black theology is Christian theology. First, there can be no theology of the gospel which does not arise from an oppressed community. This is so because God is revealed in Jesus as a God whose righteousness is inseparable from the weak and helpless in human society. The goal of black theology is to interpret God's activity as related to the oppressed black community.

Secondly, black theology is Christian theology because it centers on Jesus Christ. There can be no Christian theology which does not have Jesus Christ as its point of departure. Though black theology affirms the black condition as the primary datum of reality to be reckoned with, this does not mean that it denies the absolute revelation of God in Jesus Christ. Rather it affirms it. Unlike white theology, which tends to make the Jesus-event an abstract, unembodied idea, black theology believes that the black community itself is precisely where Jesus Christ is at work. The Jesus-event in twentieth-century America is a black-event—that is, an event of liberation taking place in the black community in which blacks recognize that it is incumbent upon them to throw off the chains of white oppression by whatever means they regard as suitable. This is what God's revelation means to black and white America, and why black theology is an indispensable theology for our time.

It is to be expected that some will ask, "Why black theology? Is it not true that God is color-blind? Is it not true that there are others who suffer as much as, if not in some cases more than, blacks?" These questions reveal a basic misunderstanding of black theology, and also a superficial view of the world at large. There are at least three points to be made here.

First, in a revolutionary situation there can never be nonpartisan theology. Theology is always identified with a particular community. It is either identified with those who inflict oppression or with those who are its victims. A theology of the latter is authentic Christian theology, and a theology of the former is a theology of the Antichrist. Insofar as black theology is a theology arising from an identification with the oppressed black community and seeks to interpret the gospel of Jesus Christ in the light of the liberation of that community, it is Christian theology. American white theology is a theology of the Antichrist insofar as it arises from an identification with the white community, thereby placing God's approval on white oppression of black existence.

Secondly, in a racist society, God is never color-blind. To say God is color-blind is analogous to saying that God is blind to justice and injustice, to right and wrong, to good and evil. Certainly this is not the picture of God revealed in the Old and New Testaments. Yahweh takes sides. On the one hand, Yahweh sides with Israel against the Canaanites in the occupancy of Palestine. On the other hand, Yahweh sides with the poor within the community of Israel against the rich and other political oppressors. In the New Testament, Jesus is not for *all*, but for the oppressed, the poor and unwanted of society, and against oppressors. The God of the biblical tradition is not uninvolved or neutral regarding human affairs; God is decidedly involved. God is active in human history, taking sides with the oppressed of the land. If God is not involved in human history, then all theology is useless, and Christianity itself is a mockery, a hollow, meaningless diversion.

The meaning of this message for our contemporary situation is clear: the God of the oppressed takes sides with the black community. God is not color-blind in the black-white struggle, but has made an unqualified identification with blacks. This means that the movement for black liberation is the very work of God, effecting God's will among men.

Thirdly, there are, to be sure, many who suffer, and not all of them are black. Many white liberals derive a certain joy from reminding black militants that two-thirds of the poor in America are white. Of course I could point out that this means that there are five times as many poor blacks as there are poor whites, when the ratio of each group to the total population is taken into account.

But it is not my intention to debate white liberals on this issue, for it is not the purpose of black theology to minimize the suffering of others, including whites. Black theology merely tries to discern the activity of the Holy One in achieving the purpose of the liberation of humankind from the forces of oppression.

We *must* make decisions about where God is at work so we can join in the fight against evil. But there is no perfect guide for discerning God's movement in the world. Contrary to what many conservatives would say, the Bible is not a blueprint on this matter. It is a valuable symbol for pointing to God's revelation in Jesus, but it is not self-interpreting. We are thus placed in an existential situation of freedom in which the burden is on us to make decisions without a guaranteed ethical guide. This is the risk of faith. For the black theologian God is at work in the black community, vindicating black victims of white oppression. It is impossible for the black theologian to be indifferent on this issue. Either God is for blacks in their fight for liberation from white oppressors, or God is not. God cannot be both for us and for white oppressors at the same time.

In this connection we may observe that black theology takes seriously Paul Tillich's description of the symbolic nature of all theological speech.[3] We cannot describe God directly; we must use symbols that point to dimensions of reality that cannot be spoken of literally. Therefore to speak of black theology is to speak with the Tillichian understanding of symbol in mind. The focus on blackness does not mean that *only* blacks suffer as victims in a racist society, but that blackness is an ontological symbol and a visible reality which best describes what oppression means in America.

The extermination of Amerindians, the persecution of Jews, the oppression of Mexican-Americans, and every other conceivable inhumanity done in the name of God and country—these brutalities can be analyzed in terms of the white American inability to recognize humanity in persons of color. If the oppressed of this land want to challenge the oppressive character of white society, they must begin by affirming their identity in terms of the reality that is antiwhite. Blackness, then, stands for all victims of oppression who realize that the survival of their humanity is bound up with liberation from whiteness.[4]

This understanding of blackness can be seen as the most adequate symbol of the dimensions of divine activity in America. And insofar as this country is seeking to make whiteness the dominating power throughout the world, whiteness is the symbol of the Antichrist. Whiteness characterizes the activity of deranged individuals intrigued by their own image of themselves, and thus unable to see that they are what is wrong with the world. Black theology seeks to analyze the satanic nature of whiteness and by doing so to prepare all nonwhites for revolutionary action.

In passing, it may be worthwhile to point out that whites are in no position whatever to question the legitimacy of black theology. Questions like "Do you think theology is black?" or "What about others who suffer?" are the product of minds incapable of *black* thinking. It is not surprising that those who reject blackness in theology are usually whites who do not question the blue-eyed white Christ. It is hard to believe that whites are worried about black theology on account of its alleged alienation of other sufferers. Oppressors are not genuinely concerned about *any* oppressed group. It would seem rather that white rejection of black theology stems from a recognition of the revolutionary implications in its very name: a rejection of whiteness, an unwillingness to live under it, and an identification of whiteness with evil and blackness with good.

Black Theology and the Black Community

Most theologians agree that theology is a church discipline—that is, a discipline which functions within the Christian community. This is one aspect which distinguishes theology from philosophy of religion. Philosophy of religion is not committed to a community; it is an individualistic attempt to analyze the nature of ultimate reality through rational thought alone, using elements of many religions to assist in the articulation of the ultimate.

Theology by contrast cannot be separated from the community which it represents. It assumes that *truth* has been given to the community at the moment of its birth. Its task is to analyze the implications of that truth, in order to make sure that the community remains committed to that which defines its existence. Theology is the continued attempt of the community to define in every generation its reason for being in the world. A community that does not analyze its existence theologically is a community that does not care what it says or does. It is a community with no identity.

Applying this description, it is evident that white American theology has served oppressors well. Throughout the history of this country, from the Puritans to the death-of-God theologians, the theological problems treated in white churches and theological schools are defined in such a manner that they are unrelated to the problem of being black in a white, racist society. By defining the problems of Christianity in isolation from the black condition, white theology becomes a theology of white oppressors, serving as a divine sanction from criminal acts committed against blacks.

No white theologian has ever taken the oppression of blacks as a point of departure for analyzing God's activity in contemporary America. Apparently white theologians see no connection between whiteness and evil or blackness and God. Even those white theologians who write books about blacks invariably fail to say anything relevant to the black community as it seeks to break the power of white racism. They usually think that writing books makes them experts on black humanity. As a result they are as arrogant as George Wallace in telling blacks what is "best" for them. It is no surprise that the "best" is always nonviolent, posing no threat to the political and social interests of the white majority.

Because white theology has consistently preserved the integrity of the community of oppressors, I conclude that it is not Christian theology at all.[5] When we speak about God as related to humankind in the black-white struggle, Christian theology can only mean black theology, a theology that speaks of God as related to black liberation. If we agree that the gospel is the proclamation of God's liberating activity, that the Christian community is an oppressed community that participates in that activity, and that theology is the discipline arising from within the Christian community as it seeks to develop adequate language for its relationship to God's liberation, then black theology is Christian theology.

It is unthinkable that oppressors could identify with oppressed existence and thus say something relevant about God's liberation of the oppressed. In order to be Christian theology, white theology must cease being *white* theology and become black theology by denying whiteness as an acceptable form of human existence and affirming blackness as God's intention for humanity. White theologians will find this difficult, and it is to be expected that some will attempt to criticize black theology precisely on this point. Such criticism will not reveal a weakness in black theology but only the racist character of the critic.

Black theology will not spend too much time trying to answer its critics, because it is accountable only to the black community. Refusing to be separated from that community, black theology seeks to articulate the theological self-determination of blacks, providing some ethical and religious categories for the black revolution in America. It maintains that all acts which participate in the destruction of white racism are Christian, the liberating deeds of God. All acts which impede the struggle of black self-determination—black power—are anti-Christian, the work of Satan.

The revolutionary context forces black theology to shun all abstract principles dealing with what is the "right" and "wrong" course of action. There is only one principle which guides the thinking and action of black theology: an unqualified commitment to the black community as that community seeks to define its existence in the light of God's liberating work in the world. This means that black theology refuses to be guided by ideas and concepts alien to blacks. It assumes that whites encountering black thought will judge it "irrational." Not understanding what it means to be oppressed, the oppressor is in no position to understand the methods which the oppressed use in liberation. The logic of liberation is always incomprehensible to slave masters. From their position of power, masters never understand what slaves mean by "dignity." The only dignity they know is that of killing slaves, as if "superior" humanity depended on the enslavement of others. Black theology does not intend to debate with whites who have this perspective. Speaking for the black community, black theology says with Eldridge Cleaver, "We shall have our manhood. We shall have it, or the earth will be leveled by our attempts to gain it."

Black Theology as Survival Theology

To speak of black theology as survival theology refers to the *condition* of the community out of which black theology arises. We can delineate three characteristics of the black condition: the tension between life and death, identity crisis, and white social and political power.

1. The Tension between Life and Death. Black theology is the theology of a community whose daily energies must be focused on physical survival in a hostile environment. The black community spends most of its time trying "to make a living" in a society labeled "for whites only." Therefore, the central question for blacks is "How are we going to survive in a world which deems black humanity an illegitimate form of human existence?" That white America has issued a death warrant for being black is evident in the white brutality inflicted on black persons. Though whites may deny it, the ghettos of this country say otherwise. Masters always pretend that they are not masters, insisting that they are only doing what is best for society as a whole, including the slaves. This is, of course, the standard rhetoric of an oppressive society. Blacks know better. They know that whites have only one purpose: the destruction of everything which is not white.

In this situation, blacks are continually asking, often unconsciously, "When will the white overlord decide that blackness in any form must be exterminated?" The genocide of Amerindians is a reminder to the black community that white oppressors are capable of pursuing a course of complete annihilation of everything black. And the killing and the caging of black leaders make us think that black genocide has already begun. It seems that, from the white cop on his beat to the high government official, whites are not prepared for a real encounter with black reality, and thus the black community knows that whites may decide at any moment that the extermination of all blacks is indispensable for continued white existence and hegemony.

This is the content of "the tension between life and death." By white definitions, whiteness is "being" and blackness is "nonbeing." Blacks live under sentence of death. They know that whites will kill them rather than permit the beauty and the glory of black humanity to be manifested in its fullness. Over three hundred and fifty years of black slavery is evidence of that fact, and blacks must carve out a free existence in this situation. To breathe in white society is dependent on saying yes to whiteness, and blacks know it.

It is only natural to cling to life; no one wants to die. But there is such a thing as living physically while being dead spiritually. As long as blacks let whiteness define the limits of their being, blacks are dead. "To be or not to be" is thus a dilemma for the black community: to assert one's humanity and be killed, or to cling to life and sink into nonhumanity.

It is in this situation that black theology seeks to speak the word of God. It says that the God who was revealed in the life of oppressed Israel and who came to us in the incarnate Christ and is present today as the Holy Spirit has made a decision about the black condition. God has chosen to make the black condition *God's* condition! It is a continuation of the incarnation in twentieth-century America. God's righteousness will liberate the oppressed of this nation and "all flesh shall see it together." It is this certainty that makes physical life less than ultimate and thus enables blacks courageously to affirm blackness and its liberating power as ultimate. When persons feel this way, a revolution is in the making.

With the assurance that God is on our side, we can begin to make ready for the inevitable—the decisive encounter between black and white existence. White appeals to "wait and talk it over" are irrelevant when children are dying and men and women are being tortured. We will not let whitey cool this one with his pious love ethic but will seek to enhance our hostility, bringing it to its full manifestation. Black survival is at stake here, and we blacks must define and assert the conditions necessary for our being-in-the-world. Only we can decide how much we can endure from white racists. And as we make our decision in the midst of life and death, being and nonbeing, the role of black theology is to articulate this decision by pointing to the revelation of God in the black liberation struggle.

2. Identity Crisis. There is more at stake in the struggle for survival than mere physical existence. You have to be *black,* with a knowledge of the history of this country, to know what America means to black persons. You also have to know what it means to be a nonperson, a nothing, a person with no past, to know what black power is all about. Survival as a person means not only food and shelter, but also belonging to a community that remembers and understands the meaning of its past. Black consciousness is an attempt to recover a past deliberately destroyed by slave masters, an attempt to revive old survival symbols and create new ones.

Herbert Aptheker has written:

> History's potency is mighty. The oppressed need it for iden-
> tity and inspiration; oppressors for justification, rationaliza-
> tion and legitimacy. Nothing illustrates this more clearly than
> the history writing on the American Negro people.[6]

White Americans try to convince themselves that they have been
innocent onlookers of that history, but black Americans evaluate
the history of this country differently. For them, white Americans
have pursued two principal courses of action with regard to blacks.
First, they decreed that blacks were outside the realm of humanity,
that blacks were animals and that their enslavement was best both
for them and for society as a whole. And as long as black labor was
needed, slavery was regarded as the only appropriate "solution" to
the "black problem." But when black labor was no longer needed,
blacks were issued their "freedom," the freedom to live in a society
which attempted to destroy them physically and spiritually. There is
no indication before or after the Civil War that this society recognized the humanity of black persons.

The second course of action that whites have taken is to try to
"integrate" blacks into white society. Before the Supreme Court
decision in 1954, whites sought to destroy black identity by segre-
gating blacks from the mainstream of society, decreeing that this
world is not for blacks. Then, under the banner of liberalism
(compounded of white guilt and black naivety), "integration"
became the watchword. The implications of the term are now all
too clear: the destruction of black identity through assimilation.
Whites wanted to integrate blacks into white society—straight hair,
neckties, deodorant, the whole package—as if blacks had no existence apart from whiteness.

In such a situation, there is only one course of action for the
black community, and that is to destroy the oppressor's definition
of blackness by unraveling new meanings in old tales so that the
past may emerge as an instrument of black liberation. If the
oppressed are to preserve their personhood, they must create a new
way of looking at history independent of the perspective of the
oppressor.

Black theology is survival theology because it seeks to provide the theological dimensions of the struggle for black identity. It seeks to reorder religious language, to show that all forces supporting white oppression are anti-Christian in their essence. The essence of the gospel of Christ stands or falls on the question of black humanity, and there is no way that a church or institution can be related to the gospel of Christ if it sponsors or tolerates racism in any form. To speak of a "racist Christian" or a "segregated church of Christ" is blasphemy and the antithesis of the Christian gospel.

In another connection, Paul Tillich wrote:

> Man discovers himself when he discovers God; he discovers something that is identical with himself although it transcends him infinitely, something from which he is estranged, but from which he never has been and never can be separated.[7]

Despite the pantheistic implications, there is some truth here that can be applied to the black identity crisis. The search for black identity is the search for God, because God's identity is revealed in the black struggle for freedom. For black theology, this is not pantheism; it is the conviction that the transcendent God who became immanent in Israelite history and incarnate in the man Jesus is also involved in black history, bringing about liberation from white oppressors. This is what black theology means for black persons who are in search of new ways of talking about God, ways that will enhance their understanding of themselves.

3. White Social and Political Power. Black theology is the theological expression of a people deprived of social and political power. Poverty-stricken whites can manage to transcend the oppression of society, but there is nothing blacks can do to escape the humiliation of white supremacy except to affirm the very attribute which oppressors find unacceptable. It is clear to blacks why they are unwanted in society, and for years they tried to make themselves acceptable by playing the game of human existence according to white rules, hoping that some day whites would not regard the color of their skins as the ultimate or only criterion for human relationships. But to this day, there is little evidence that whites can deal with the reality of physical blackness as an appropriate form of human existence. For this reason, blacks are oppressed socially even if they have economic and intellectual power. Jews in Nazi Germany found out the hard way that economic power was no security against an insane government that had the political and social power to determine the fate of Jewish existence.

Realizing that white racism is an insanity comparable to Nazism, black theology seeks to articulate a theological ethos consistent with the black revolutionary struggle. Blacks know that there is only one possible authentic existence in this society, and that is to force a radical revolutionary confrontation with the structures of white power by saying yes to the essence of their blackness. The role of black theology is to tell blacks to focus on their own self-determination as a community by preparing to do anything the community believes necessary for its existence.

To be human in a condition of social oppression involves affirming that which the oppressor regards as degrading. In a world in which the oppressor defines right in terms of whiteness, humanity means an unqualified identification with blackness. Black, therefore, is beautiful; oppressors have made it ugly. We glorify it because they despise it; we love it because they hate it. It is the black way of saying, "To hell with your stinking white society and its middle-class ideas about the world. I will have no part in it."

The white view of black humanity also has *political* ramifications. That is why so much emphasis has been placed on "law and order." Blacks live in a society in which blackness means criminality, and thus "law and order" means "get blacky." To live, to stay out of jail, blacks are required to obey laws of humiliation. "Law and order" is nothing but an emphasis on the stabilization of the status quo, which means telling blacks they cannot be black and telling whites that they have the moral and political right to see to it that black persons "stay in their place." Conversely the development of black power means that the black community will define its own place, its own way of behaving in the world, regardless of the consequences to white society. We have reached our limit of tolerance, and if it means death with dignity or life with humiliation, we will choose the former. And if that is the choice, we will take some honkies with us. What is to be hoped is that there can be a measure of existence in dignity in this society for blacks so that we do not have to *prove* that we have reached the limits of suffering.

The person in political power is a strange creature, and it is very easy for such a one to believe that human dignity has no real meaning. In André Malraux's *Man's Fate*, Konig, chief of Chiang Kai-shek's police, illustrates the inability of the man in political power to understand the condition of the oppressed. Intrigued by Kyo's participation in the Shanghai insurrection, Konig asks his prisoner:

> "I have been told that you are a communist through dignity. Is that true?" Kyo replies: "I think that communism will make dignity possible for those with whom I am fighting." But Konig asks, "What do you call dignity? It doesn't mean anything." "The opposite of humiliation," says Kyo. "When one comes from where I come, that means something."[8]

Because oppressors do not come from the land of the oppressed, they do not have to attach any meaning to the demands of the oppressed.

We can conclude, then, that survival is a way of life for the black community. Black theology is a theology of survival because it seeks to interpret the theological significance of the being of a community whose existence is threatened by the power of nonbeing. We are seeking meaning in a world permeated with philosophical and theological absurdities, where hope is nonexistent. In existential philosophy the absurd is "that which is meaningless":

> Thus man's existence is absurd because his contingency finds no external justification. His projects are absurd because they are directed toward an unattainable goal.[9]

This is certainly the feeling of blacks as they seek to make sense out of their existence in a white society. What can we say to a community whose suffering and humiliation is beyond rational explication? The black condition is inflicted by the white condition and there is no rational explanation of it.

Speaking to the black condition characterized by existential absurdities, black theology rejects the tendency of classic Christianity to appeal to divine providence. To suggest that black suffering is consistent with the knowledge and will of God and that in the end everything will happen for the good of those who love God is unacceptable to blacks. The eschatological promise of a distant, future heaven is insufficient to account for the earthly pain of black suffering. We cannot accept a God who inflicts or tolerates black suffering for some inscrutable purpose.

Black theology also rejects those who counsel blacks to accept the limits which this society places on them, for it is tantamount to suicide. In existential philosophy suicide is the ultimate expression of despair. If we accept white definitions of blackness, we destroy ourselves.

Black theology, responding to the black condition, takes on the character of rebellion against things as they are. In the writings of Camus, the rebel is the one who refuses to accept the absurd conditions of things but fights against them in spite of the impossibility of arriving at a solution. In black theology, blacks are encouraged to revolt against the structures of white social and political power by affirming blackness, but not because blacks have a chance of "winning." What could the concept of "winning" possibly mean? Blacks do what they do because and only because they can do no other; and black theology says simply that such action is in harmony with divine revelation.

Black Theology as Passionate Language

Because black theology is survival theology, it must speak with a passion consistent with the depths of the wounds of the oppressed. Theological language is passionate language, the language of commitment, because it is language which seeks to vindicate the afflicted and condemn the enforcers of evil. Christian theology cannot afford to be an abstract, dispassionate discourse on the nature of God in relation to humankind; such an analysis has no ethical implications for the contemporary forms of oppression in our society. Theology must take the risk of faith, knowing that it stands on the edge of condemnation by the forces of evil. Paul Tillich calls this an "existential risk":

> The risk of faith is an existential risk, a risk in which the meaning and fulfillment of our lives is at stake, and not a theoretical judgment which may be refuted sooner or later.[10]

Blacks know what it means to have their lives at stake, for their lives are at stake every moment of their existence. In the black world no one takes life for granted: every moment of being is surrounded with the threat of nonbeing. If black theology is to relate itself to this situation, it too must take the risk of faith and speak with a passion in harmony with the revolutionary spirit of the oppressed.

The sin of American theology is that it has spoken without passion. It has failed miserably in relating its work to the oppressed in society by refusing to confront the structures of this nation with the evils of racism. When it has tried to speak for the poor, it has been so cool and calm in its analysis of human evil that it implicitly disclosed whose side it was on. Most of the time American theology has simply remained silent, ignoring the condition of the victims of this racist society. How else can we explain the theological silence during the period of white lynching of black humanity in this nation? How else can we explain the inability of white religionists to deal relevantly with the new phenomenon of black consciousness? And how else can we explain the problem white seminaries are having as they seek to respond to radical black demands? There is really only one answer: American theology is racist; it identifies theology as dispassionate analysis of "the tradition," unrelated to the sufferings of the oppressed.

Black theology rejects this approach and views theology as a participation in passion in behalf of the oppressed. Seeking to be Christian theology in an age of societal dehumanization, it contemplates the ultimate possibility of nonbeing (death) with the full intention of affirming the ultimate possibility of being (life). In the struggle for truth in a revolutionary age, there can be no principles of truth, no absolutes, not even God. For we realize that, though the reality of God must be the presupposition of theology (the very name implies this—*theos* and *logos*), we cannot speak of God at the expense of the oppressed.

Insistence on a passionate theology is a call for an anthropocentric point of departure in theology. I realize that such a call must raise the eyebrows of all who have felt the impact of Karl Barth. But let me state clearly that this approach is not a return to nineteenth-century liberalism with its emphasis on the goodness and worth of humanity (which always meant white European humanity). Every black intellectual is aware that when liberals spoke of "inevitable progress" and the "upward movement of Western culture," it was realized at the expense of blacks who were enslaved and colonized to secure "progress." My concern is altogether different. Though my perspective begins with humanity, it is not humanity in general, not some abstract species of Platonic idealism. I am concerned with concrete humanity, particularly with oppressed humanity. In America that means black humanity. This is the point of departure of black theology, because it believes that oppressed humanity is the point of departure of Christ himself. It is this concern that makes theological language a language of passion.

My characterization of black theology as passionate theology is analogous to Paul Tillich's analysis of "the existential thinker." Quoting Feuerbach, he writes:

> Do not wish to be a philosopher in contrast to being a man . . . do not think as a thinker . . . think as a living, real being . . . think in Existence. Love is passion, and only passion is the mark of Existence.

In fact, Tillich quotes Feuerbach as saying, "Only what is as an object of passion—really is."[12] The existential thinker is a thinker who not only relates thought to existence but whose thought arises out of a passionate encounter with existence. As Kierkegaard put it in his definition of truth:

> An objective uncertainty held fast in the most passionate personal experience is the truth, the highest truth attainable for an Existing individual.[13]

Relating this to black theology, we can say that the definition of truth for the black thinker arises from a passionate encounter with black reality. Though that truth may be described religiously as God, it is not the God of white religion but the God of black existence. There is no way to speak of this objectively; truth is not objective. It is subjective, a personal experience of the ultimate in the midst of degradation. Passion is the only appropriate response to this truth.

To be passionate, black theology may find it necessary to break with traditional theological concerns. Such concerns are often unrelated to oppressed existence. Like the pre-Civil War black preachers, it believes that racism is incompatible with the gospel of Christ, and it must, therefore, do everything it can to reveal the satanic nature of racism, so that it can be destroyed. It will be difficult for white theologians to participate in this reality—because of their identification with unreality. Creative theological reflection about God and God's movement in the world is possible only when one frees oneself from the powers that be. The mind must be freed from the values of an oppressive society. It involves prophetic condemnation of society so that God's word can be clearly distinguished from the words of human beings. Such a task is especially difficult in America, a nation demonically deceived about what is good, true, and beautiful. The oppression in this country is sufficiently camouflaged to allow many Americans to believe that things are not really too bad. White theologians, not having felt the sting of oppression, will find it most difficult to criticize this nation, for the condemnation of America entails their own condemnation.

Black thinkers are in a different position. They cannot be black *and* identified with the powers that be. To be black is to be committed to destroying everything this country loves and adores. Creativity and passion are possible when one stands where the black person stands, the one who has visions of the future because the present is unbearable. And the black person will cling to that future as a means of passionately rejecting the present.

2

The Sources and Norm of Black Theology

The Function of the Sources and Norm

Though I have alluded already to some of the factors which shape the perspective of black theology, it is necessary to say a word about what are often designated as the sources and the norm in systematic theology. Sources are the "formative factors" that determine the character of a given theology.[1] The norm is "the criterion to which the sources . . . must be subjected."[2] That is, the sources are the relevant data for the theological task, whereas the norm determines how the data will be used. It is often the case that different theologies share the same sources, and it is the theological norm which elevates one particular source (or sources) to a predominant role.

Karl Barth and Paul Tillich provide useful examples. Both agree that the Bible and culture are important data for theology. But an examination of their work shows that culture plays a much larger role in Tillich's theology, whereas the Bible is crucial for Barth. For Barth scripture is the witness to the word of God and thus is indispensable to doing theology. Tillich, on the other hand, agrees that the Bible is important, but holds that the task of making the gospel relevant to the contemporary mind is equally important. If pressed, Barth (at least in his later years) would not deny that Tillich's concern for relevance is a legitimate concern; yet Barth is skeptical about regarding culture as a point of departure for theology. God is still God and humankind is still humankind, even for the later Barth. That being the case, the only legitimate starting point of theology is the man Jesus who is the revelation of God. Whatever is said about culture must be said in the light of this prior perspective.

But this style of theology worries Tillich. He wonders whether kerygmatic theologians like Barth are giving answers to questions that the modern world is not asking. Culture—that is, the situation of modern man—must be the point of relevant theology. For Tillich the danger of confusing the divine and the human, which is so important for Barth, is not nearly so important as the danger of giving answers that are irrelevant. In fact, divine-human identification is the risk of faith:

> The risk of faith is based on the fact that the unconditional element can become a matter of ultimate concern only if it appears in a concrete embodiment.[3]

It is the "concrete embodiment" of the infinite which must be taken seriously. Culture, then, is the medium through which the human person encounters the divine and thus makes a decision.

Barth and Tillich illustrate the role that sources and norm play in shaping the character of a theology. Though their sources are similar, they do not agree on the norm. It is clear in Tillich's writings that the apologetic situation is decisive in defining the norm of systematic theology, and he identifies the norm as "New Being in Jesus as the Christ," which is the only answer to human estrangement. Tillich appeals to the cultural situation regarding the norm, but Barth is kerygmatic in that he defines the man Jesus as witnessed to in the holy scriptures as the only norm for God-talk.

It is clear, therefore, that the most important decisions in theology are made at this juncture. The sources and norm are presuppositions that determine the questions that are to be asked, as well as the answers that are to be given. Believing that the biblical Christ is the sole criterion for theology, Barth not only asks questions about human nature that arise from a study of christology, but he also derives answers from the man Jesus. Tillich, on the other hand, deals with questions that arise from the cultural situation of humankind, and endeavors to shape his answers according to that situation. Both approaches are conditioned by their theological perspectives.

Because a perspective refers to the whole of a person's being in the context of a community, the sources and norm of black theology must be consistent with the perspective of the black community. Inasmuch as white American theologians do not belong to the black community, they cannot relate the gospel to that community. Invariably, when white theology attempts to speak to blacks about Jesus Christ, the gospel is presented in the light of the social, political, and economic interests of the white majority. (One example of this is the interpretation of Christian love as nonviolence.) Black theologians must work to destroy the corruptive influence of white thought by building theology on sources and a norm that are appropriate to the black community.

The Sources of Black Theology

There are many factors which shape the perspective of black theology. Black consciousness is a relatively new phenomenon, and it is too early to identify all the sources participating in its creation. The black community as a self-determining people, proud of its blackness, has just begun, and we must wait before we can describe what its fullest manifestation will be. "We are God's children now; it does not yet appear what we shall be . . . " (I John 3:2a). Even so, at this stage, a word must be said about the present manifestation. What are the sources in black theology?

1. Black Experience. There can be no black theology which does not take seriously the black experience—a life of humiliation and suffering. This must be the point of departure of all God-talk which seeks to be black-talk. This means that black theology realizes that it is human beings who speak of God, and when those human beings are black, they speak of God only in the light of the black experience. It is not that black theology denies the importance of God's revelation in Christ, but blacks want to know what Jesus Christ means when they are confronted with the brutality of white racism.

The black experience prevents us from turning the gospel into theological catch phrases, and makes us realize that they must be clothed in black flesh. The black experience forces us to ask, "What does revelation mean when one's being is engulfed in a system of white racism cloaking itself in pious moralities?" "What does God mean when a police officer whacks you over the head because you are black?" "What does the church mean when white churchmen say they need more time to end racism?"

The black experience should not be identified with inwardness, as implied in Schleiermacher's description of religion as the "feeling of absolute dependence." It is not an introspection in which one contemplates one's own ego. Blacks are not afforded the luxury of navel gazing. The black experience is the atmosphere in which blacks live. It is the totality of black existence in a white world where babies are tortured, women are raped, and men are shot. The black poet Don Lee puts it well:

> The true black experience in most cases is very concrete . . . sleeping in subways, being bitten by rats, six people living in a kitchenette.[4]

The black experience is existence in a system of white racism. The black person knows that a ghetto is the white way of saying that blacks are subhuman and fit only to live with rats. The black experience is police departments adding more recruits and buying more guns to provide "law and order," which means making a city safe for its white population. It is politicians telling blacks to cool it or *else*. It is George Wallace, Hubert Humphrey, and Richard Nixon running for president. The black experience is college administrators defining "quality" education in the light of white values. It is church bodies compromising on whether blacks are human. And because black theology is a product of that experience, it must talk about God in the light of it. The purpose of black theology is to make sense of black experience.

The black experience, however, is more than simply encountering white insanity. It also means blacks making decisions about themselves—decisions that involve whites. Blacks know that whites do not have the last word on black existence. This realization may be defined as black power, the power of the black community to make decisions regarding its identity. When this happens, blacks become aware of their blackness; and to be aware of self is to set certain limits on the others' behavior toward oneself. The black experience means telling whitey what the limits are.

The power of the black experience cannot be overestimated. It is the power to love oneself precisely because one is black and a readiness to die if whites try to make one behave otherwise. It is the sound of James Brown singing, "I'm Black and I'm Proud" and Aretha Franklin demanding "respect." The black experience is catching the spirit of blackness and loving it. It is hearing black preachers speak of God's love in spite of the filthy ghetto, and black congregations responding Amen, which means that they realize that ghetto existence is not the result of divine decree but of white inhumanity. The black experience is the feeling one has when attacking the enemy of black humanity by throwing a Molotov cocktail into a white-owned building and watching it go up in flames. We know, of course, that getting rid of evil takes something more than burning down buildings, but one must start somewhere.

Being black is a beautiful experience. It is the sane way of living in an insane environment. Whites do not understand it; they can only catch glimpses of it in sociological reports and historical studies. The black experience is possible only for black persons. It means having natural hair cuts, wearing African dashikis, and dancing to the sound of Johnny Lee Hooker or B. B. King, knowing that no matter how hard whitey tries there can be no real duplication of black soul. Black soul is not learned; it comes from the totality of black experience, the experience of carving out an existence in a society that says you do not belong.

The black experience is a source of black theology because this theology seeks to relate biblical revelation to the situation of blacks in America. This means that black theology cannot speak of God and God's involvement in contemporary America without identifying God's presence with the events of liberation in the black community.

2. Black History. Black history refers to the way blacks were brought to this land and the way they have been treated in this land. This is not to say that only American whites participated in the institution of slavery. But there was something unique about American slavery—namely, the white attempt to define blacks as nonpersons. In other countries slaves were allowed community, and there were slave rights. Slaves were human beings, and their humanity was protected (to some degree) by certain civil laws. Black history in North America meant that whites used every conceivable method to destroy black humanity. As late as 1857 the highest court of this land decreed that blacks "had no rights which the white man was bound to respect." The history of slavery in this country reveals how low human depravity can sink. And the fact that this country still, in many blatant ways, perpetuates the idea of the inferiority of blacks poignantly illustrates the capabilities of human evil. If black theology is going to speak to the condition of black persons, it cannot ignore the history of white inhumanity committed against them.

But black history is more than what whites did to blacks. More importantly black history is black persons saying no to every act of white brutality. Contrary to what whites say in *their* history books, black power is not new. It began when black mothers decided to kill their babies rather than have them grow up to be slaves. Black power is Nat Turner, Denmark Vesey, and Gabriel Prosser planning a slave revolt. It is slaves poisoning masters, and Frederick Douglass delivering an abolitionist address. This is the history that black theology must take seriously before it can begin to speak about God and black humanity.

Like black power, black theology is not new either. It came into being when the black clergy realized that killing slave masters was doing the work of God. It began when the black clergy refused to accept the racist white church as consistent with the gospel of God. The organizing of the African Methodist Episcopal Church, the African Methodist Episcopal Zion Church, the Christian Methodist Church, the Baptist churches, and many other black churches is a visible manifestation of black theology. The participation of black churches in the black liberation struggle from the eighteenth to the twentieth century is a tribute to the endurance of black theology.

Black theology focuses on black history as a source for its theological interpretation of God's work in the world because divine activity is inseparable from black history. There can be no comprehension of black theology without realizing that its existence comes from a community which looks back on its unique past, visualizes the future, and then makes decisions about possibilities in the present. Taking seriously the reality of God's involvement in history, black theology asks, "What are the implications of black history for the revelation of God? Is God active in black history or had God withdrawn and left blacks to the mercy of white insanity?" Although answers to these questions are not easy, black theology refuses to accept a God who is not identified totally with the goals of the black community. If God is not for us, if God is not against white racists, then God is a murderer, and we had better kill God. The task of black theology is to kill gods that do not belong to the black community; and by taking black history as a source, we know that this is neither an easy nor a sentimental task but an awesome responsibility.

3. Black Culture. The concept of black culture is closely related to black experience and black history. We could say that the black experience is what blacks feel when they try to carve out an existence in dehumanized white society. It is black "soul," the pain and the joy of reacting to whiteness and affirming blackness. Black history is the record of joy and pain. It is those experiences that the black community remembers and retells because of the mythic power inherent in the symbols for the present revolution against white racism.

Black culture consists of the creative forms of expression as one reflects on history, endures pain, and experiences joy. It is the black community expressing itself in music, poetry, prose, and other art forms. The emergence of the concept of the revolutionary black theater with such writers as LeRoi Jones, Larry Neal, Ed Bullins, and others is an example of the black community expressing itself culturally. Aretha Franklin, James Brown, Charlie Parker, John Coltrane, and others are examples in music. Culture refers to the way persons live and move in the world; it molds their thought forms.

Black theology must take seriously the cultural expressions of the community it represents so that it will be able to speak relevantly to the black condition. Of course, black theology is aware of the danger of identifying the word of human beings with the word of God, the danger Karl Barth persuasively warned against in the second decade of this century:

Form believes itself capable of taking the place of content. . . . Man has taken the divine in his possession; he has brought [God] under his management.[5]

Such a warning is necessary in a situation alive with satanic creatures like Hitler, and it is always the task of the church to announce the impending judgment of God against state power which seeks to destroy the weak. This is why Bonhoeffer said, "When Christ calls a man, he bids him come and die." Suffering is the badge of true discipleship. But is it appropriate to speak the same words to the oppressed?

To apply Barth's words to the black-white context and interpret them as a warning against identifying God's revelation with black culture is to misunderstand Barth. His warning was appropriate for the situation in which it was given, but not for blacks in America. Blacks need to see some correlations between divine salvation and black culture. For too long Christ has been pictured as a blue-eyed honky. Black theologians are right: we need to dehonkify him and thus make him relevant to the black condition.

Paul Tillich wrote:

I am not unaware of the danger that in this way [the method of relating theology to culture] the substance of the Christian message may be lost. Nevertheless, this danger must be risked, and once one has realized this, one must proceed in this direction. Dangers are not a reason for avoiding a serious demand.[6]

Though Tillich was not speaking of the black situation, his words are applicable to it. To be sure, as Barth pointed out, God's word is alien to humanity and thus comes to it as a "bolt from the blue"— but which humanity? For oppressors, dehumanizers, the analysis is correct. However, when we speak of God's revelation to the oppressed, the analysis is incorrect. God's revelation comes to us in and through the cultural situation of the oppressed. God's word is our word; God's existence, our existence. This is the meaning of black culture and its relationship to divine revelation.

Black culture, then, is God's way of acting in America, God's participation in black liberation. Speaking of black art, Don Lee writes:

Black art will elevate and enlighten our people and lead them toward an awareness of self, *i.e.,* their blackness. It will show them mirrors. Beautiful symbols. And will aid in the destruction of anything nasty and detrimental to our advancement as a people.[7]

This is black liberation, the emancipation of black minds and black souls from white definitions of black humanity. Black theology does not ignore this; it participates in this experience of the divine.

4. Revelation. Some religionists who have been influenced by the twentieth-century Protestant theologies of revelation will question my discussion of revelation as the fourth source rather than the *first.* Does this not suggest that revelation is secondary to the black experience, black history, and black culture? Is not this the very danger which Karl Barth pointed to?

I should indicate that the numerical order of the discussion is not necessarily in order of importance. It is difficult to know which source is more important: all are interdependent and thus a discussion of one usually involves the others. No hard-and-fast line can be drawn between them. A perspective is an expression of the way a community perceives itself and its participation in reality, and this is a *total* experience. It is not possible to slice up that experience and rate the pieces in terms of importance. Inasmuch as being refers to the whole of reality, reference to one aspect of being necessitates consideration of the totality of being. I have tried to choose the method of discussion that best describes the encounter of the black community with reality.

I do not think that revelation is comprehensible from a black theological perspective without a prior understanding of the concrete manifestation of revelation in the black community as seen in the black experience, black history, and black culture. For Christian faith, revelation is an event, a happening in human history. It is God's self-revelation to the human race through a historical act of human liberation. Revelation is what Yahweh *did* in the event of the exodus; it is Yahweh tearing down old orders and establishing new ones. Throughout the entire history of Israel, to know God is to know what God is doing in human history for the oppressed of the land.

In the New Testament, God's revelatory event takes place in the person of Jesus. He is the event of God, telling us who God is by what God does for the oppressed. In Christian thinking the man Jesus must be the decisive interpretive factor in everything we say about God because he is the plenary revelation of God.

This analysis of the meaning of revelation is not new in Protestant circles; Karl Barth popularized it. The weakness of white American theology is that it seldom gets beyond the first century in its analysis of revelation. If I read the New Testament correctly, the resurrection of Jesus means that he is present today in the midst of all societies effecting his liberation of the oppressed. He is not confined to the first century, and thus our talk of him in the past is important only insofar as it leads us to an *encounter* with him *now*. As a black theologian, I want to know what God's revelation means right now as the black community participates in the struggle for liberation. The failure of white theology to speak to the black liberation struggle only reveals once again the racist character of white thought.

For black theology, revelation is not *just* a past event or a contemporary event in which it is difficult to recognize the activity of God. *Revelation is a black event*—it is what blacks are doing about their liberation. I have spoken of the black experience, black history, and black culture as theological sources because they are God at work liberating the oppressed.

I am aware of a possible pantheistic distortion of my analysis. But this risk must be taken if theological statements are going to have meaning in a world that is falling apart because white racists think that God has appointed them to rule over others, especially over blacks. Besides, religionists who are unduly nervous about pantheism inevitably move toward a deistic distortion of faith, and the god of deism may as well be dead. Our risk is no greater than the risk inherent in Hebrew prophecy; and do I need to mention the risk taken by Jesus? Christian theology, if it is going to have relevance in a revolutionary situation, must take the risk of pointing to the contemporary manifestation of God, and this necessarily involves taking sides. Should God's work in the world be identified with the oppressors or the oppressed? There can be no neutrality on this issue; neutrality is nothing but an identification of God's work with the machinations of oppressors.

Black theology takes the risk of faith and thus makes an unqualified identification of God's revelation with black liberation. There can be no other medium for encountering the contemporary revelatory event of God in this society.

5. Scripture. Black theology is biblical theology. That is, it is theology which takes seriously the importance of scripture in theological discourse. There can be no theology of the Christian gospel which does not take into account the biblical witness. It is true that the Bible is not the revelation of God; only Jesus is. But it is an indispensable witness to God's revelation and is thus a primary source for Christian thinking about God. As John Macquarrie says, "It is one important way . . . by which the community of faith keeps open its access to that primordial revelation on which the community has been founded."[8] By taking seriously the witness of scripture, we are prevented from making the gospel into private moments of religious ecstasy or into the religious sanctification of the structures of society. The Bible can serve as a guide for checking the contemporary interpretation of God's revelation, making certain that our interpretation is consistent with the biblical witness.

It is indeed the *biblical* witness that says that God is a God of liberation, who speaks to the oppressed and abused, and assures them that divine righteousness will vindicate their suffering. It is the Bible that tells us that God became human in Jesus Christ so that the kingdom of God would make freedom a reality for all human beings. This is the meaning of the resurrection of Jesus. The human being no longer has to be a slave to anybody, but must rebel against all the principalities and powers which make human existence subhuman. It is in this light that black theology is affirmed as a twentieth-century analysis of God's work in the world.

From this, however, we should not conclude that the Bible is an infallible witness. God was not the author of the Bible, nor were its writers mere secretaries. Efforts to prove verbal inspiration of the scriptures result from the failure to see the real meaning of the biblical message: human liberation! Unfortunately, emphasis on verbal infallibility leads to unimportant concerns. While churches are debating whether a whale swallowed Jonah, the state is enacting inhuman laws against the oppressed. It matters little to the oppressed who authored scripture; what is important is whether it can serve as a weapon against oppressors.

There is a close correlation between political and religious conservatism. Whites who insist on verbal infallibility are often the most violent racists. If they can be sure, beyond any doubt, of their views of scripture, then they can be equally resolute in imposing their views on society as a whole. With God on their side there is nothing that will be spared in the name of "the laws of God and men." It becomes an easy matter to kill blacks, Amerindians, or anybody else who questions their right to make decisions on how the world ought to be governed.

Literalism thirsts for the removal of doubt in religion, enabling believers to justify all kinds of political oppression in the name of God and country. During slavery blacks were encouraged to be obedient slaves because it was the will of God. After all, Paul did say "slaves obey your masters"; and because of the "curse of Ham," blacks have been considered inferior to whites. Even today the same kind of literalism is being used by white scholars to encourage blacks to be nonviolent, as if nonviolence were the only possible expression of Christian love. It is surprising that it never dawns on these white religionists that oppressors are in no moral position to dictate what a Christian response is. Jesus' exhortations to "turn the other cheek" and "go the second mile" do not mean that blacks should let whites walk all over them. We cannot use Jesus' behavior in the first century as a *literal* guide for our actions in the twentieth century. To do so is to fall into the same trap that fundamentalists fall into. It destroys Christian freedom, the freedom to make decisions patterned on, but not dictated by, the example of Jesus.

Scripture, then, does not make decisions for us. On the contrary, it is a theological source because of its power to "renew for us the disclosure of the holy which was the content of the primordial revelation."[9] The God who is present today in our midst is the same God who was revealed in Jesus Christ as witnessed in the scriptures. By reading an account of God's activity in the world as recorded in scripture, it is possible for a community in the twentieth century to experience the contemporary work of God in the world. The meaning of scripture is not to be found in the words of scripture as such but only in its power to point beyond itself to the reality of God's revelation—and in America, that means black liberation. Herein lies the key to the meaning of biblical inspiration. The Bible is inspired: by reading it a community can encounter the resurrected Jesus and thus be moved to risk everything for earthly freedom.

6. Tradition. Tradition refers to the theological reflection of the church upon the nature of Christianity from the time of the early church to the present day. It is impossible for any student of Christianity to ignore tradition; the New Testament itself is a result of it. The possibility of going back to the Bible without taking into account the tradition which gave rise to it and which defines our contemporary evaluation of it is unthinkable; tradition controls (in part) both our negative and positive thinking about the nature of the Christian gospel.

Though tradition is essential for any theological evaluation of Christianity, black theology is not uncritical of it, particularly the history of Western Christianity since the fourth century. The "conversion" of Constantine to Christianity and his subsequent acceptance of it as the official religion of the Roman empire raise some serious questions about Christendom, especially the possibility of its remaining true to its origin and mandate. It can be argued that this was the beginning of the decline of Christianity so evident in contemporary American society. Is it possible for the church to be the church (committed unreservedly to the oppressed in society) and at the same time be an integral part of the structure of a society? I think not. If the gospel of Jesus is the gospel of and for the oppressed in society, the church of Christ cannot be the religion of society. But the official church, which has been most responsible for the transmission of the gospel tradition, has also played a role as the political enforcer of "law and order" against the oppressed by lending divine sanction to the laws of the state and thus serving as the "redemptive" center of an established order. The long bloody history of Christian anti-Semitism is a prominent case in point.

The Protestant Reformation in the sixteenth century did little to change this emphasis. Luther's identification with the oppressors in society enabled him to speak of the state as a servant of God at the same time that the oppressed were being tortured by the state. It is impossible for the oppressed who are seeking liberation to think of the state as God's servant. In most cases, the state is responsible for human enslavement and is thus the enemy of all who strive for human freedom.

Luther's concern for "law and order" in the midst of human oppression is seriously questioned by black theology. Although it may be doubtful whether his doctrine of the relationship between church and state prepared the way for Hitler's massacre of Jews, it did little to prevent it. In fact, his condemnation of the Peasant Revolt sounds very much like white churchmen's condemnation of ghetto rebellions.[10]

Other Protestants reformers, especially Calvin and Wesley, did little to make Christianity a religion for the politically oppressed in society. Though no one can be responsible for everything that is done in their name, one may be suspicious of the easy affinity among Calvinism, capitalism, and slave trading.[11] John Wesley also said little about slaveholding and did even less.[12] We are told that Wesley's Methodism prevented a revolution in England, but I am not sure whether we should praise or condemn him on that account. The stance of the white Methodist Church in America, with its vacillation on slavery and colonization, is consistent with Wesley's less than passionate approach to the issues.

Black theology believes that the spirit of the authentic gospel is often better expressed by "heretics" than by the "orthodox" tradition. Certainly the so-called radical reformers were closer to the truth of Christianity in their emphasis on Christian discipleship through identification with the oppressed of the land than was Luther, who called on the state to put down peasants.

Regarding what is often called tradition, black theology perceives *moments* of authentic identification with the ethical implications of the gospel of Jesus, but they are rare. When black theology speaks of the importance of tradition, it focuses primarily on the history of the black church in America and secondarily on white western Christianity. It believes that the authentic Christian gospel as expressed in the New Testament is found more in the pre–Civil War black church than in its white counterpart. Richard Allen, Daniel Payne, and Highland Garnet are more important in analyzing the theological implications of black liberation than are Luther, Calvin, and Wesley. This is partially true because they are black but more importantly because inherent in their interpretation of the gospel is political, economic, and social liberation. These men recognized the incompatibility between Christianity and slavery. While the white church in America was rationalizing slavery by recourse to fallacious exegesis, black ministers were preaching freedom and equality.

The black church in America was founded on the belief that God condemned slavery and that Christian freedom meant political emancipation. Highland Garnet even argued that it was both a political and Christian right that slaves should rise in revolt against their white masters by taking up arms against them:

Brethren, it is as wrong for your lordly oppressors to keep you in slavery, as it was for the man-thief to steal our ancestors from the coast of Africa. You should therefore now use the same manner of resistance, as would have been just in our ancestors, when the bloody footprints of the first remorseless soul-thief was placed upon the shores of our fatherland.[13]

Black theology is concerned only with the tradition of Christianity that is usable in the black liberation struggle. As it looks over the past, it asks: "How is the Christian tradition related to the oppression of blacks in America?"

The Norm of Black Theology

In the previous section, I attempted to set forth the basic sources of black theology. It is appropriate now to analyze the hermeneutical principle or norm which is operative in black theology as it makes a theological determination regarding the sources. Sometimes it is possible to perceive the norm of a particular theology by an evaluation of the selection and analysis of its sources; but this is not always the case, because most theologies share common sources. As I have pointed out, the difference between Barth and Tillich does not lie in their choice of sources. The crucial difference is in their use of sources, which is traceable to the definition of their theological norm.

The theological norm is the hermeneutical principle which is decisive in specifying how sources are to be used by rating their importance and by distinguishing relevant data from irrelevant. For example, most theologians would agree that the Bible is important for the work of theology. But there are sixty-six books in the Bible, and how are we going to decide which books are more important than others? The answers to this question range from the fundamentalist's verbal-inspiration view to the archliberal view that the Bible is merely one of many records of religious experiences. In all cases, the importance and use of the Bible are determined by the theological norm which is brought to the scripture. Theologies with a kerygmatic consciousness would like to think that the norm arises from scripture itself, but this is not always easy to determine.

What is certain is that the theologian brings to the scripture the perspective of a community. Ideally, the concern of that community is consistent with the concern of the community that gave us the scriptures. It is the task of theology to keep these two communities (biblical and contemporary) in constant tension in order that we may be able to speak meaningfully about God.

Black theology seeks to create a theological norm in harmony with the black condition and biblical revelation. On the one hand, the norm must not be a private norm of a particular theologian but must arise from the black community itself. This means that there can be no norm for the black community which does not take seriously its reality in the world and what that means in a white racist society. Theology cannot be indifferent to the importance of blackness by making some kind of existential leap beyond blackness to an undefined universalism. It must take seriously the questions which arise from black existence and not even try to answer white questions, questions coming from the lips of those who know oppressed existence only through abstract reflections.

If theology is to be relevant to the human condition which created it, it must relate itself to the questions which arise out of the community responsible for its reason for being. The very existence of black theology is dependent on its ability to relate itself to the human situation unique to oppressed persons generally and blacks particularly. If black theology fails to do this adequately, then the black community will and should destroy it. Blacks have heard enough about God. What they want to know is what God has to say about the black condition. Or, more importantly, what is God doing about it? What is the relevance of God in the struggle against the forces of evil which seek to destroy black being? These are the questions which must shape the character of the norm of black theology.

On the other hand, black theology must not overlook biblical revelation. This means that black theology should not devise a norm which ignores the encounter of the black community with the revelation of God. Whatever it says about liberation must be said in the light of the black experience of Jesus Christ. The failure of many black radicals to win the enthusiasm of the black community may be due to their inability to take seriously the religious character inherent in that community. It is not possible to speak meaningfully to the black community about liberation unless it is analyzed from a Christian perspective which centers on Jesus Christ. This accounts for the influence of Martin Luther King, Jr.

As a prophet, with a charisma never before witnessed in this century, King preached black liberation in the light of Jesus Christ and thus aroused the spirit of freedom in the black community. To be sure, one may argue that his method of nonviolence did not meet the needs of the black community in an age of black power; but it is beyond question that it was King's influence and leadership in the black community which brought us to the period in which we now live, and for that we are in debt. His life and message demonstrate that the "soul" of the black community is inseparable from liberation but always liberation grounded in Jesus Christ. The task of black theology is to build on the foundation laid by King by recognizing the theological character of the black community, a community whose being is inseparable from liberation through Jesus Christ.

This is an awesome task for black theology. It is so easy to sacrifice one for the other. There is a tendency, on the one hand, to deny the relevance of Jesus Christ for black liberation, especially in view of white prostitution of the gospel in the interests of slavery and white supremacy. One can be convinced that Jesus Christ is the savior and God of whites and thus can have nothing to do with black self-determination. And yet, what other name is there? The name of Jesus has a long history in the black community. Blacks know the source from which the name comes, but they also know the reality to which that name refers. Despite its misuse in the white community (even the devil is not prohibited from adopting God's name), the black community is convinced of the reality of Jesus Christ's presence and his total identification with their suffering. They never believed that slavery was his will. Every time a white master came to his death, blacks believed that it was the work of God inflicting just judgment in recompense for the suffering of God's people. Black theology cannot ignore this spirit in the black community if it is going to win the enthusiasm of the community it serves.

Black theology must also avoid the opposite error of speaking of Jesus Christ without reference to black liberation. The post–Civil War black church committed this error. It turned to the white Jesus who always speaks to blacks in terms of white interest and power. He tells blacks that love means turning the other cheek; that the only way to win political freedom is through nonviolence; he even praises Martin Luther King, Jr., for his devotion to him, though he knows that King was always his enemy in spirit and that he chose King because he thought King was the least of the evils available. The white Jesus tries to convince us that there is no difference between American democracy and Christian freedom, that violence is no way to respond to inhumanity.

Black theology must realize that the white Jesus has no place in the black community, and it is our task to destroy him. We must replace him with the black messiah, as Albert Cleage would say, a messiah who sees his existence as inseparable from black liberation and the destruction of white racism.

The norm of black theology must take seriously two realities, actually two aspects of a single reality: the liberation of blacks and the revelation of Jesus Christ. With these two realities before us, what is the norm of black theology? *The norm of all God-talk which seeks to be black-talk is the manifestation of Jesus as the black Christ who provides the necessary soul for black liberation.* This is the hermeneutical principle for black theology which guides its interpretation of the meaning of contemporary Christianity. Black theology refuses to accept any norm which does not focus on Jesus Christ, because he is the essence of the Christian gospel. But when we speak of the Christian gospel, we have merely scratched the surface by saying Jesus is at its center. It is so easy to make his name mean intellectual analysis, and we already have too much of that garbage in seminary libraries. What is needed is an application of the name to concrete human affairs. What does the name mean when black people are burning buildings and white people are responding with riot-police control? Whose side is Jesus on? The norm of black theology, which identifies revelation as a manifestation of the black Christ, says that he is those very blacks whom white society shoots and kills. The contemporary Christ is in the black ghetto, making decisions about white existence and black liberation.

Of course, this interpretation of theology will seem strange to most whites, and even some blacks will wonder whether it is really true that Christ is black. But the truth of the statement is not dependent on white or black affirmation, but on the reality of Christ himself who is presently breaking the power of white racism. This and this alone is the norm for black-talk about God.

3

The Meaning of Revelation

If we are going to speak about God and God's movement in the world, it will be necessary to analyze the methodological procedure which enables us to recognize God's activity. This raises the question concerning the epistemological justification of the Christian faith. How do we know who God is or even that God is involved in our history? The rise of analytical philosophy, with its investigation of the relationship between language and truth, has caused many theological nightmares as religionists have sought to defend the validity of theological speech. Religionists can be thankful to the philosophy of language for subjecting theological speech to the analytical test. Even though we insist that truth is determined only by an oppressed community asserting its existence in an oppressive world, and not by an "uncommitted" philosopher of language applying an "objective" test, the logic of analytical philosophy does make us more sensitive in our use of language and forces us to subject our own language to tests devised by the community itself. Every community must ask, How do we know that our claims about God are valid? Every community which speaks about God must analyze the meaning of that speech by subjecting it to analytical tests which are in harmony with the perspective of the community. It is the task of theology to explicate coherently the validity of the knowledge of God claimed by a community.

Of course, this does not mean that theology should be able to prove that Christianity is superior to other worldviews. In this world of ours, with so many sharply divergent perspectives, it is not possible to know what constitutes proof or superiority. We are living in an immensely complex world, and our finite existence cannot qualify us to postulate absolute value judgments. We should be especially suspicious of religionists who claim that their view of things is better than that of others. In the words of Pascal, "Men never do evil so fully and so happily as when they do it for conscience's sake."[1] What authentic Christians know (and do not know—an element which enables them to act with *conviction* but never dogmatism) is their unwillingness to accept the world as it is. Children were not created for torture, and men and women were not created to have their dignity crushed. We believe that the Christian gospel offers all sincere persons an authentic response to inhumanity by assuring them of God's participation in the struggle to end human suffering. The knowledge of God frees believers to live for their neighbor without having to worry about storing up treasures on earth.

As pointed out in an earlier chapter, the gospel offers no assurance of winning. Again, what could "winning" possibly mean? If it means what white racists mean by it—enslavement of human beings on the alleged basis of white supremacy—then, "God deliver us!" The idea of winning is a hang-up of liberal whites who want to be white and Christian at the same time; but they fail to realize that this approach is a contradiction in terms—Christianity and whiteness are opposites. Therefore, when whites say, "That approach will not win out," our reply must be: "What do you mean? Who's trying to win?"

The only real question for Christians is whether their actions are in harmony with their knowledge of God. And the only ones who are in a position to answer the question concerning the epistemological justification of the knowledge of God are the members of a given Christian community. Others, with some empathy, may give an intellectual evaluation of the perspective of the community, but they cannot tell the community what is or is not true and expect the community to take it seriously. This is especially true for whites who are in the habit of telling blacks what is and is not the appropriate response to white racism, white religionists not excluded. Intrigued by their own expertise in Christian theology, white religionists think they have the moral and intellectual right to determine whether black churches are Christian. They fail to realize that their analysis of Christianity is inseparable from their oppressor-mentality, which shapes everything they say about God.

The development of black theology is an attempt of the black community itself to define what the knowledge of God means for its existence in a white racist society. To ask about the epistemological justification of our claim to the knowledge of God is to ask about the concept of revelation. When a religious community is asked, "How do you know that your assertions about God are valid?" the only reply is, "We know because of revelation." Revelation, then, is the epistemological justification of the claims of a community about ontological reality.

Tillich, of course, is correct when he reminds us that "every epistemological assertion is implicitly ontological."[2] Nevertheless, it is necessary to make rational sense out of the ontological assertions of a community, so that its members will understand more clearly the meaning of their commitment to the ultimate. Therefore, if the theologian is going to make intelligible the community's view of God and humankind, it is necessary to begin with a rational analysis of revelation so that the presuppositional character of Christian theology will be clear from the outset.

Revelation and American Theology

In Protestant Christianity, because of the influence of the so-called Barthian school,[3] the first half of this century will be remembered for the radical reinterpretation of the idea of revelation. Before this period, revelation was largely understood as divine information *about* God communicated to humankind either through reason (natural theology) or through faith (assent to biblical truths). The major exception to this interpretation was Friedrich Schleiermacher's interpretation of religion as a "feeling of absolute dependence." Theology, according to him, rests neither on truths found by reason nor on authoritatively communicated truths of scripture but on the religious self-consciousness of the Christian community. For Schleiermacher, theology was an explication of the meaning of communal self-consciousness.

This approach earned Schleiermacher the title "the father of modern Protestant theology," because his view transcended the old dichotomy between Protestant dogmatism and philosophic rationalism. But there were other problems with this view of the knowledge of God. Ludwig Feuerbach pointed out the dangers of this approach.[4] By using human self-consciousness as a point of departure for God-talk, theology gave credence to the Feuerbachian claim that theology is nothing but anthropology, the idea of God being a projection of human consciousness of its own greatness. Recent studies in Schleiermacher have challenged this view of him; but it is beyond question that he was the most influential religious thinker in the nineteenth century, and that was the century that put its confidence in human nature and human progress. I cannot help but think that Schleiermacher's anthropological point of departure was partly responsible for this. It certainly did not challenge it.

Through the rediscovery of Kierkegaard, the impact of World War I, the failure of the Social Gospel, and the irrelevancy of orthodox views of the verbal infallibility of scripture, the Barthians were led to a new understanding of God's revelation. All agreed that revelation had nothing to do with truths about God communicated through the church, scripture, or reason. Revelation is rather the disclosure of God in the person of Jesus Christ. Revelation is not a rational articulation of human self-consciousness, but an existential encounter in a situation of concern, as Tillich would say. Of course, there were differences among them in their views of revelation. Emil Brunner preferred to speak of the divine-human encounter, which does not deny the reality of general revelation. For Barth, revelation was the Wholly Other God descending on humankind like a bolt from the blue, radically transforming the human situation. Tillich wanted to preserve the cultural relevancy of revelation by emphasizing the "concrete situation of concern." For Bultmann, with his existential orientation, revelation was the means by which human nature attains its own authenticity. But for all these theologians revelation meant a manifestation of God in human history.

Unfortunately the European analysis has done little in helping American theology focus on the central meaning of God's revelation in this country. Barth, Bonhoeffer, and other members of the Confessing Church of Germany were able to relate God's self-disclosure to the existing situation of oppression during the reign of Hitler. Revelation meant that no human order is synonymous with God's order, and that it is better to choose death than assent to the evils of the state. Even Bultmann, with his view of revelation as essentially a spiritual self-understanding and not political discourse, spoke out against the dangers implied in Nazism. In a public lecture, May 2, 1933, he said:

> Ladies and gentlemen! I have made a point never to speak about current politics in my lectures, and I think I also shall not do so in the future. However, it would seem to me unnatural were I to ignore today the political situation in which we begin this new semester. The significance of the political happenings for our entire existence has been brought home to us in such a way that we cannot evade the duty of reflecting on the meaning of our theological work in this situation.[5]

He went on to emphasize the dangers in referring to the state as an "ordinance" of God. To know God as creator is to know the inherent potentiality and actuality of sin, which characterizes every human act. Complete obedience belongs only to God, not to the state.

What is strange, though perhaps understandable, is the silence of American theology regarding God's revelation and the oppressed of the land. Why is it that the idea of *liberation* (inseparable from the biblical view of revelation) is conspicuously absent in theological discussions about the knowledge of God? No sensitive religionist has endeavored to apply the contemporary manifestation of God's revelation to the situation of black humanity. To be sure, American religionists have informed us that God's revelation is a self-disclosure to humankind, in human history, effecting human salvation. But for some reason the contemporary significance of the biblical meaning has been sidestepped.

It seems that white theology has made revelation and redemption into an esoteric word game without much meaning for the world at large. Some of Reinhold Niebuhr's early writings may be an exception, especially his *Moral Man and Immoral Society*.[6] But for the most part, theological discourse in this country has been nothing but a participation in the structures of political oppression under the disguise of freedom and democracy. It is sad that the most blatant expressions of human oppression (the enslavement of black

Americans) have been overlooked in American theology. And that gross sin cannot be forgiven.

Revelation and Black Theology

Black theology agrees with contemporary theology that God's self-disclosure is the distinctive characteristic of divine revelation. Divine revelation is not the rational discovery of God's attributes, or the assent to infallible biblical propositions, or an aspect of human self-consciousness. Rather, revelation has to do with God as God is in personal relationship with humankind effecting the divine will in our history.

But black theology cannot stop here. There is a need to define revelation in such a manner that the definition will, on the one hand, retain the essence of the biblical emphasis and, on the other, be relevant to the situation of oppressed blacks. In the zeal to be biblical, we cannot lose sight of the contemporary situation and what this situation means to the oppressed of the land. If we fail, by ignoring the poor and the unwanted, we become antibiblical. Racists will accept the view of revelation which stresses the self-disclosure of God as long as the interpretation remains antibiblical and thus does not challenge their right to define the limits of black humanity. The fact that racists can also agree on this view of revelation means that there is something lacking in the contemporary interpretation of it.

According to black theology, revelation must mean more than just divine self-disclosure. Revelation is God's self-disclosure to humankind *in the context of liberation*. To know God is to know God's work of liberation in behalf of the oppressed. God's revelation means liberation, an emancipation from death-dealing political, economic, and social structures of society. This is the essence of biblical revelation.

There is no revelation of God without a condition of oppression which develops into a situation of liberation. Revelation is only for the oppressed of the land. God comes to those who have been enslaved and abused and declares total identification with their situation, disclosing to them the rightness of their emancipation on their own terms. God not only reveals to the oppressed the divine right to break their chains by any means necessary, but also assures them that their work in their own liberation is God's own work.

When we apply this view of God's revelation to the existing situation of blacks in America, we immediately realize that the black revolution in America is the revelation of God. Revelation means black power—that is, the "complete emancipation of black people from white oppression by whatever means black people deem necessary."[7] It is blacks telling whites where to get off, and a willingness to accept the consequences.

God's revelation has nothing to do with white suburban ministers admonishing their congregation to be nice to black persons. It has nothing to do with voting for open occupancy or holding a memorial service for Martin Luther King, Jr. God's revelation means a radical encounter with the structures of power which King fought against to his death. It is what happens in a black ghetto when the ghettoized decide to strike against their enemies. In a word, God's revelation means *liberation*—nothing more, nothing less.

The Biblical View of Revelation

The emphasis that black theology puts on liberation as an indispensable ingredient of revelation is inherently biblical. The biblical emphasis on liberation may be approached through an analysis of the relationship of revelation, faith, and history.

In the Bible revelation is inseparable from history and faith. History is the arena in which God's revelation takes place. Unlike many non-Christian religions, the God of the Bible makes the divine will and purpose known through participation in human history. That is why Christianity has been described as a historical religion. It is a religion which affirms that we know who God is by what God does in human history. In fact, there is no revelation of God without history. The two are inseparable.

It is this realization that led Wright and Fuller to publish *The Book of the Acts of God*.[8] They encouraged other biblical scholars to speak of Israelite history as "the history of salvation." In the same vein Rudolf Bultmann's hermeneutical method of demythologizing[9] received some sharp criticism because it seemed to challenge the place of history in Christianity. Most scholars believe that it is not possible to retain the essence of biblical religion without seeing God as a God who is involved in human affairs.

It is important to note the history in which God chose to grant a self-disclosure. It was granted to an oppressed people, and the nature of the revelatory deed was synonymous with the emancipation of that people. The exodus of Israel from Egypt was a revelation-liberation. In this revelatory event, Israel came to know God as the liberator of the oppressed, and also realized that its being as a people was inseparable from divine concomitance. Thus Yahweh was known primarily for the deeds done for Israel when other political powers threatened its existence as a community.

The biblical writers expressed Israel's view of God's revelation by describing Yahweh as a warrior:

> I will sing to the Lord, for he has triumphed gloriously;
>> the horse and his rider he has thrown into the sea.
> The Lord is my strength and my song,
>> and he has become my salvation;
> this is my God, and I will praise him,
>> my father's God, and I will exalt him.
> The Lord is a man of war;
>> the Lord is his name [Exodus 15:1b–3].

In this passage God's revelation means political emancipation, which involves destruction of an enemy. In view of God's overwhelming defeat of the Egyptians, a covenant is made with Israel. The covenant is an expression of God's identification with Israel and the will to be its God and of Israel's will to be God's people. The entire history of Israel is a history of what God has done, is doing, and will do in moments of oppression.

Though God acts in history, only the community of *faith* is able to perceive God's revelation. Revelation, in the bibilical perspective, is inseparable from those with faith to perceive it. Faith, then, is the perspective which enables human beings to recognize God's actions in human history. Other persons could have been aware of the exodus of a small band of Hebrews from Egypt and their subsequent entering into the land of Canaan, thereby establishing themselves as a recognizable community from about the twelfth century B.C.; but only those with the faith of Israel would know that those liberative events were God's self-revelation. They did not happen by chance, nor can they be explained in terms of human capabilities. The only explanation in the eyes of Israel is Yahweh, who saw its affliction in Egypt, took pity on it, and set it free. This is Israel's faith, its way of interpreting its existence as a people. Faith, then, is the existential recognition of a situation of oppression and a participation in God's liberation.

By making revelation a historical happening, the Bible makes faith something other than an ecstatic feeling in moments of silent prayer, or an acceptance of inerrant propositions. Faith is the response of the community to God's act of liberation. It means saying yes to God and no to oppressors. Faith is the existential element in revelation—that is, the community's perception of its being and the willingness to fight against nonbeing.

It is not difficult to make a contemporary application of this view to the plight of black Americans today. Indeed it is difficult to ignore. How could we speak about God's revelation in the exodus, the conquest of Palestine, the role of the judges of Israel without seeing parallels in black history? In Israel the judge was a charismatic leader, endowed with the spirit of Yahweh; he led his people in battle against the enemy. Is it really hard for us to believe that black examples of this would be Nat Turner, Denmark Vesey, and Malcolm X? These leaders represent the "soul" of blackness, and what blacks mean by black liberation. They are the black judges endowed with the spirit of Yahweh for the sole purpose of creating a spirit of freedom among their people.

General and Special Revelation

In the history of theology, it is not uncommon to make a distinction between general revelation and special revelation. General revelation refers to the knowledge of God independent of biblical revelation. Special revelation refers to the knowledge of God through biblical revelation, focusing primarily on Jesus Christ as the sole criterion for knowledge of God.

1. General Revelation. Every student of theology knows of Karl Barth's merciless attack on natural theology, which he believed failed to take due notice of the infinite qualitative distinction between God and the human being. God is God and human beings are human beings and there *is* a difference, according to Barth.

Any form of natural theology which attempts to decide *a priori* what God ought to do is presumption—that is, sin. A passage from Barth's *Epistle to the Romans* reveals the vehemence of his rejection of natural theology:

> God, the pure and absolute boundary and beginning of all that we are and have and do; God, who is distinguished qualitatively from men and from everything human, and must never be identified with anything which we name, or experience, or conceive, or worship, as God; God, who confronts all human disturbance with an unconditional command "Halt," and all human rest with an equally unconditional command "Advance"; God the "Yes" in our "No" and the "No" is our "Yes"; the First and the Last, and, consequently, the Unknown, who is never a known thing in the midst of other known things; God, the Lord, the Creator, the Redeemer:—this is the living God.[10]

Barth is attacking any form of natural theology expounded by liberal theology, as well as all forms of mysticism, especially that form in which persons sink within themselves to find God. In opposition to these views, he affirms that God and human beings are on different levels; they do not move in the same dimensions. If there is to be any relationship between the two, the initiative cannot come from the human side, as the exponents of natural theology assume, but only from God, by God's coming down to the human level, because humans cannot of themselves ascend to God. "God must," writes Barth, "strike down perpendicularly as the vertical line to the horizontal."

Some of Barth's colleagues thought he was going too far. Emil Brunner, once an avid follower, severed his ties with Barth on the issue of general revelation. If we are going to assess Barth's unequivocal stance on general revelation, it will be necessary to take into consideration the *times* in which he lived. His theological stand against general revelation took place during the 1920s and 1930s, the time of Hitler, Stalin, and Roosevelt. It was a time when natural theology tended toward glorification of the state and persecution of Jews. It is noteworthy that when the world situation changed, Barth began to speak about the *Humanity of God*.[11] It was about the same time that blacks in America and other oppressed groups throughout the world began to affirm their being by striking against their oppressors.

The theoretical question, "Is there knowledge of God independent of the Bible?" is irrelevant. It is not the theologian's task to settle logical problems unrelated to human affairs. It is the theologian's task to speak to the times, pointing to God's revelation in current events.

According to black theology, the idea of general revelation is primarily applicable to oppressed peoples. To the extent that we are creatures who rebel against ungodly treatment, God's self-revelation is granted. All human acts against alienative powers of enslavement are acts of God. We do not need to read the Bible to know that human enslavement is ungodly, and that slaves will do everything possible to break their chains. God has created all persons in such a way that none will cooperate contentedly in their own oppression. We are not creatures who can be domesticated. In this sense, whether all persons know what some Christians call special revelation, they nevertheless know God—that is, it is their identity with the divine that makes all slaves rebel against their masters.

Emil Brunner emphasized the idea of general revelation in order to show that all persons are responsible for their sin:

> We distinguish categorically: formally the *imago* is not in the least touched—whether sinful or not, man is a subject and is responsible. Materially the *imago* is completely lost, man is a sinner through and through and there is nothing in him which is not defiled by sin.[12]

For black theology this is especially applicable to oppressors. They are held accountable for their enslavement of the oppressed, and no measure of rationalistic alibis can free them of this responsibility. But we have to be careful in trying to make this aspect of general revelation applicable to the oppressed. In what sense are the oppressed sinners?

In an attempt to speak to this question, I must point out quite clearly that oppressors are in no position to speak about the sinfulness of the oppressed. Black theology rejects categorically white comments about the sins of blacks, suggesting that we are partly responsible for our plight. Not only does such talk provide an ungodly method for easing the guilt of white oppressors, but it also suggests that whites and blacks are one community. Sin is a concept which is meaningful only within the context of a Christian community. It is community recognition that some have lost their *identity* for being. Inasmuch as whites and blacks do not share a common identity, whites cannot possibly know what sin is from a black perspective.

Black theology does not deny that all persons are sinners. What it denies is white reflections on the sin of blacks. Only blacks can speak about sin in a black perspective and apply it to black and white persons. The white vision of reality is too distorted and renders whites incapable of talking to the oppressed about their shortcomings.

According to black theology, the sin of the oppressed is not that they are responsible for their own enslavement—far from it. Their sin is that of trying to "understand" enslavers, to "love" them on their own terms. As the oppressed now recognize their situation in the light of God's revelation, they know that they should have killed their oppressors instead of trying to "love" them.

To summarize general revelation from the perspective of black theology, to say that all persons know God means that human oppression is contradictory to the idea of the holy, and every blow for liberation is the work of God. God will not be without a witness.

2. Special Revelation. Special revelation has always occupied the central role in Christian theology. It means that there has been a self-revelation of God in biblical history and decisively in Jesus Christ. It is this conviction that Karl Barth takes seriously by using christology as the point of departure of his *Church Dogmatics.* God has been fully revealed in the man Jesus so that the norm of all existence is determined exclusively by him. He is *the* revelation of God. For the oppressed this means that authentic movement in the world and one's rebellion against the enemy is found in Christ.

Gordon Kaufmann, who writes systematic theology from a historicist perspective, comments:

To say God's act in Christ is revelatory . . . means that the event of Jesus Christ was an occurrence in and through which God spoke and man heard; that is, here God communicated himself with sufficient effectiveness that man was enabled to appropriate the meaning and respond to it, his existence thus being radically transformed.[13]

When that existence is black existence, such an analysis has far-reaching implications. Through Christ blacks are able to perceive the nature of black being and destroy the forces of nonbeing (white racism). The transformed existence is the new sense of self-evaluation and a new determination to say no to oppressors, and mean it. This is the meaning of special revelation for black theology.

Bultmann's View of New Testament Revelation

Contemporary New Testament scholarship is indebted to Rudolf Bultmann and the form-critical school for seeking to make the New Testament Jesus relevant for today. Like Barth, Bultmann rejected the nineteenth-century liberal attempt to find the Jesus of history so that he could be our contemporary model for the "good" life. Using the hermeneutical method of demythologization, Bultmann abandons all attempts to find the so-called historical Jesus. In his book entitled *Jesus and the Word*, he writes:

I do indeed think that we can know almost nothing concerning the life and personality of Jesus, since the early Christian sources show no interest in either, are moreover fragmentary and often legendary; and other sources about Jesus do not exist.[14]

Forsaking all attempts to locate the Jesus of history, Bultmann seeks to interpret the New Testament in such a way that it *must* become relevant to the existential situation of contemporary humankind. Thus, according to Bultmann:

Revelation is *an occurrence that puts me in a new situation as a self*, in which, to be sure, there is also given the possibility of knowledge (namely, about myself in my new situation). . . . [15]

There can be no revelation which does not provide us with an understanding of our own authenticity:

> The meaning of revelation consists in its being the means whereby we achieve our authenticity, which we cannot achieve by our resources. Therefore, to know about revelation means to know about our own authenticity—and, at the same time, thereby to know our limitations. [16]

It is not hard to recognize existentialist influences upon Bultmann's interpretation, especially that of Martin Heidegger. In Bultmann's view, revelation is not an alien substance which descends on the human situation. It is human beings coming to their own self-understanding, whereby they see both the freedom and the limits of their own existence. Revelation is self-knowledge, a knowledge in which human beings make a decision about their own existence in the world. That is why Bultmann says revelation is a *"personal address."* There can be no revelation which does not involve an existential decision.

By interpreting revelation as a transformation of the self in an existential moment of decision, Bultmann is able to make it something other than a *past* event. "It is precisely an 'eschatological' fact, i.e., the kind of fact in which the world comes to an end." [17] This means that revelation "is understood in its true character only when it is understood as something that takes place in the present, in my particular present." [18] Bultmann believes that revelation becomes contemporary through the preaching of the word in the form of an address. Here the contemporary person has to make a decision: either live or die.

Black theology can agree with some aspects of Bultmann's interpretation. The idea that revelation changes my own self-understanding is crucial for black theology and biblical revelation. It is impossible to view the exodus as an act of God without at the same time seeing it as an act that changes Israel's view of itself as a people. The resurrection of Jesus certainly changed the self-understanding of the disciples. When persons encounter God's self-disclosure, they not only know who God is but also who they are. This is also what the black revolution in America is all about. It is not enough to say that God's revelation is a Christ-event; it is a *black-event*—that is, black persons expressing their being in spite of three hundred and fifty years of white oppression. This is the reality that shapes the black perspective. To know God is to know about ourselves, our beautiful black selves. This is what revelation means to blacks. It is a contemporary decision about a contemporary event, the event of black and white beings.

My major difficulty with Bultmann's view is that it does not take seriously the irreducibly historical character of revelation. If we do not keep revelation within the context of history, then we are free to make it whatever we please. History is inseparable from the biblical view of revelation. Although history is not the "proof" of revelation, it is the context in which the person of faith perceives God's activity. Therefore, revelation is not only my own individualistic self-understanding; it is the self-understanding of a community which sees God at work in history.

Equally important, Bultmann's view fails to express the idea of *liberation*. Revelation is a historical liberation of an oppressed people from slavery. When an oppressed people comes to know who it is, it will not tolerate oppression. This is the key to self-understanding. This is what Paul Tillich calls the courage to be—that is, the courage to affirm one's being in spite of those elements of existence which threaten being.[19] It is the courage to be black in spite of white racists. This is what revelation means in our times.

4

God in Black Theology

The reality of God is presupposed in black theology. Black theology is an attempt to analyze the nature of that reality, asking what we can say about the nature of God in view of God's self-disclosure in biblical history and the oppressed condition of black Americans.

If we take the question seriously, it becomes evident that there is no simple answer to it. To speak of God and God's participation in the liberation of the oppressed of the land is a risky venture in any society. But if the society is racist and also uses God-language as an instrument to further the cause of human humiliation, then the task of authentic theological speech is even more dangerous and difficult.

It is *dangerous* because the true prophet of the gospel of God must become both "anti-Christian" and "unpatriotic." It is impossible to confront a racist society, with the meaning of human existence grounded in commitment to the divine, without at the same time challenging the very existence of the national structure and all its institutions, especially the established churches. All national institutions represent the interests of society as a whole. We live in a nation which is committed to the perpetuation of white supremacy, and it will try to exterminate all who fail to support this ideal. The genocide of the Amerindian is evidence of that fact. Black theology represents that community of blacks who refuse to cooperate in the exaltation of whiteness and the degradation of blackness. It proclaims the reality of the biblical God who is actively destroying everything that is against the manifestation of black human dignity.

Because whiteness by its very nature is against blackness, the black prophet is a prophet of national doom. He proclaims the end of the "American Way," for God has stirred the soul of the black community, and now that community will stop at nothing to claim the freedom that is three hundred and fifty years overdue. The black prophet is a rebel with a cause, the cause of over twenty-five million American blacks and all oppressed persons everywhere. It is God's cause because God has chosen the blacks as God's own people. And God has chosen them not for redemptive suffering but for freedom. Blacks are not elected to be Yahweh's suffering people. Rather we are elected because we are oppressed against our will and God's, and God has decided to make our liberation God's own undertaking. We are elected to be free now to do the work for which we were called into being—namely, the breaking of chains. Black theologians must assume the dangerous responsibility of articulating the revolutionary mood of the black community. This means that their speech about God, in the authentic prophetic tradition, will always move on the brink of treason and heresy in an oppressive society.

The task of authentic theological speech is *difficult* because all religionists in society claim to be for God and thus for humankind. Even executioners are for God. They carry out punitive acts against certain segments of society because "decent" citizens need protection against undesirables. That is why blacks were enslaved and Amerindians exterminated—in the name of God and freedom. That is why today blacks are forced into ghettos and shot down like dogs if they raise a hand in protest.

When George Washington, Thomas Jefferson, Lyndon Johnson, Richard Nixon, and other "great" Americans can invoke the name of God at the same time that they are shaping society for whites only, then black theology knows it cannot approach the God-question too casually. It must ask, "How can we speak of God without being associated with oppressors?" White racism is so pervasive that oppressors can destroy the revolutionary mood among the oppressed by introducing a complacent white God into the black community, thereby quelling the spirit of freedom.

Therefore if blacks want to break their chains, they must recognize the need for going all the way if liberation is to be a reality. The white God will point to heavenly bliss as a means of detouring blacks away from earthly rage. Freedom comes when we realize that it is against our interests, as a self-determining black community, to point out the "good" elements in an oppressive structure. *There are no assets to slavery!* Every segment of society participates in black oppression. To accept the white God, to see good in evil, is to lose sight of the goal of the revolution—the destruction of everything "masterly" in society. "All or nothing" is the only possible attitude for the black community.

Must We Discard God-Language?

Realizing that it is very easy to be co-opted by the enemy and the enemy's God-language, it is tempting to discard all references to God and seek to describe a way of living in the world that could not possibly be associated with "Christian" murderers. Some existentialist writers—Camus and Sartre—have taken this course, and many black revolutionaries find this procedure appealing. Reacting to the ungodly behavior of white churches and the timid, Uncle Tom approach of black churches, many black militants have no time for God and the deadly prattle about loving your enemies and turning the other cheek. Christianity, they argue, participates in the enslavement of black Americans. Therefore an emancipation from white oppression means also liberation from the ungodly influences of white religion.

This approach is certainly understandable, and the merits of the argument warrant a serious investigation. As black theologians seeking to analyze the meaning of black liberation, we cannot ignore this approach. Indeed, it is quite intellectually tempting. Nevertheless two observations are in order at this juncture.

(1) Black theology affirms that there is nothing special about the English word "God" in itself. What is important is the dimension of reality to which it points. The word "God" is a symbol that opens up depths of reality in the world. If the symbol loses its power to point to the meaning of black liberation, then we must destroy it. Black theology asks whether the word "God" has lost its liberating power. Must we say that as a meaningful symbol the word "God" is hopelessly dead and cannot be resurrected?

Certainly black theology realizes that, when a society performs ungodly acts against the poor in the name of God, there may come a time when the oppressed might have to renounce all claims to that kind of "faith" in God in order to affirm authentic faith in God. Sometimes because of the very nature of oppressed existence, the oppressed must define their being by negating everything oppressors affirm, including belief in the God of oppressors. The oppressed must demonstrate that all communications are cut off. In Camus's words:

> There is, in fact, nothing in common between a master and a slave; it is impossible to speak and communicate with a person who has been reduced to servitude.[1]

Oppressed and oppressors cannot possibly mean the same thing when they speak of God. The God of the oppressed is a God of revolution who breaks the chains of slavery. The oppressors' God is a God of slavery and must be destroyed along with the oppressors. The question then, as black theology sees it, is not whether blacks believe in God, but whose God?

(2) In response to those inclined to discard God-language, black theology also believes that the destiny of blacks is inseparable from the religious dimensions inherent in the black community. Theologically, one way of describing this reality is to call it general revelation. This means that all human beings have a sense of the presence of God, a feeling of awe, and it is precisely this experience that makes them creatures who always rebel against domestication. The black community is thus a religious community, a community that views its liberation as the work of the divine.

It is important to note that every significant black liberation movement has had its religious dimensions. Black liberation as a movement began with the pre-Civil War black churches which recognized that Christian freedom grounded in Jesus Christ was inseparable from civil freedom. That is why black preachers were the leaders in the struggle for the abolition of slavery, and why southern slave owners refused to allow the establishment of independent black churches in the south. It is true, however, that the post-Civil War black church lost its emphasis on civil freedom and began to identify Christianity with moral purity. But this does not mean that religion is irrelevant altogether; it only means that religion unrelated to black liberation is irrelevant.

To try to separate black liberation from black religion is a mistake, because black religion is authentic only when it is identified with the struggle for black freedom. The influence of Marcus Garvey, Elijah Muhammed, Malcolm X, and Martin Luther King, Jr., demonstrates the role of religion in the black community.

It is not the task of black theology to remove the influence of the divine in the black community. Its task is to interpret the divine element in the forces and achievements of black liberation. Black theology must retain God-language despite its perils, because the black community perceives its identity in terms of divine presence. Black theology cannot create new symbols independent of the black community and expect blacks to respond. It must stay in the black community and get down to the real issues at hand ("cutting throats" to use LeRoi Jones's phrase) and not waste too much time discussing the legitimacy of religious language.

The legitimacy of any language, religious or otherwise, is determined by its usefulness in the struggle for liberation. That the God-language of white religion has been used to create a docile spirit among blacks so that whites could aggressively attack them is beyond question. But that does not mean that we cannot kill the white God, so that the presence of the black God can become known in the black-white encounter. The white God is an idol created by racists, and we blacks must perform the iconoclastic task of smashing false images.

Hermeneutical Principle for the Doctrine of God

Every doctrine of God is based on a particular theological methodology. For instance, Karl Barth's theological point of departure is the word of God as revealed in the man Jesus. We know who God is, according to Barth, because we know who Christ is. To look for the knowledge of God other than in Christ is to look in the wrong place, and thus end up constructing images which reflect human pride rather than divine revelation. "The knowledge of God occurs in the fulfillment of the revelation of His Word by the Holy Spirit."[2]

Paul Tillich, on the other hand, does not share Barth's kerygmatic emphasis. His theological methodology is a "method of correlation," in which he seeks to relate the changeless gospel to changing cultural situations. Culture, according to Tillich, is indispensable for God-talk.

Relying heavily on existential philosophy and its analysis of the human condition (a condition best described by the word "estrangement"), Tillich describes God as being-itself, which provides the only answer to human estrangement from self and neighbor. Because being-itself is free from the threat of nonbeing or nothingness, it is the source of human courage—the ability to affirm being in spite of the presence of nonbeing. Therefore "God" is a symbolic word pointing to the dimension of reality which is the answer to the human condition.

Inasmuch as the perspective of black theology differs from that of both Barth and Tillich, there is also a difference in its approach to the doctrine of God. The point of departure of black theology is the biblical God as related to the black liberation struggle. It asks, "How do we *dare* speak of God in a suffering world, a world in which blacks are humiliated because they are black?" This question, which occupies the central place in our theological perspective, forces us to say nothing about God that does not participate in the emancipation of black humanity. God-talk is not Christian-talk unless it is *directly* related to the liberation of the oppressed. Any other talk is at best an intellectual hobby, and at worst blasphemy.

There are, then, two hermeneutical principles which are operative in the black theology analysis of the doctrine of God.

(1) The Christian understanding of God arises from the biblical view of revelation, a revelation of God that takes place in the liberation of oppressed Israel and is completed in the incarnation, in Jesus Christ. This means that whatever is said about the nature of God and God's being-in-the-world must be based on the biblical account of God's revelatory activity. We are not free to say anything we please about God. Although scripture is not the only source that helps us to recognize divine activity in the world, it cannot be ignored if we intend to speak of the Holy One of Israel.

(2) The doctrine of God in black theology must be of the God who is participating in the liberation of the oppressed of the land. This hermeneutical principle arises out of the first. Because God has been revealed in the history of oppressed Israel and decisively in the Oppressed One, Jesus Christ, it is impossible to say anything

about God without seeing him as being involved in the contemporary liberation of all oppressed peoples. The God in black theology is the God of and for the oppressed, the God who comes into view in their liberation. Any other approach is a denial of biblical revelation.

New Wine in New Wineskins

Because black theology is the theology of black liberation, it must break with traditional theological speech when that speech softens the drive for black self-determination. It cannot run the risk of putting "new wine into old wineskins" (Mark 2:22). When Jesus used the phrase, he was referring to the kingdom of God and its relationship to the conventional Judaism of his time.

When black theologians analyze the doctrine of God, seeking to relate it to the emerging black revolution in America, they must be especially careful not to put this new wine (the revelation of God as expressed in black power) into old wineskins (white folk-religion). The black theology view of God must be sharply distinguished from white distortions of God. This does not mean that black theology rejects white theology entirely. Unfortunately, this cannot be done, for oppression always means that the communication skills of an oppressed community are determined to a large degree by the oppressors. That is precisely the meaning of oppression! Because black theologians are trained in white seminaries, and white thinkers make decisions about the structure and scope of theology, it is not possible for black religionists to separate themselves immediately and completely from white thought.

When Jesus spoke of the gospel as new wine, it did not mean a total rejection of Judaism. What he meant was that the revolutionary message could not be restricted to the possibilities available in the old structure.

Similarly, because our knowledge of Christianity came from white oppressors, the black theology view of God is in part dependent on white theologians, but this does not mean white theologians set the criteria for black theology. Liberation means that the oppressed must define the structure and scope of reality for themselves; they do not take their cues from oppressors. If there is one brutal fact that the centuries of white oppression have taught blacks, it is that whites are incapable of making any valid judgment about human existence. The goal of black theology is the destruction of *everything* white, so that blacks can be liberated from alien gods.

The God of black liberation will not be confused with a blood-thirsty white idol. Black theology must show that the black God has nothing to do with the God worshiped in white churches whose primary purpose is to sanctify the racism of whites and to daub the wounds of blacks. Putting new wine in new wineskins means that the black theology view of God has nothing in common with those who prayed for an American victory in Vietnam or who pray for a "cool" summer in the ghetto.

The refusal of black theology to put new wine in old wineskins also means that it will show that the God of the black community cannot be confused with the God of white seminaries. With their intellectual expertise, it is inevitable that white scholars fall into the racist error of believing that they have the right to define what is and what is not orthodox religious talk. Because they have read so many of their own books and heard themselves talk so often, it is not surprising that they actually believe most of the garbage they spout out about God. They therefore think that all authentic God-talk must meet their approval before it can be called theology. But black theology rejects their standards, for we know they speak for oppressors, and thus will inevitably analyze the nature of God in the interests of white society as a whole.

Black theology must also be suspicious of so-called white revolutionary theologians. What is most disturbing about their self-proclaimed identification with black power is their inability to let *us* speak for ourselves. They still insist on defining what black power is, and not only in private conversations but also in print. And to make it worse, they invariably miss the whole point of black power. They should know by now that, in view of white brutality against blacks and church participation in it, no white person who is halfway sensitive to black self-determination should have the audacity to speak for blacks. That is the problem! *Too many whites think they know how we feel about them.* If whites were really serious about their radicalism in regard to the black revolution and its theological implications in America, they would keep silent and take instructions from blacks. Only blacks can speak about God in

"There is no place in black theology for a colorless ~~object~~ God in a society where human beings suffer precisely because of their color" (Cone 63).

- Goes onto say that if God doesn't accept blacks for who they are and praises whites for who they are, then God is a racist. A black God takes the suffering into his own hands

er year and suggests feasible
udies.

nent and implementation of two quality
ing and evaluation studies and follow-
ent outcomes per year. Helps develop
it quality improvement plan.

ment quality improvement plan, but
follow through with development and
iitoring and evaluation studies.

ility and department quality
s.

14

relationship to their liberation. And those who wish to join us in this divine work must be willing to lose their white identity—indeed, destroy it.

Black theology also rejects any identification with the "death of God" theology. The death-of-God question is a white issue which arises out of the white experience. Questions like "How do we find meaning and purpose in a world in which God is absent?" are questions of an affluent society. Whites may wonder how to find purpose in their lives, but our purpose is forced upon us. We do not want to know how we can get along without God, but how we can survive in a world permeated with white racism.

God Is Black

Because blacks have come to know themselves as *black,* and because that blackness is the cause of their own love of themselves and hatred of whiteness, the blackness of God is the key to our knowledge of God. The blackness of God, and everything implied by it in a racist society, is the heart of the black theology doctrine of God. There is no place in black theology for a colorless God in a society where human beings suffer precisely because of their color. The black theologian must reject any conception of God which stifles black self-determination by picturing God as a God of all peoples. Either God is identified with the oppressed to the point that their experience becomes God's experience, or God is a God of racism.

As Camus has pointed out, authentic identification

[Is not] a question of psychological identification—a mere subterfuge by which the individual imagines that it is he himself who is being offended. . . . [It is] identification of one's destiny with that of others and a choice of sides.[3]

Because God has made the goal of blacks God's own goal, black theology believes that it is not only appropriate but necessary to begin the doctrine of God with an insistence on God's blackness.

The blackness of God means that God has made the oppressed condition God's own condition. This is the essence of the biblical revelation. By electing Israelite slaves as the people of God and by becoming the Oppressed One in Jesus Christ, the human race is made to understand that God is known where human beings experience humiliation and suffering. It is not that God feels sorry and takes pity on them (the condescending attitude of those racists who need their guilt assuaged for getting fat on the starvation of others); quite the contrary, God's election of Israel and incarnation in Christ reveal that the *liberation* of the oppressed is a part of the innermost nature of God. Liberation is not an afterthought, but the essence of divine activity.

The blackness of God means that the essence of the nature of God is to be found in the concept of liberation. Taking seriously the Trinitarian view of the Godhead, black theology says that as Creator, God identified with oppressed Israel, participating in the bringing into being of this people; as Redeemer, God became the Oppressed One in order that all may be free from oppression; as Holy Spirit, God continues the work of liberation. The Holy Spirit is the Spirit of the Creator and the Redeemer at work in the forces of human liberation in our society today. In America, the Holy Spirit is black persons making decisions about their togetherness, which means making preparation for an encounter with whites.

It is the black theology emphasis on the blackness of God that distinguishes it sharply from contemporary white views of God. White religionists are not capable of perceiving the blackness of God, because their satanic whiteness is a denial of the very essence of divinity. That is why whites are finding and will continue to find the black experience a disturbing reality.

White theologians would prefer to do theology without reference to color, but this only reveals how deeply racism is embedded in the thought forms of their culture. To be sure, they would *probably* concede that the concept of liberation is essential to the biblical view of God. But it is still impossible for them to translate the biblical emphasis on liberation to the black-white struggle today. Invariably they quibble on this issue, moving from side to side, always pointing out the dangers of extremism on both sides. (In the black community, we call this "shuffling.") They really cannot make a decision, because it has already been made for them.

How scholars would analyze God and blacks was decided when black slaves were brought to this land, while churchmen sang

"Jesus, Lover of My Soul." Their attitude today is no different from that of the bishop of London who assured slaveholders that:

> Christianity, and the embracing of the Gospel, does not make the least Alteration in Civil property, or in any Duties which belong to Civil Relations; but in all these Respects, it continues Persons just in the same State as it found them. The Freedom which Christianity gives, is a Freedom from the Bondage of Sin and Satan, and from the dominion of Man's Lust and Passions and inordinate Desires; but as to their outward Condition, whatever that was before, whether bond or free, their being baptized and becoming Christians, makes no matter of change in it.[4]

Of course white theologians today have a "better" way of putting it, but what difference does that make? It means the same thing to blacks. "Sure," as the so-called radicals would say, "God is concerned about blacks." And then they would go on to talk about God and secularization or some other white problem unrelated to the emancipation of blacks. This style is a contemporary white way of saying that "Christianity . . . does not make the least alteration in civil property."

In contrast to this racist view of God, black theology proclaims God's blackness. Those who want to know who God is and what God is doing must know who black persons are and what they are doing. This does not mean lending a helping hand to the poor and unfortunate blacks of society. It does not mean joining the war on poverty! Such acts are sin offerings that represent a white way of assuring themselves that they are basically "good" persons. Knowing God means being on the side of the oppressed, becoming *one* with them, and participating in the goal of liberation. *We must become black with God!*

It is to be expected that whites will have some difficulty with the idea of "becoming *black* with God." The experience is not only alien to their existence as they know it to be, it appears to be an impossibility. "How can whites become black?" they ask. This question always amuses me because they do not really want to lose their precious white identity, as if it is worth saving. They know, as everyone in this country knows, blacks are those who say they are black, regardless of skin color. In the literal sense a black person is anyone who has "even one drop of black blood in his or her veins."

But "becoming black with God" means more than just saying "I am black," if it involves that at all. The question "How can white persons become black?" is analogous to the Philippian jailer's question to Paul and Silas, "What must I do to be saved?" The implication is that if we work hard enough at it, we can reach the goal. But the misunderstanding here is the failure to see that blackness or salvation (the two are synonymous) is the work of God, not a human work. It is not something we accomplish; it is a gift. That is why Paul and Silas said, "Believe in the Lord Jesus and you will be saved."

To *believe* is to receive the gift and utterly to reorient one's existence on the basis of the gift. The gift is so unlike what humans expect that when it is offered and accepted, we become completely new creatures. This is what the Wholly Otherness of God means. God comes to us in God's blackness, which is wholly unlike whiteness. To receive God's revelation is to become black with God by joining God in the work of liberation.

Even some blacks will find this view of God hard to handle. Having been enslaved by the God of white racism so long, they will have difficulty believing that God is identified with their struggle for freedom. Becoming one of God's disciples means rejecting whiteness and accepting themselves as they are in all their physical blackness. This is what the Christian view of God means for blacks.

The Love and Righteousness of God

The theological statement "God is love" is the most widely accepted assertion regarding the nature of God. All theologians would agree that it is impossible to speak of the Christian understanding of God without affirming the idea of love as essential to the divine nature. Anders Nygren's *Agape and Eros*[5] is the classic treatment of the subject, and he shows, perhaps conclusively, that *agape* is inseparable from the authentic Christian view of God. When religionists deviated from the *agape* motif, the result was always a distortion of the authentic Christian conception of God.

Though religionists have agreed that love is indispensable to the

Christian view of God's nature, there has been much disagreement on how the idea of the *wrath* of God is reconciled with the love of God.

Marcion was one of the first to face this problem head-on. According to him, it is impossible to reconcile the Old Testament idea of the righteous God with the New Testament idea of the God of love.[6] The concept of law *(nomos)* is a complete denial of love *(agape)*. Marcion's solution was to insist that the gospel of Christ is completely new and thus has nothing to do with the concept of righteousness (including wrath) as presented in the Old Testament. This led him to posit two Gods, the Creator God of the Old Testament who stressed obedience to the law of righteousness, and the Redeemer God of the New Testament who is the "good" God, the God of love. Interpreting Marcion's view, Nygren writes:

> The message of Christ is marked by the spontaneous love and mercy of the Highest God, shown to strangers, unmotivated and uncalculated. In the Old Testament, on the other hand, man's relation to God is dominated by the idea of retribution, of reward and punishment.[7]

It was to be expected that the church would reject Marcion's view: the early Christian community did not understand its existence as being completely new in the sense of negating the God of the Old Testament. The early Christians believed that they were the authentic continuation of the old Israel, not its denial. Jesus, therefore, did not destroy the Old Testament; he fulfilled it.

Although the church rejected Marcion's sharp dichotomy between the Old Testament view of God's righteousness and the New Testament view of God's love in Jesus Christ, there is still much confusion about the precise relationship between the two "symbols"[8] when applied to God's nature. The most common procedure is to emphasize God's love as the dominant motif of Christianity and then interpret God's righteousness in the light of it. But this approach fails to take seriously the concept of God's righteousness and tends to make God's love mere sentimentality. By emphasizing the love of God to the exclusion of a meaningful encounter of God's righteousness, we could argue that the approach is basically Marcionite, except that Marcion was more honest. Marcion claimed that the idea of righteousness is *basic* to the Old Testament view of God, and he was right in this. He further suggested that the idea of love as revealed in Christ is a negation of the Old Testament view of righteousness, and he was wrong in this.

Most religionists, although rejecting the Marcion dichotomy, proceed to analyze the concept of the love of God without relating it to God's righteousness. Marcion's position presents us with two alternatives. Either we agree with him and his view of the two Gods, Righteousness and Love, or we affirm the basic oneness of God's righteousness and love, and that means that God's love is inexplicable without equal emphasis on God's righteousness and vice versa. Contemporary theology seems to want to have its cake and eat it too—that is, reject the Marcionite view and also accept a view of love that ignores righteousness, and that is not possible.

Gordon Kaufmann's work, *Systematic Theology: A Historicist Perspective,* seems to be open to this criticism. Particularly concerned about protecting the idea of love in God's nature, Kaufmann says that it is improper to speak of the "wrath" of God as an expression of the being of God. Love is essential, but the idea of wrath is an expression of human disobedience and can be understood only by looking at human nature, not God's nature:

> The wrath of God is a symbol more appropriate to discussion of the nature (and plight) of *man* than God. . . . The man hanging on the cross . . . reveals God's nature as long-suffering love, not vengeance or wrath in any sense. . . . Hence, in our direct exposition of the doctrine of God such symbols as "wrath" would only be misleading and should be avoided: God reveals himself as love and faithfulness, and this it is that we must seek to grasp here.[9]

Black theology agrees that the idea of love is indispensable to the Christian view of God. The exodus, the call of Israel into being as the people of the covenant, the gift of the promised land, the rise of prophecy, the second exodus, and above all the incarnation reveal God's self-giving love to oppressed humanity.

We do not read far in the biblical tradition without recognizing that the divine-human fellowship is to be understood exclusively in terms of what God does for humankind and not what humankind does for itself or for God. That is why Nygren is correct in describing God's *agape* as the "initiation of the fellowship with God,"[10] and why it is appropriate for Barth to emphasize the complete freedom of God in the divine-human encounter. If the incarnation means anything in Christian theology, it must mean that "God so loved the world that he gave his only Son, that whoever believes in him should not perish but have eternal life" (John 3:16).

The love of God is the heart of the Christian gospel. As the writer of I John puts it, "God is love" (4:8, 16). Commenting on the theological implications of this phrase, C. H. Dodd writes:

> To say "God is love" implies that *all* His activity is loving activity. If He creates, He creates in love; if He rules, He rules in love; if He judges, He judges in love. All that He does is the expression of His nature which is—to love.[11]

Black theology, then, asks not whether love is an essential element of the Christian interpretation of God, but whether the love of God itself can be properly understood without focusing equally on the biblical view of God's righteousness. Is it possible to understand what God's love means for the oppressed without making *wrath* an essential ingredient of that love? What could love possibly mean in a racist society except the righteous condemnation of everything racist? Most theological treatments of God's love fail to place the proper emphasis on God's wrath, suggesting that love is completely self-giving without any demand for obedience. Bonhoeffer called this "cheap grace":

> Cheap grace means grace as a doctrine, a principle, a system. It means forgiveness of sins proclaimed as a general truth, the love of God taught as the Christian "conception" of God.[12]

The difficulty with Kaufmann's view and others like his is not so much his explicit statements but their false implications. By removing wrath as a symbol of the nature of God, his interpretation weakens the central biblical truth about God's liberation of the oppressed from oppressors. A God without wrath does not plan to do too much liberating, for the two concepts belong together. A God minus wrath seems to be a God who is basically not against anything. All we have to do is behave nicely, and everything will work out all right.

Such a view of God leaves us in doubt about God's role in the black-white struggle. Blacks want to know whose side God is on and what kind of decision God is making about the black revolution. We will not accept a God who is on everybody's side—which means that God loves everybody in spite of who they are, and is working (through the acceptable channels of society, of course) to reconcile all persons to the Godhead.

Black theology cannot accept a view of God which does not represent God as being for oppressed blacks and thus against white oppressors. Living in a world of white oppressors, blacks have no time for a neutral God. The brutalities are too great and the pain too severe, and this means we must know where God is and what God is doing in the revolution. There is no use for a God who loves white oppressors *the same as* oppressed blacks. We have had too much of white love, the love that tells blacks to turn the other cheek and go the second mile. What we need is the divine love as expressed in black power, which is the power of blacks to destroy their oppressors, here and now, by any means at their disposal. Unless God is participating in this holy activity, we must reject God's love.

The interpretation of God's love without righteousness also suggests that white "success" is a sign of God's favor, of God's love. Kaufmann's view is open to the ungodly assumption that all is well with the way whites live in the world, because God loves them, and their material success is the evidence. But according to black theology, it is blasphemy to say that God loves white oppressors unless that love is interpreted as God's wrathful activity against them and everything that whiteness stands for in American society. If the wrath of God is God's almighty no to the yes of human beings, then blacks want to know where the no of God is today in white America. We believe that the black community's no as expressed in the black revolution is God's no, showing God's rejection of oppressors and acceptance of the oppressed.

Kaufmann's view also suggests that there is knowledge of God as God is *in se*. Theologically this seems impossible. We can know God only in relationship to the human race, or more particularly in God's liberating activity in behalf of oppressed humanity. The attempt to analyze God independently of God's liberating work is analogous to the theological attempt to understand human nature *before* the fall. The fall itself renders such knowledge impossible: there is no way to get behind the human condition as we know it to be.

The limitation of human knowledge is equally true in regard to God as God is *in se*. We are not permitted to transcend our finiteness and rise to a vision of God unrelated to the human condition. If this is true, what merit is there in saying that God's wrath is not a part of the divine nature? If God is a God of the oppressed of the land, as the revelation of Christ discloses, then wrath is an indispensable element for describing the scope and meaning of God's liberation of the oppressed. The wrath of God is the love of God in regard to the forces opposed to liberation of the oppressed.

Love without righteousness is unacceptable to blacks: this view of God is a product of the minds of enslavers. By emphasizing the complete self-giving of God in Christ, without seeing also the content of righteousness, oppressors could then demand that the oppressed do likewise. If God freely enters into self-donation, then in order to be godlike we must give ourselves to our oppressors in like manner. If God has loved us in spite of our revolt against God, then to be like God we too must love those who revolt against or enslave us. For blacks this would mean letting whites crowd us into ghettos where rats and filth eat away at our being, and not raising a hand against them.

This view of love places no obligation on white oppressors. The existing laws of society protect them, and their white skins are badges of acceptance. In fact, they are permitted to do whatever they will against blacks, assured that God loves them as well as the ones they oppress. Love means that God will accept white oppressors, and blacks will not seek reprisal.

Black theology rejects this view, saying that those who oppress others are in no position to define what love is. How could white scholars know that love means turning the other cheek? They have never had to do so. Only those who live in an oppressed condition can know what their love-response ought to be to their oppressors. Their oppressors certainly cannot answer that question for them!

This means that all white intellectual disputation about blacks and God is a religious lie. If oppressors themselves, who claim to be followers of the love-ethic, would actually practice what they preach, then the oppressed condition would no longer exist. There is something demonic about whites who have the protection of the state but advise blacks to go the second mile for them. They have not moved even an inch for blacks: how can they claim to be speaking from a common perspective called Christianity?

It takes a special kind of reasoning to conclude that God's love means that God is no respecter of persons in a society filled with hate, where some think they have the right to define the course of human history for all. Ungodly in their very relationship to blacks, they want to tell us what God's love means. There is only one explanation for this attitude. They are white and can think only in white thought-patterns, even in reference to God. How else do we explain that the white theological view of God's love invariably complements or shores up outrageous socio-political structures that want blacks to be complacent and obedient to white enemies? Can they really expect blacks to take them seriously?

The oppressor's view of God's love is rejected by black theologians because they represent a people that shares Frantz Fanon's feelings about the world:

> All the native has seen in his country is that they can freely arrest him, beat him, starve him: and no professor of ethics, no priest has ever come to be beaten in his place, nor to share their bread with him. As far as the native is concerned, morality is very concrete; it is to silence the settler's defiance, to break his flaunting violence—in a word, to put him out of the picture.[13]

Black theology will accept only a love of God which participates in the destruction of the white oppressor. With Fanon, black theology takes literally Jesus' statement, "the last will be first, and the first last." Black power "is the putting into practice of this sentence."[14]

Blacks cannot adhere to a view of God that will weaken their drive for liberation. This means that in a racist society, we must insist that God's love and God's righteousness are two ways of talking about the same reality. Righteousness means that God is addressing the black condition; love means that God is doing so in the interests of both blacks and whites. The blackness of God points to the righteousness of God, as well as to the love of God.

Paul Tillich, in another connection, has placed a similar emphasis. Though he refuses to say that wrath is a part of God's being, it is to his credit that he has insisted that divine love and justice should not be separated:

> Justice is that side of love which affirms the independent right to object and subject within the love relation. [Because love is the reunion of the estranged, it] does not destroy the freedom of the beloved and does not violate the structures of the beloved's individual and social existence.[15]

This means that justice is the structure necessary for the human expression of human freedom. To be God, God must protect both the freedom and the structure of human behavior. That is why Tillich rejects sentimental misinterpretations of love as emotion, which suggest that there is a conflict between divine love and its relationship to power and justice. The three are inseparable, according to Tillich:

> It must be emphasized that it is not divine power as such which is thought to be in conflict with the divine love. The divine power is the power of being-itself, and being-itself is actual in the divine life whose nature is love. A conflict can be imagined only in relation to the creature who violates the structure of justice and so violates love itself. When this happens . . . judgment and condemnation follow. . . . Condemnation then is not the negation of love but the negation of the negation of love.[16]

What, then, can we conclude about the meaning of God's love in a racist society? Using blackness as the point of departure, black theology believes that God's love of humankind is revealed in God's willingness to become black. God's love is incomprehensible apart from blackness. This means that to love blacks God takes on black oppressed existence, becoming one of us. God is black because God loves us; and God loves us because we are black.

Righteousness is that side of God's love which expresses itself through black liberation. God makes black what humans have made white. Righteousness is that aspect of God's love which prevents it from being equated with sentimentality. Love is a refusal to accept whiteness. To love is to make a decision against white racism. Because love means that God meets our needs, God's love for white oppressors could only mean wrath—that is, a destruction of their whiteness and a creation of blackness.

For black theology love cannot be discussed in the abstract. It must be concrete because black suffering is concrete. Black suffering is whites making decisions about our place in the world, telling us what we can or cannot do in society. Love must be brought down to this level, the reality of white inhumanity against the black community. As Fanon says, "no phraseology can be a substitute for reality."[17] That is why black theology says that God's love is God's liberation of blacks as expressed in black power.

Traditional Theological Language and the Black God

One of the major tasks of black theology is that of making sense out of the traditional theological talk about God. It asks, in regard to every theological assertion, "What are its implications for the oppressed?" Or, more specifically, "Does it have any meaning in the struggle for black liberation in America?" Believing that the biblical God is made known through the liberation of the oppressed, the black theology analysis of God begins with an emphasis on God's blackness.

But now we must ask, How is the concept of the blackness of God related to such traditional divine symbols as creator, transcendence, immanence, and providence?

1. God as Creator. The biblical view of God as creator is expressed in the priestly assertion, "In the beginning God created the heavens and the earth" (Genesis 1:1). To speak of God as creator means that the world and everything that is *is* because of the creative will of God. In traditional theological language, God as creator expresses aseity—that is, the total independence of God from creation. God is self-existent, meaning that the source of God's existence is found in God.

In order to emphasize the absolute sovereignty of God over creation, traditional theology introduced the idea of creation out of nothing *(ex nihilo)*. The purpose is to deny that God used an eternal substance (as in Plato) in the creation of the universe. The existence of an eternal substance would compromise the complete lordship of God over creation. God is fully free, Being without limitations.

Black theology is not interested in debating the philosophical and theological merits of God's aseity except as it can be related to the earthly emancipation of the oppressed. What has the idea of God's self-existence to do with the existence of the oppressed? First it is necessary to point out that the biblical view of God as creator is not a paleontological statement about the nature and origin of the universe, but a theological assertion about God and God's relationship to the oppressed of the land.

It is important to remember that the priestly narrative was put together during the Babylonian exile as an attempt to make theological sense of the history of Israel as an oppressed people. Therefore, it is impossible to remain faithful to the biblical viewpoint without seeing the doctrine of creation as a statement about God and the oppressed of the land. God as creator means that humankind is a creature; the source of its meaning and purpose in the world is not found in oppressors but in God. This view of God undoubtedly accounts for the exclusivism of Israel in a situation of political oppression.

Though white theologians have emphasized that God as creator is a statement about the divine-human relationship, they have not pointed out the political implications of this theological truth for blacks. God as creator has not been related to the oppressed in society. If creation "involves a bringing into existence of something that did not exist before,"[18] then to say God is creator means that *my being* finds its source in God. *I am black because God is black!* God as creator is the ground of my blackness (being), the point of reference for meaning and purpose in the universe.

If God, not whiteness, is the ground of my being, then God is the only source for reference regarding how I should behave in the world. Complete obedience is owed only to God, and every alien loyalty must be rejected. Therefore, as a black person living in a white world that defines human existence according to white inhumanity, I cannot relax and pretend that all is well with black humanity. Rather it is incumbent upon me by the freedom granted by the creator to deny whiteness and affirm blackness as the essence of God.

That is why it is necessary to speak of the black revolution rather than reformation. The idea of reformation suggests that there is still something "good" in the system itself, which needs only to be cleaned up a bit. This is a false perception of reality. The system is based on whiteness, and what is necessary is a replacement of whiteness with blackness. God as creator means that oppressed humanity is free to revolutionize society, assured that acts of liberation are the work of God.

2. *Immanence and Transcendence of God.* The immanence of God means that God always encounters us in a situation of historical liberation. That is why Christianity is called a historical religion. God is not a symbol referring to the interior religious experiences of humankind. Nor is God to be thought of in the manner of the deist philosophers, who pictured God as performing the initial act of creation but refraining from any further involvement in the world. According to biblical religion, God is involved in the concrete affairs of human history, liberating the oppressed. Therefore to ask, "Who is God?" is to focus on what God is doing; and to look at what God is doing is to center on human events as they pertain to the liberation of suffering humanity.

God, then, is not that pious feeling in our hearts, nor is God a being "out there" or "up there." It is not possible to speak of the reality of the divine in scientific categories. Like the symbol transcendence, immanence is not a causal term. It refers to the depths of liberation in human society, affirming that God is never less than our experience of liberation.

The immanence of God is the infinite expressing itself in the finite. It is God becoming concrete in finite human existence. We are able to speak of the divine because the divine is revealed in the concreteness of this world. The immanence of God forces us to look for God in the world and to make decisions about the Ultimate in terms of present historical reality. We cannot postpone our decision about God or condition it in terms of a future reality. The finality of God is God's involvement in human now-experiences. For blacks this means that God has taken on blackness, has moved into the black liberation struggle.

Though black theology stresses the immanence of God, it does not deny the reality of God's transcendence. The transcendence of God prevents us from deifying our own experiences, which results in pantheism. God is neither nature nor our highest aspirations. God is always more than our experience of God. This means that truth is not limited to human capabilities. It is this reality that frees the rebel to give all for the liberation struggle without having to worry about the Western concept of winning.

When blacks say that "all is in God's hand," this should not be equated with the trite expression "We should do nothing." It should be taken to mean that blacks are now free to be for the black community, to make decisions about their existence in the world without an undue preoccupation with white ideas about "odds" (we have all the guns) or victory (you cannot win). Ultimately (and this is what God's transcendence means) black humanity is not dependent on our power to win. Despite the empirical odds, our involvement in our liberation is not pointless; it is not absurd. It refers to the depth and meaning of our being-in-the-world.

It is interesting that, although white "Christians" say they adhere to the meaning of Jesus Christ's existence in the world, they are especially concerned about "winning." The military budget of this country is evidence of this fact. When confronted with the uncompromising demands of the black community, they quickly remind us that they have all the guns, as if that fact itself is supposed to make blacks "stay in their place." Being "Christian," they should know that Jesus was crucified because he did not "stay in his place."

In fact, that is what authentic Christian existence is all about, *the refusal to stay in one's place.* Of course, this may mean physical death, but death is beside the point when one knows that there is a depth to existence that transcends death. The death and resurrection of Christ were an expression of God's transcendence—that is, human beings do not have to live on the basis of mere physical existence. They are free to transcend it, free to encounter the presence of the infinite, which transcends physical reality. This is why blacks do not have to cling to physical life as if it were the ultimate.

Like immanence, transcendence is not a spatial concept. God is not "above" or "beyond" the world. Rather, transcendence refers to human purpose as defined by the infinite in the struggle for liberation. For blacks this means that their humanity is not defined by sociological reports and scientific studies. There is a transcendent value in blackness that makes us all human and to which blacks must appeal as ultimate. Human dignity transcends human calculation.

Whites try to tell blacks what is "best" for them in scientific terms—as if blackness were subject to white measurements. But to the surprise of whites, blacks reject their definitions, because blacks know that they are not "things" to be computerized and limited according to white predeterminations. We are *free,* free to defy the oppressor's laws of human behavior, because we have encountered the concreteness of the divine in our liberation, which has revealed to us the transcendence of our cause beyond all human definitions.

The tension between the transcendence and immanence of God is what Paul Tillich calls the risk of faith. To speak of God is to speak, on the one hand, of the presence of the infinite in the finite concrete world. On the other hand, the infinite can never be reduced to the finite. Though the infinite is not equated with finite existence, yet because human beings can encounter the infinite only in their finiteness, they must speak of the finite as if it were the ultimate. Tillich calls this "the infinite tension between the absoluteness of its claim and the relativity of its life."[19]

Relating this to black humanity, black theology interprets it to mean that our struggle for liberation is the infinite participating in the concrete reality of human existence. But because God is always more than our experience of God, the reality of God cannot be limited to a particular human experience. However, just because God is more than our encounter of the divine in a particular moment of liberation, this should not be interpreted to mean that we must qualify our assertions about God. Just the opposite. Because God is not less than our experience of the divine, we must speak with an absoluteness that does not compromise with evil, despite the relativity of our claims.

3. Providence. It is difficult to talk about divine providence when men and women are dying and children are tortured. Richard Rubenstein pointed out the dangers of this concept in his excellent book *After Auschwitz.*[20] Whether or not we agree with his conclusion about the death of God, we can appreciate his analysis, based as it is on his identification with an oppressed people. Like black theology, Rubenstein refuses to affirm any view of God which contributes to the oppression of the Jewish people. If God is the Lord of history, directing the course of events toward a final goal, and if the Jews are God's elected people, then there is no way to avoid divine responsibility for the death of six million Jews in Germany, according to Rubenstein. Therefore, rather than accept a view of God that incorporates Jewish blood in the divine plan, he concludes that God is dead. The argument is cogent and certainly advances the death-of-God theology beyond white Christian views as represented in the thinking of William Hamilton and Thomas Altizer.

Rubenstein was not the first to recognize the difficulty of reconciling human suffering and divine participation in history. Without focusing on the God of history, the writer of Job recognized this problem. In more recent writing Albert Camus and the existentialists have dealt with it also. In the thinking of Camus, if God is omnipotent and permits human suffering, then God is a murderer. That is why he quotes Bakunin with approval: "If God did exist, we would have to abolish Him."

Traditional Christian theology somehow fails to take this problem seriously. Although agreeing that human suffering is a reality which appears to conflict with God's love, theologians still insist on quoting Paul with approval: "We know that in everything God works for good with those who love him, who are called according to his purpose" (Romans 8:28).

Emil Brunner's view of divine providence is perhaps representative. He begins by distinguishing between God as creator and God's providential care of the world. Avoiding both pantheism and deism, he writes:

> There is an existence which is not that of God, but is a creaturely existence, one therefore which is distinguished from the existence of God. Without a certain independent existence the creature cannot stand over against God, and if it does not do so, then it is not a creature as contrasted with the Creator. Even if we do not speak of a *creatio continua* we imply that even now God does not cease to create an existence distinct from His own, a manner of existence which is differ-

ent from His. If this be so, then there is also an activity of God in and on this existence which is distinct from himself, in and on the world He has created, which is not the activity of the Creator, but of the Preserver, the Ruler.[21]

After distinguishing providence from God's activity as creator, Brunner proceeds to define the meaning of divine providence. Providence, he says, means that "all that is, and all that happens, takes place within the knowledge and the will of God." There is nothing that happens that does not fit into God's ultimate plan.

> All that happens is connected with the divine Purpose; all is ordered in accordance with, and in subordination to, the divine plan and the final divine purpose.[22]

If providence means what Brunner says, it is difficult, if not impossible, to avoid the conclusion that all human suffering is in accordance with the divine plan. This would mean that the death of six million Jews, the genocide of Amerindians, the enslavement and lynching of blacks, and every other inhumanity, happened "within the knowledge and will of God." Only oppressors can make such a claim.

Of course, my opponents could reply that this view of providence does not mean that God *wills* human suffering. It simply means that God permits it in order to protect human freedom. It means further that, although there is oppression in this world, God does not let humankind have the last word about human existence, but translates human evil into the divine purpose. Quoting Paul with approval, Brunner says, "I reckon that the sufferings of this present time are not worthy to be compared with the glory which shall be revealed in us" (Romans 8:18). The believer looks beyond suffering to the final goal which it must serve; compared with that promised glory, suffering does not count. Suffering becomes the way to eternal life. No human suffering is overlooked by God, and thus providence means that it is redeemable. Thus "the real solution to the problem of theodicy is redemption."[23]

Despite the emphasis on future redemption in present suffering, black theology cannot accept any view of God that even *indirectly* places divine approval on human suffering. The death and resurrection of Jesus does not mean that God promises us a future reality in order that we might tolerate present evil. The suffering that Jesus accepted and which is promised to his disciples is not to be equated with the easy acceptance of human injustice inflicted by white oppressors. God cannot be the God of blacks *and* will their suffering. To be elected by God does not mean freely accepting the evils of oppressors. The suffering which is inseparable from the gospel is that style of existence that arises from a decision to *be* in spite of nonbeing. It is that type of suffering that is inseparable from freedom, the freedom that affirms black liberation despite the white powers of evil. It is suffering in the struggle for liberation.

Providence, then, is not a statement about the future. It does not mean that all things will work out for the best for those who love God. Providence is a statement about present reality—the reality of the liberation of the oppressed. For blacks it is a statement about the reality of blackness and what it means in the liberation struggle against whites. As Tillich says:

> Faith in providence is faith "in spite of"—in spite of the . . . meaninglessness of existence. . . . [Special providence] gives the individual the certainty that under any circumstances, under any set of conditions, the divine "factor" is active and that therefore the road to his ultimate fulfillment is open.[24]

Black theology interprets this to mean that in spite of whiteness a way is open to blackness, and we do not have to accept white definitions.

It is within this context that divine omnipotence should be interpreted. Omnipotence does not refer to God's absolute power to accomplish what God wants. As John Macquarrie says, omnipotence is "the power to let something stand out from nothing and to be."[25] Translating this idea into the black experience, God's omnipotence is the power to let blacks stand out from whiteness and to be. It is what happens when blacks make ready for the black-white encounter with the full determination that they shall have their freedom or else. In this situation, divine providence is seeing divine reality in the present reality of black liberation—no more, no less.

5

The Human Being in Black Theology

Although Christian theology is essentially God-talk, we must not forget who it is that speaks of God. Human finiteness means that we cannot transcend human existence even when we speak of the transcendent God. We know who God is, not because we can move beyond our finiteness but because the transcendent God has become immanent in our history, transforming human events into divine events of liberation. It is the *divine* involvement in historical events of liberation that makes theology God-centered; but because God participates in the historical liberation of humanity, we can speak of God only in relationship to human history. In this sense, theology is anthropology.

In order to clarify the black perspective on theological anthropology, it will be useful to compare it with certain examples of American theology and of existential philosophy.

American Theology, Existentialism, and Black Theology

The weakness of most "Christian" approaches to anthropology stems from a preoccupation with (and distortion of) the God-problem, leaving concrete, oppressed human beings unrecognized and degraded. This is evident, for instance, in fundamentalist and orthodox theologies when they view the infallibility of the Bible as the sole ground of religious authority and fail to ask about the relevance of the inerrancy of scripture to the wretched of the earth. If the basic truth of the gospel is that the Bible is the infallible word of God, then it is inevitable that more emphasis will be placed upon "true" propositions about God than upon God as active in the liberation of the oppressed of the land. Blacks, struggling for survival, are not interested in abstract truth, "infallible" or otherwise. Truth is concrete.

The same God-emphasis is evident among American Barthians, who talk about the absolute sovereignty of God in self-revelation, but say nothing about God's self-revelation to blacks who are forced to live in rat-infested ghettos. These theologians are silent on the real human issues.

It may be interesting in a seminary class to talk about God's self-disclosure and how this view of revelation renders the traditional proofs of God's existence invalid. But most blacks never heard of Aristotle, Anselm, Descartes, or Kant, and they do not care about the interrelationship of theology and philosophy. Unless God's revelation is related to black liberation, blacks must reject it. The Barthians have confused God-talk with white-talk, and thus have failed to see that there is no real speech about God except in relationship to the liberation of the oppressed.

Unfortunately, liberal theologians have been guilty of the same error. Though they may have stressed God's love and neighborly love in human relations, it was done with a white emphasis. They stressed God's love at the expense of black liberation, failing to articulate the right of blacks to defend themselves against white racists. They asked blacks to turn the other cheek (so they could be "like" Jesus) when whites were destroying them.

It is true that some liberals "helped" blacks by persuading whites to be nice to them, and this probably prevented some lynchings. But blacks know that a person can be lynched in other ways than by hanging from a tree. What about depriving blacks of their humanity by suggesting that white humanity is humanity as God intended it to be? What about the liberal emphasis on human goodness at the same time whites were doing everything they could to destroy blacks?

It is disappointing, though perhaps understandable, that the death-of-God theology and secular theologies follow the same pattern. They ask us to embrace humanity and its urban manifestation, but fail miserably in relating this "new humanism" to the inhumanity committed against blacks. "God is dead," they tell us, but blacks are not impressed: they know that this is a white attempt to make life meaningful for whites in spite of their brutality to the black community.

Because black theology begins with the black condition as the fundamental datum of human experience, we cannot gloss over the significance and the concreteness of human oppression in the world in which blacks are condemned to live. In its concern for concreteness, black theology resembles existentialism, with its conviction that "existence precedes essence" (to use Sartre's phrase). This means that the concrete human being must be the point of departure of any phenomenological analysis of human existence. According to Sartre, there is no essence or universal humanity independent of persons in the concreteness of their involvement in the world. All persons define their own essence by participating in the world, making decisions that involve themselves and others.

Sartre's emphasis on human concreteness and the awesome responsibility of making decisions that include others has led him to deny the reality of God. To speak of human freedom necessarily means the exclusion not only of God but also of every appeal to a common human nature. Sartre's humanism excludes God and universals because they enslave human beings and deprive them of the possibilities inherent in the future.[1]

Unlike Sartre, Camus (who refused to refer to himself as an existentialist) appeals to a common value among human beings, a value capable of recognition by all and responsible for revolt against human oppression. The affirmation of a common value accounts for Camus's popularity among religionists. He appears to leave open the question of God. That, however, was not his intention: like Sartre, he denies the relevance of God to human existence. The experience of the absurd as disclosed in the reality of human suffering cannot be reconciled with belief in an omnipotent God.[2]

Black theology, though declining to enter the debate on human nature between Camus and Sartre, concurs in the intensity with which they focus on oppressed human beings. And although we see no need to deny the existence of God, we are glad for the presence of Camus and Sartre to remind theologians that the God-problem must never be permitted to detract from the concern for real human beings. The sole purpose of God in black theology is to illuminate the black condition so that blacks can see that their liberation is the manifestation of God's activity.

We believe, then, that we can learn more about God, and therefore about human nature, by studying blacks as they get ready to "do their thing" than by reading some erudite discourse on human nature by a white theologian. God in Jesus meets us in the situation of our oppressed condition and tells us not only who *God* is and what *God* is doing about our liberation, but also who *we* are and what *we* must do about white racism. If blacks can take christology seriously, then it follows that the meaning of our anthropology is also found in and through our oppressed condition, as we do what we have to about the presence of white racism.

Some readers will object to the absence of the "universal note" in the foregoing assertions, asking, "How can you reconcile the lack of universalism regarding human nature with a universal God?" The first reply is to deny that there is a "universal God" in the normal understanding of the term. As pointed out in the previous chapter, God is black.

Secondly, black theology is suspicious of those who appeal to a universal, ideal humanity. Oppressors are ardent lovers of humanity. They can love all persons in general, even black persons, because intellectually they can put blacks in the category called Humanity. With this perspective they can participate in civil rights and help blacks purely on the premise that they are part of a universal category. But when it comes to dealing with particular blacks, statistics transformed into black encounter, they are at a loss. They remind us of Dostoevski's doctor, who said, "I love humanity, but I wonder at myself. The more I love humanity in general, the less I love man in particular."[3]

The basic mistake of our white opponents is their failure to see that God did not become a universal human being but an oppressed Jew, thereby disclosing to us that both human nature and divine nature are inseparable from oppression and liberation. To know who the human person *is* is to focus on the Oppressed One and what he does for an oppressed community as it liberates itself from slavery.

Jesus is not a human being for all persons; he is a human being for oppressed persons, whose identity is made known in and through their liberation. Therefore our definition of the human being must be limited to what it means to be liberated from human oppression. Any other approach fails to recognize the reality of suffering in an inhuman society.

Black theology cannot affirm a higher harmony of the universe which sidesteps the suffering of blacks. We are reminded of Dostoevski's Ivan Karamazov and his rejection of God because of the suffering of children:

> I renounce the higher harmony altogether. It's not worth the tears of that one tortured child who beat itself on the breast with its little fist and prayed in its stinking outhouse, with its unexpiated tears to "dear kind God!"

To experience the sufferings of little children is to reject the universal human being in favor of particular human beings. It forces you to say something that takes seriously the meaning of human suffering. Whites can move beyond particular human beings to the universal human being because they have not experienced the reality of *color*. This is the meaning of Maulana Ron Karenga's comment:

> Man is only man in a philosophy class or a biology lab. In the world he is African, Asian or South American. He is a Chinese making a cultural revolution, or an Afro-American with soul. He lives by bread and butter, enjoys red beans and rice, or watermelon and ice cream.[4]

The inability of American theology to define human nature in the light of the Oppressed One and of particular oppressed peoples stems from its identity with the structures of white power. The human person in American theology is George Washington, Thomas Jefferson, and Abraham Lincoln rolled into one and polished up a bit. It is a colorless person, capable of "accepting" blacks as sisters and brothers, which means that it does not mind the blacks living next door *if* they behave themselves.

It is at this very point that American theology ceases to speak of the human person in any real sense. Actually, only the oppressed know what human personhood is because they have encountered both the depravity of human behavior from oppressors and the healing powers revealed in the Oppressed One. Having experienced the brutality of human pride, they will speak less of human goodness; but also having encountered the meaning of liberation, they can and must speak of human worth as revealed in the black community itself affirming its blackness.

I have defined my point of departure as the manifestation of the Oppressed One as he is involved in the liberation of an oppressed community. It is now appropriate to ask, "What is the human person?" That is, what is it that makes human beings what they are, thereby distinguishing them essentially from everything else that exists?[5]

The question about the human person is not answered by enumerating a list of properties; a person is not a collection of properties that can be scientifically analyzed. Rather to speak of the human being is to speak about its being-in-the-world-of-human-oppression. With the reality of human suffering as our starting point, what can black theology say about human nature?

The Human Being as Endowed with Freedom

1. Freedom as Liberation. If the content of the gospel is liberation, human existence must be explained as "being in freedom," which means rebellion against every form of slavery, the suppression of everything creative. "A slave," writes LeRoi Jones, "cannot be a man."[6] To be human is to be free, and to be free is to be human. The liberated, the free, are the ones who define the meaning of their being in terms of the oppressed of the land by participating in their liberation, fighting against everything that opposes integral humanity. Only the oppressed are truly free!

This is the paradox of human existence. *Freedom is the opposite of oppression, but only the oppressed are truly free*. How can this be? On the one hand, the concreteness of human existence reveals that human beings are not (fully) human when their creativity is enslaved by alien powers. To be (fully) human is to be separated from everything that is evil, everything that is against the "extension of the limits of humanity."[7] But on the other hand, human existence also discloses that the reality of evil is an ever-present possibility in our finite world, and to be (fully) human means to be identified with those who are enslaved as they fight against human evil. Being human means being against evil by joining sides with those who are the victims of evil. Quite literally, it means becoming oppressed with the oppressed, making their cause one's own cause by involving oneself in the liberation struggle. *No one is free until all are free.*

Paul Tillich expresses this paradox in his analysis of the relationship between being and nonbeing. On the one hand, being is the opposite of nonbeing. To *be* is to participate in Being, which is the source of everything that is. To exist is to exist in freedom—that is, stand out from nonbeing and *be*.[8] But, on the other hand, finite being "does not stand completely out of non-being."[9] Always present is the threat of nothingness, the possibility of ceasing to be.

The human person, therefore, is a creature who seeks to be in spite of nonbeing. The power to be in spite of nonbeing is what Tillich calls courage:

> The courage to be is the ethical act in which man affirms his being in spite of those elements of his existence which conflict with essential self-affirmation.[10]

Inherent in freedom is the recognition that there is something wrong with society, and those who are free will not be content until all members of society are treated as persons. There comes a time in life when persons realize that the world is not as they dreamt, and they have to make a choice: submit or risk all.[11] Being free means that the only real choice is risking all. Those who are prepared to risk all when they perceive the true nature of society and what it means to the oppressed. Those who come to this recognition also realize, as does Ignazio Silone's Pietro Spina in *Bread and Wine*, that freedom must be *taken*:

> Freedom is not something you get as a present. . . . You can live in a dictatorship and be free—on one condition: that you fight the dictatorship. The man who thinks with his own mind and keeps it uncorrupted is free. The man who fights for what he thinks is right is free. But you can live in the most democratic country on earth, and if you're lazy, obtuse or

servile within yourself, you're not free. Even without any violent coercion, you're a slave. You can't beg your freedom from someone. You have to seize it—everyone as much as he can.[12]

It is not difficult for the oppressed to understand the meaning of freedom. They are forced by the very nature of their condition to interpret their existence in the world contrary to the value-structures of an oppressive society. For the oppressed, to be is to be in revolt against the forces that impede the creation of the new person.

This is what Karl Marx had in mind in his definition of the human being as praxis, which means "directed activity."[13] Praxis expresses human freedom. "Freedom," writes Marx, "is the essence of man."[14] It *"is not something outside one who freely is, it is the specific mode or structure of being,"*[15] and inherent in it is action. Marx says: "The coincidence of the changing circumstances and of human activity can be conceived and rationally understood only as revolutionizing practice [praxis]."[16] He elaborates on the inseparable relationship of freedom and liberative activity. To be (fully) human is to be involved, participating in societal structures for human liberation.

As Petrović puts it:

> *The question of the essence of freedom*, like the question of the essence of man, *is not only a question*. It is *at once participation in production of freedom*. It is an activity through which freedom frees itself.[17]

Freedom, then, is not an abstract question. It deals with human existence in a world of societal enslavement. We cannot solve the question of freedom in a college classroom, theoretically debating the idea of "freedom versus determinism." Freedom is an existential reality. It is not a matter of rational thought but of human confrontation. It is not solved by academic discussion but by risky human encounter. As Silone's Spina says, "Man doesn't really exist unless he's fighting against his own limits."[18]

To be free means that human beings are not an object, and they will not let others treat them as an "it." They refuse to let limits be

Oppression dehumanizes people

put on their being. They are at once a part of nature (subject to laws of the universe) and are independent of nature. Dostoevski makes this point in his *Notes from the Underworld:* "Great Heavens, what are the laws of nature to me! . . . Obviously I cannot pierce this wall with my forehead . . . but neither will I reconcile myself to it just because it is a stone wall." Or again, he writes: "The whole human enterprise consists exclusively in man proving to himself every moment that he is man and not a cog." Those who insist on treating human beings as cogs must be made to realize that the human being is not a robot but is a free, living organism, capable of making the most of human creativity. Liberation is nothing but putting into practice the reality of human freedom.

2. Freedom and the Image of God. The being of the human person as freedom is expressed in the Bible in terms of the image of God. Even though there has been much talk about the *imago Dei* in the history of theology, most religionists have not given proper attention to the concept of existential freedom and its relationship to the image of God. Theologians seem to have a way of making simple ideas obscure by spending their energies debating fine points. (It is little wonder that nonprofessionals think that theology is unrelated to ordinary human involvement in the world.)

In the history of theology, the image of God is generally conceived of in terms of *rationality* and *freedom*.[19] Justin's statement is representative of the patristic period:

> In the beginning He made the human race with the power of thought and of choosing the truth and doing right, so that all men are without excuse before God; for they have been born rational and contemplative.[20]

It is significant that freedom and rational reflection go hand in hand, without any connection to the rebellion of the oppressed. Medieval thought was similarly defective, as the image was interpreted in terms of an *analogia entis*, which means that the being of the human persons as such is in the likeness of the being of God.

The Reformation reinterpreted the image to include the personal encounter between God and the human person, and deemphasized the capacity of reason to know God. Luther even speaks of reason as a "whore" that deceives persons by causing a creature to think that it is God. To say that humankind was created in the image of God meant, for Luther, that "man was in a relation to God that was wholly based on and governed by God's grace, to which man responded with faith."[21] It was a relationship analogous to a child's relationship to its father. Just as the child responds to its father in obedience and trust, the image of God responds to God with trustful obedience.

Commenting on Luther's view of the original righteousness of human nature (image of God), P. S. Watson says:

> It was a state in which his whole life was so centered in God, that in thought, will and action he was governed solely by the good and gracious will of God. It was as if he had "no will of his own," no desire but to do the will of God, whose word of command and promise he implicitly believed. That was what constituted man's "original righteousness"—the right relationship to God, and therefore to all else, for which and in which he was created.[22]

It is to Luther's credit that he added the personal dimension in contrast to the rationalistic approach of medieval theology. But it is to his discredit that he failed to relate this concept to the social and political conditions of the oppressed. Luther's identification with the structures of power weakened his view of the image of God. The idea of freedom to challenge the state with force when it resorts to oppression is not present in his thinking.

Modern theology, following Schleiermacher's unhappy clue to the relationship of theology and anthropology, forgot about Luther's emphasis on human depravity and proceeded once again to make appeals to human goodness. The nineteenth century is known for its confidence in the rational person, who not only knew what was right but was capable of responding to it. The image of God in human nature was the guarantee that the world was moving in a desirable direction. It never occurred to these "Christian" thinkers that they had missed some contrary evidence: this was the period of black enslavement and Amerindian extermination, as well as European colonial conquests in Africa and Asia.

World War I did much to shatter this ungodly view of human nature. Karl Barth with his *Epistle to the Romans* commentary,

Rudolf Bultmann with his existential, form-critical approach, Paul Tillich with his ontology, Emil Brunner with his own brand of neo-orthodoxy, and Reinhold Niebuhr with his ethical orientation made such an impact on liberalism that we are likely never to see it again the way it used to be. These thinkers did not share the liberalist confidence in human nature; like the reformers, they emphasized human depravity, the inability of the creature to transcend finite existence. The image of God in human nature was not to be identified with abstract rationality or freedom. Although all the so-called neo-orthodox theologians had unique approaches to the idea of the image, they all agreed that it involved the whole person in a divine-human encounter.

Refuting the Thomistic concept of an *analogia entis*, Bonhoeffer says:

> There is no analogy between God and man, if only because God—the only One existing in and for himself in his underived being, yet at the same time existing for his creatures, binding and giving his freedom to man—must not be thought of as being alone; in-as-much as he is the God who in Christ bears witness to his "being for man."[23]

Bonhoeffer prefers to speak of an *analogia relationis*, which is neither a part of human nature, nor a structure of its being, nor a capacity. It is a given relationship in which human beings are free to be for God because God is free for them in Christ.

> The analogy, the likeness must be understood strictly as follows: the likeness has its likeness *only* from the original. It always refers us only to the original, and is "like" only in this way. *Analogia relationis* is therefore the relation given by God. . . . The relation of creature with creature is a God-given relation because it exists in freedom and freedom originates from God.[24]

Black theology can appreciate the new emphasis, but it is not enough to identify the image with *analogia relationis*, as Bonhoeffer himself apparently realized later when Hitler's pretensions to deity became evident. If the image of God includes freedom, as is definitely implied in the divine-human encounter, then it must also include *liberation*.

Even though Karl Barth was opposed to them, the liberals were right in their stress on freedom as an essential element of the *imago Dei*, though they had the wrong idea of freedom. Freedom is not a rational decision about possible alternatives; it is a participation of the whole person in the liberation struggle. The Barthians were correct on the personal aspect of freedom in the divine-human encounter, but they failed to place due emphasis on the role of liberation in an oppressive society.

The biblical concept of image means that human beings are created in such a way that they cannot obey oppressive laws and still be human. To be human is to be in the image of God—that is, to be creative: revolting against everything that is opposed to humanity. Therefore, whatever we say about sin and the human inability to know God because of the fall, it must not in any way diminish the human freedom to revolt against oppression. As Gerhard von Rad says:

> The Priestly account of man's creation . . . speaks less of the nature of God's image than of its purpose. There is less said about the gift itself than about the task . . . [that task is] domination in the world, especially over the animals.[25]

In view of the exodus we must also say that the task includes participation in the freedom of God in the liberation of God's people. Jürgen Moltmann puts it this way:

> Jahweh is . . . the God who leads his people out of the house of bondage. Thus he is a God of freedom, the God ahead of us. One acquires social, political, and world-surpassing freedom from God, not against him.[26]

It is the biblical concept of the image of God that makes black rebellion in America human. When black persons affirm their freedom in God, they must say no to white racists. By saying no, they say yes to God and their blackness, affirming at the same time the inhumanity of the white neighbor who insists on playing God. Black theology emphasizes the right of blacks to be black and by so doing to participate in the image of God.

The image of God refers to the way in which God intends human beings to live in the world. The image of God is thus more than rationality, more than what so-called neo-orthodox theologians call divine-human encounter. In a world in which persons are oppressed, the image is human nature in rebellion against the structures of oppression. It is humanity involved in the liberation struggle against the forces of inhumanity.

3. Freedom as Identification with an Oppressed Community. It is important to point out that freedom is not white middle-class individualism. It has nothing to do with reading and writing poetry or joining Students for a Democratic Society. It is not to be equated with Hippies or Yippies—the long hair and all that jazz.

This is not intended as a put-down of white young persons who are moving against their elders for one of the first times in American history; and I must say that they do appear to be quite human at times. The positive value of these "unusual" manifestations is their seeming recognition that there is something wrong with carrying on a war in Vietnam and with oppression generally—contrary to the long-standing assumptions of this society. The beginning of freedom is the perception that oppressors are the evil ones, and that we must do something about it.

But truly free adults take one more step. They also recognize that freedom becomes a reality when they throw in their lot with an oppressed community by joining with it in its cause, accepting whatever is necessary in order to be identified with the victims of evil.

The problem for many white groups is that of becoming truly identified with the black community. Like their elders, they seem to expect blacks to accept them without too much emotional feeling about the past. When blacks reject them, they quickly turn in on themselves, forming their own esoteric little groups, saying, "Blacks want in and we are trying to get out."

To be free is to participate with those who are victims of oppression. Persons are free when they belong to a free community seeking to emancipate itself from oppression. Freedom, then, is more than just making decisions in the light of one's individual taste during moments of excitement. It always involves making decisions within the context of a community of persons who share similar goals and are seeking the same liberation. Freedom means taking sides in a crisis situation, when a society is divided into oppressed and oppressors. In this situation we are not permitted the luxury of being on neither side by making a decision that only involves the self. Our decision affects the whole of society, and it cannot but be made in view of either oppressed or oppressors. There is no way to transcend this alternative.

The truly free are identified with the humiliated because they know that their own being is involved in the degradation of their brothers and sisters. They cannot stand to see them stripped of their humanity. This is so not because of pity or sympathy, but because their own existence is being limited by another's slavery. They do not need to ask whether their fellow human being is at fault. All they know is that there is a fight going on, and they must choose sides, without any assurance of who is right in the "Christian" sense of future victory.

Mathieu, the protagonist in Sartre's *The Age of Reason*, recognized the difficulty of being truly free by renouncing a false freedom. Thinking to himself during his encounter with Brunet, who was trying to persuade him to join the communist party, he says:

> "At this moment, at this very moment, there are men firing point-blank at one another in the suburbs of Madrid, there are Austrian Jews agonizing in concentration camps, there are Chinese burning under the ruins of Nanking, and here I am, in perfect health, I feel quite free, in a quarter of an hour I shall take my hat and go for a walk in the Luxembourg." He turned towards Brunet and looked at him with bitterness. "I am one of the *irresponsibles*," he thought.[27]

Freedom is something more than intellectual articulation of an existential philosophical attitude. It involves the commitment of one's whole being for the cause of the oppressed. That is why Brunet says:

> "You're all the same, you intellectuals: everything is cracking and collapsing, the guns are on the point of going off, and you stand there calmly claiming the right to be convinced. If only you could see yourselves with my eyes, you would understand that time presses."[28]

But that is just the point: oppressors never see themselves as the oppressed see them. Brunet is wasting his time. If persons always have to be *told* about the inhumanity around them, there is little hope for them. Even Mathieu knows intellectually that Brunet is right and that he ought to make a choice. At one moment he says to himself regarding Brunet: "He is freer than I: he is in harmony with himself and with the party."[29]

In order to be free, a person must be able to make choices that are not dependent on an oppressive system. Mathieu is able to live an irresponsible life that some might call "freedom" because he participates in a society that protects him. He is insensitive to the suffering of others, even that of his own mistress, Marcelle. If he cannot choose a freedom that involves his intimate friend, it is not likely that he will be able to choose a freedom that involves unknown sufferers. As Sartre says: "The only way of helping the enslaved out there is to take sides with those who are here."

It seems that this is the major weakness of whites who say that they are concerned about humanity. With all due respect to white concern for the war in Vietnam, the authenticity of their response must be questioned. The destruction of black humanity began long before the Vietnam war and few whites got upset about it. It is therefore appropriate to ask, "Is it because white boys are dying in the war that whites get so upset? Can we expect them to be equally involved in the destruction of their racism when the war is over? In view of their lack of concern for the oppression of blacks before and during the ungodly massacre of Vietnam, is it likely that whites will turn their energies toward the oppressed in America?" In light of the past attitudes of whites, we could have expected that after the war was over and the troops withdrawn, white America would be free to deal with the "black problem" the same way it always deals with any problem: tell blacks what is required for them to exist, for their presence, and then proceed to destroy everyone who thinks otherwise.

It is an interesting miscarriage of logic that white religionists can get so perturbed about the Vietnam war but are not particularly concerned about blacks. In regard to the oppression of blacks, they can always make excuses and even suggest that black suffering is not too severe. The only way I can understand this logic is to see it for what it is—the logic of oppressors. Being white, it is only natural that their taste for humanity will arouse their sensitivities when they watch white boys leave for a war and come back in boxes. No one likes to see any member of *their own community* destroyed.

The whiteness of whites enhances their protest against wars in other parts of the world, but it only increases their own determination to keep blacks down. Being white excludes them from the black community and thus whatever concern they have for blacks will invariably work against black freedom. What whites fail to recognize is the fact that all decisions made with regard to what is important or worthwhile are made in the context of participation in a community. It is in the community that values are chosen, because the community provides the structure in which our being as persons is realized. It is not possible to transcend the community; it frames our being because being is always *being in relation to others*.

Is it possible to change communities? To change communities involves a change of *being*. It is a radical movement, a radical reorientation of one's existence in the world. Christianity calls this experience conversion.

Certainly if whites expect to be able to say anything relevant to the self-determination of the black community, it will be necessary for them to destroy their whiteness by becoming members of an oppressed community. Whites will be free only when they become new persons—when their white being has passed away and they are created anew in black being. When this happens, they are no longer white but free, and thus capable of making decisions about the destiny of the black community.

4. Freedom and Suffering. Because being free means participating in the liberation of an oppressed community, freedom is inevitably associated with suffering. Socially and existentially free persons will count their losses.

To assert one's freedom always involves encountering the economic and social structures of oppression. When rulers first perceive dissent—a threat to "their" society—their initial response is to try to silence the dissenters by cutting off the sources of physical existence and social involvement. This is to remind the rebels who is boss. Oppressors hope that by making it difficult to live, rebels will come around to seeing the world as oppressors see it.

Coupled with economic oppression is social ostracism. The intention is to demonstrate the perversity of rebel involvement by picturing them as destroyers of "the good." At no time are the rebels given the opportunity to define their way of looking at the world, because the mass media belong to the oppressors who will not permit the seditious presence to extend itself.

If economic and social oppression fail to bring the rebels into line, the structures of power begin to devise political means of silencing them. Rebels expect this because they know that liberation always involves fighting against the powers that be. To go against the "keepers of peace" is to take a political risk, the risk of being shot, imprisoned, or exiled. That is why Silone's Spina says, "Freedom is not something you get as a present. . . . You can't beg your freedom from someone. You have to seize it—everyone as much as he can."

Reinhold Niebuhr makes this point convincingly in *Moral Man and Immoral Society*, observing that those in power will never admit that society rewards them far out of proportion to the services they render; and this attitude inevitably makes them enslave all who question their interests. Appeals to reason and religion do not change the balance of power, because both are used to defend the interests of oppressors. Change will take place, according to Niebuhr, when the enslaved recognize that power must be met with power. The black community is aware of this; and the black revolution is nothing but a will to spread the decision among blacks to seize their freedom—any way they can. No black person will ever be good enough in the eyes of whites to *merit* equality. Therefore, if blacks are to have freedom, they must *take* it, by any means necessary. For we now know as even Sartre's Mathieu recognized: "No one can be a man who has not discovered something for which he is prepared to die."[30]

Without minimizing the horror of social, economic, and political losses, it may at least be noted that these are expected by the oppressed, and that one's life can be adjusted to accommodate physical pain. It is not possible to be black and not know what white people do to black people. The presence of the black ghettos in every city where blacks live is a visible manifestation of white cruelty. But existential suffering is not easily recognized or readily dealt with. It refers to the pain associated with the absurdity of being black in a white racist world and with the responsibility of doing something about it.

Growing up in America is an absurd experience for blacks. At first, they do not know what is going on. They cannot figure out what they have done to merit the treatment accorded them. But then they realize that white brutality is not related to their particular actions. It is white society's way of telling blacks that they are not persons. Now they must make a decision: either accept their place or resolve to call down upon themselves white indignation by revolting against the world as it is.

It is important to note that the absurdity arises not from black persons' perceptions of themselves, but only from the attempt to reconcile their being with the white world. It is analogous to Albert Camus's philosophical analysis of absurdity. The absurd is the "strangeness of the world" when the wronged try to make sense out of it in relation to their existence. The absurd, writes Camus, is "the confrontation of this irrational and wild longing for clarity whose call echoes in the human heart."[31] There is suffering because there is no *hope* that reconciliation will be possible, and the only authentic response is to face the reality of the absurdity in rebellion.

In another context, Sartre describes freedom in terms of anguish, forlornness, and despair. The three together point to the suffering which is inseparable from being-in-the-world. Anguish is the recognition that one's actions involve all humanity. "Man is anguish," writes Sartre, in that we are creatures capable of involvement, realizing that it is not possible to accept responsibility for all and not have some anxiety about it. We are thrown into the world with a multiplicity of possibilities but with no guide for correctness in choice. But whatever choice we make, it is not simply a choice for us; it is a choice for all human beings. We assume the responsibility for humanity and declare what we consider to be humanly possible. Who can make such a choice without feeling at the same time a deep sense of anxiety? This is the choice that blacks make. They are alone and yet not alone, and there is no way to evade the seriousness of their responsibility.

Forlornness, writes Sartre, means that "God does not exist and that we have to face all the consequences of this."[32] The purpose is to deny "values in heaven" or an "*a priori* good." It is taking

Dostoevski seriously, "If God didn't exist, everything would be possible." We know that that is our situation, "and as a result man is forlorn, because neither within him nor without does he find anything to cling to."[33] We have no universal ethic to guide our existence in the world, and thus we are condemned to make our choices without any assurances. We choose our existence.

Sartre's analysis of forlornness is especially appropriate for the oppressed. Oppression means that society has defined truth in terms of human slavery; and liberation means the denial of that truth. The God of society must be destroyed so that the oppressed can define existence in accordance with their liberation. In the moment of liberation, there are no universal truths; there is only the truth of liberation itself, which the oppressed themselves define in the struggle for freedom. To be forlorn is to accept the task of choosing humanity without any certainty beyond the existing moment.

It is not possible to experience oppression without also experiencing despair. Despair means that "we shall confine ourselves to reckoning only with what depends upon our will, or on the ensemble of probabilities which make our action possible."[34] We cannot move beyond our earthly possibilities. Again in Sartre's words:

> I am left in the realm of possibility; but possibilities are to be reckoned with only to the point where my action comports with the ensemble of these possibilities and no further.[35]

It is illegitimate to point to the *future* unless the pointing includes the recognition that "I am my future." To avoid this dimension of existence is to move to a false security. It is necessary for the oppressed to carve out the meaning of existence without appealing to alien values.

The relationship between freedom and suffering is also evident in the biblical tradition. The election of Israel is a call to share in Yahweh's liberation. It is not a position of privilege but of terrible responsibility. To be Yahweh's people, Israel must be willing to fight against everything that is against this liberation. Therefore, the whole of its history is a description of the movement of this people in relation to God's liberating work. This involves suffering because liberation means a confrontation between evil and the will of the God who directs history.

The life of Jesus also discloses that freedom is bound up with suffering. It is not possible to be for him and not realize that one has chosen an existence in suffering. "Blessed are you when men revile you and persecute you . . . falsely on my account" (Matthew 5:11). The very character of human existence as defined in his life is enough to show that we cannot be for Jesus and for the societal humiliation of human beings. To be for him means being for the oppressed, as expressed in their self-determination. Jesus himself expresses this by limiting the kingdom of God to the poor and unwanted. The kingdom is for the poor because they represent the meaning of oppression and the certainty of liberation. Moltmann puts it well:

> If we believe the crucified Christ to be the representative of God on earth, we see the glory of God no longer in the crowns of the mighty but in the face of the man who was executed on the gallows. What the authorities intended to be the greatest humiliation—namely the cross—is thus transformed into the highest dignity. It follows that the freedom of God comes to earth not through crowns—that is to say, through the struggle for power—but through love and solidarity with the power-less.[36]

Christians can never be content as long as their sisters and brothers are enslaved. They must suffer with them, knowing that freedom for Jesus Christ is always freedom for the oppressed. Christian freedom has its beginning "in the midst of all the misery of this world," and we "can only demonstrate this freedom by using our own freedom for the actual liberation of man from his real misery."[37]

5. Freedom and Blackness. What does freedom mean when we relate it to contemporary America? Because blackness is at once the symbol of oppression and of the certainty of liberation, freedom means an affirmation of blackness. To be free is to be black—that is, identified with the victims of humiliation in human society and a participant in the liberation of oppressed humanity. The free person in America is the one who does not tolerate whiteness but fights against it, knowing that it is the source of human misery. The free person is the black person living in an alien world but refusing to behave according to its expectations.

Being free in America means accepting blackness as the only possible way of existing in the world. It means defining one's identity by the marks of oppression. It means rejecting white proposals for peace and reconciliation, saying, "All we know is, we must have justice, not next week but this minute."

Nat Turner, Gabriel Prosser, and Denmark Vesey are examples of free persons. They realized that freedom and death were inseparable. The mythic value of their existence for the black community is incalculable, because they represent the personification of the possibility of *being* in the midst of *nonbeing*—the ability to be black in the presence of whiteness. Through them we know that freedom is what happens to blacks when they decide that whitey has gone too far and that it is incumbent upon them as the victims of humiliation to do something about the encroachment of whiteness. Freedom is the black movement of a people getting ready to liberate itself, knowing that it cannot *be* unless its oppressors *cease to be*.

When blackness is equated with *freedom as a symbol* both of oppression and of the human potential, whites feel left out of things. "What about the oppression of whites?" they ask. "Is it not true that the enslaver also enslaves himself which makes him a member of the community of the oppressed?" There is a danger inherent in these questions. If white intellectuals, religionists, and assorted liberals can convince themselves that the white condition is analogous to the black condition, then there is no reason to respond to the demands of the black community. "After all, we are all oppressed," they say, rationalizing with a single stroke the whole white way of life. By equating their own condition with the condition of the black ghetto, they are able to sleep at night, assuring themselves that we are all in the same boat.

Black theology rejects this technique as the work of the white Christ whose basic purpose is to soothe the guilt feelings of white overlords. Inherent in the recognition of the oppressed condition is the rebellion against it with all one's might. To know oppression is to refuse to put up with it. This is why black oppression and liberation are a manifestation of the revelation of God. To be oppressed means that one is enslaved against one's will by alien forces; and liberation means that one is willing to pay the cost of freedom—including death. Now we put the question to our white suburbanites: "What power is keeping you out there? Is it not true that the so-called oppression of which you speak is freely accepted because you are unwilling to pay the price of real freedom?"

The basic difference between black oppression and so-called white oppression is the fact that the latter is voluntarily chosen and the former is forced upon the black community. Whites can leave their ghetto whenever they please, but blacks are confined against their will. Black suffering is not by choice but is a result of the evil of white racists, who believe that they have the first, last, and only word on how the world ought to be run.

This is not to deny that whites are enslaved. What we deny is their ability to know and analyze their slavery. The depravity of oppressors is their enslavement to their own "freedom." Because they are free to do what they will to the oppressed, the only check being their pious feelings about the world, it is not possible for them to see the oppressed as human beings. The oppressed become objects to be used to make the world more amenable to the whims of the masters. Thus oppressors are enslaved and dehumanized by their own will to power. They storm the citadel of the gods, claiming sole authority to declare what is real and right, and to shape the world accordingly. If they are to be liberated from such megalomania, it must be done by the oppressed. When the oppressed affirm their freedom by refusing to behave according to the masters' rules, they not only liberate themselves from oppression, but they also liberate oppressors from enslavement to their illusions.

The basic error of white comments about their own oppression is the assumption that they *know* the nature of their enslavement. This cannot be so, because if they really knew, they would liberate themselves by joining the revolution of the black community. They would destroy themselves and be born again as beautiful black persons.

The Human Being as a Fallen Creature

Human fallenness is expressed in the Bible as sin. Sin is a theological concept that describes separation from the source of being. Instead of affirming their identity in the source of being, sinners reject it and attempt to be what they are not. Sin is thus a definition of being in relation to nonbeing; it is a condition of estrangement from the source of meaning and purpose in the universe.

1. Sin as a Community Concept. In order to understand clearly the function of sin in the biblical tradition, it is necessary to point out that it is meaningful only in the context of the Israelite community. Sin is not an abstract idea that defines ethical behavior for all and sundry. Rather it is a religious concept that defines the human condition as separated from the essence of the community. To be in sin has nothing to do with disobeying laws that are alien to the community's existence. Quite the contrary, failure to destroy the powers that seek to enforce alien laws on the community is to be in a state of sin. It is incumbent on all members of the community to define their existence according to the community's essence and to defend the community against that which seeks to destroy it.

To be in sin, then, is to deny the values that make the community what it is. It is living according to one's private interests and not according to the goals of the community. It is believing that one can live independently of the source that is responsible for the community's existence.

For Israel sin meant alienation from the covenant of Yahweh as grounded in Yahweh's liberating activity at the exodus. If the meaning of Israel's existence is defined by the exodus and the covenant, then all other ways of living in the world must be termed a violation of its existence as the people of Yahweh. Sin in the community of Israel is nothing but a refusal to acknowledge the significance of the exodus and the covenant as God's liberating activity. It means grounding one's being on some loyalty other than Yahweh. It is counting Yahweh's activity as secondary by refusing to define the community in terms of divine liberation.

It is human existence in community that defines the meaning of sin. To be in sin means to deny the community. Nor does this definition of sin ignore the biblical claim that the fall describes the condition of *all* human beings. Indeed that is the very point: Genesis 3 is *Israel's* analysis of universal sin and thus is comprehensible only from its perspective. It is not likely that other communities, defining their being from other sources, will take too seriously Israel's condemnation of them as sinners. Genesis 3 is meaningful to those who participate in Israel's community and to no one else.

It is important to point out that Genesis 3 was probably written during the reign of Solomon, more than three centuries after the exodus. Casting his eye back across that time span, the writer sees the history of Israel as the history of alienation from the source of its being, the exodus and Sinai events. This historical and existential alienation is then projected onto a cosmic and universal screen in Genesis 3. Because Israel has not directed its existence exclusively according to divine liberation, it is separated from God and is in a condition of fallenness.

At the exodus, Yahweh appears as the God of oppressed Israel in its liberation from the Egyptians. The covenant at Sinai is the agreement between Yahweh and this people that Yahweh would continue a liberative presence if Israel would define its existence as a community on the basis of divine liberation. Sin, then, is the failure of Israel to recognize the liberating work of God. It is believing that liberation is not the definition of being in the world. When Israel tries to define its existence according to the pattern of other nations and thus believes that its existence is dependent on some source other than Yahweh's liberating activity, it is in a state of sin. To revolt against the community's reason for being is to deny the reality of the community itself.

The idea of sin is applicable to other people as they are related to the community of Israel. Because Israel believes that Yahweh is Lord of all history, those who fail to define their existence accordingly are separated from God. To fail to recognize God's activity as defined by the community of Israel is to exist in sin.

The relationship between sin and community is further evident in the character of Israelite prophecy. A prophet is one who speaks for Yahweh by reminding the community of its reason for being in the world. Nathan rebukes David because he acted for self and not for the community. Elijah challenges Ahab because he fails to recognize the absolute sovereignty of Yahweh. Amos and Hosea also remind Israel of the meaning of its existence by pointing back to the exodus and covenant. The essence of their concern is to call the community back to the source of its life. They are saying that unless we *become* what we *are*, we will no longer be. Sin is living a lie—that is, trying to be what we are not. To be is to know that one's being is grounded in God's liberating activity.

The same perspective is also found in the New Testament. Because Jesus, the Oppressed One, reveals to us what we are as God created us to be, the oppressed Christian community knows that as we actually *are*, we are fallen creatures. We are not what we ought to be. When we look at Jesus, then, we know that instead of affirming our existence in him, we have denied him and taken a course completely alien to our being.

Sin, then, is a condition of human existence in which we deny the essence of God's liberating activity as revealed in Jesus Christ. It is a way of life in which we cease to be fully human and we make choices according to our private interests, identifying the ultimate with an alien power. It is accepting slavery as a condition of human existence by denying the freedom grounded in God's activity. Sin is an alienation from the source of humanity in the world, resulting in human oppression and misery.

2. Sin and the Black and White Communities. What does sin mean for the black and white communities in contemporary America? Because sin is a concept that is meaningful only for an oppressed community as it reflects upon its liberation, it is not possible to make a universal analysis that is meaningful for both black and white persons. Black theology believes that the true nature of sin is perceived only in the moment of oppression and liberation. This means that blacks, like Israel of old, know what sin is because they have experienced the source of their being and are now able to analyze their own existence in relation to the world at large. They know what nonbeing (sin) is because they have experienced being (black power). We are now in a position to say what the world ought to be in relation to what it is.

Because sin is inseparable from revelation, and because revelation is an event that takes place in the moment of liberation from oppression, there can be no knowledge of the sinful condition except in the movement of an oppressed community claiming its freedom. This means that whites, despite their self-proclaimed religiousness, are rendered incapable of making valid judgments on the character of sin. That is why American theology discusses sin in the abstract, debating it in relation to universal humankind. In white theology, sin is a theoretical idea, not a concrete reality. No white theologian has been able to relate sin to the black-white encounter in America.

Generally, white fundamentalists have identified sin with moral purity. More sophisticated liberal and neo-orthodox thinkers have spoken in hushed solemnity about our broken relationship with God—but that is all they say. We are still waiting for an interpretation of sin in relation to the world at large. Invariably, white theologians analyze sin as if blacks and whites represent one community. On the one hand, Billy Graham and his cohorts are saying that the trouble with the world is that humankind needs God; we need to turn from our wicked ways. The wicked ways, of course, refer to the failure to live according to the rules of white society. On the other hand, other whites are saying that the problem stems from his broken relation with God—a far more serious analysis than Graham's simplistic one. But we are still waiting for the meaning of this, as blacks get ready for revolution. We wait in vain because oppressors do not wish to know what is wrong with the world. Only the oppressed know what is wrong, because they are both the victims of evil and the recipients of God's liberating activity.

What, then, does sin mean for whites from the black perspective? The sin of whites is the definition of their existence in terms of whiteness. It is accepting the condition that is responsible for Amerindian reservations, black concentration camps, and the rape of Vietnam. It is believing in the American way of life as defined by its history.

Most whites, some despite involvement in protests, do believe in "freedom in democracy," and they fight to make the ideals of the Constitution an empirical reality for all. It seems that they believe that, if we just work hard enough at it, this country can be what it ought to be. But it never dawns on these do-gooders that what is wrong with America is not its failure to make the Constitution a reality for all, but rather its belief that persons can affirm whiteness and humanity at the same time. This country was founded for whites and everything that has happened in it has emerged from the white perspective. The Constitution is white, the Emancipation Proclamation is white, the government is white, business is white, the unions are white. What we need is the destruction of whiteness, which is the source of human misery in the world.

Whites, *because* they are white, fail to perceive this as the nature of sin. It is characteristic of sin that it permeates the whole of one's being, distorting one's humanity, leaving the sinner incapable of reversing the condition or indeed of truly recognizing it. If something is to be done, action must come from another source. Christianity believes that the answer to the human condition is found in the event of Jesus Christ who meets us in our wretched condition and transforms our nonbeing into being for God. If that is true, then black confrontation with white racism is Jesus Christ meeting whites, providing them with the possibility of reconciliation.

Sin warps a person's existence in the world. This is what happens when a people believes that it is God's chosen people because of its privileges in the world. It is the condition that causes ministers to compromise with slavery and to make *excuses* for white brutality against blacks. Sin is the condition that produces lynchings. It makes white theologians define the theological enterprise as the "safe" venture. Sin is white northern congregations wondering why blacks will not come to their churches, and white southern churches fearing that blacks might come. In a word, sin is whiteness—the desire of whites to play God in the realm of human affairs.

What does sin mean for blacks? Again, we must be reminded that sin is a community concept, and this means that only blacks can talk about their sin. Oppressors are not only rendered incapable of knowing their own condition, they cannot speak about or for the oppressed. This means that whites are not permitted to speak about what blacks have done to contribute to their condition. They cannot call blacks Uncle Toms; only members of the black community can do that. For whites, to do so is not merely insensitivity, it is blasphemy!

Whites cannot know us; they do not even know themselves. If we could just get "concerned" whites to recognize this fact, then we blacks could get about the business of cleaning up this society and destroying the filthy manifestations of whiteness in it.

If we are to understand sin and what it means to blacks, it is necessary to be black and also a participant in the black liberation struggle. Because sin represents the condition of estrangement from the source of one's being, for blacks this means a desire to be white. It is the refusal to be what we are. Sin, then, for blacks is loss of identity. It is saying yes to the white absurdity—accepting the world as it is by letting whites define black existence. To be in sin is to be contented with white solutions for the "black problem" and not rebel against every infringement of white being on black being.

We blacks know what that means because too long we have let whites determine the shape of the future and what the limits are. We have reinforced white values by letting whites define what is good and beautiful. But now we are being born anew; our community is being redeemed. This is so because we are perceiving the true nature of black existence. The black theology analysis of this change focuses on Jesus as the black Christ. To this we now turn in the next chapter.

6

Jesus Christ in Black Theology

Christian theology begins and ends with Jesus Christ. He is the point of departure for everything to be said about God, humankind, and the world. That is why christology is the starting point of Karl Barth's *Dogmatics* and why Wolfhart Pannenberg says that "theology can clarify its Christian self-understanding only by a thematic and comprehensive involvement with Christological problems."[1] To speak of the Christian gospel is to speak of Jesus Christ who is the content of its message and without whom Christianity ceases to be. Therefore the answer to the question "What is the essence of Christianity?" can be given in the two words: Jesus Christ.

Because Jesus Christ is the focal point for everything that is said about the Christian gospel, it is necessary to investigate the meaning of his person and work in light of the black perspective. It is one thing to assert that he is the essence of the Christian gospel, and quite another to specify the meaning of his existence in relation to the slave ships that appeared on American shores. Unless his existence is analyzed in light of the oppressed of the land, we are still left wondering what his presence means for the auction block, the Underground Railroad, and contemporary manifestations of black power. To be sure, white theology has informed us that Jesus Christ is the content of the gospel, but it has failed miserably in relating that gospel to Nat Turner, Denmark Vesey, and Gabriel Prosser. It is therefore the task of black theology to make theology relevant to the black reality, asking,

110

"What does Jesus Christ mean for the oppressed blacks of the land?"

The task of explicating the existence of Jesus Christ for blacks is not easy in a white society that uses Christianity as an instrument of oppression. White conservatives and liberals alike present images of a white Jesus that are completely alien to the liberation of the black community. Their Jesus is a mild, easy-going white American who can afford to mouth the luxuries of "love," "mercy," "long-suffering," and other white irrelevancies, because he has a multi-billion-dollar military force to protect him from the encroachments of the ghetto and the "communist conspiracy." But black existence is existence in a hostile world without the protection of the law. If Jesus Christ is to have any meaning for us, he must leave the security of the suburbs by joining blacks in their condition. What need have we for a white Jesus when we are not white but black? If Jesus Christ is white and not black, he is an oppressor, and we must kill him. The appearance of black theology means that the black community is now ready to do something about the white Jesus, so that he cannot get in the way of our revolution.

The Historical Jesus and Black Theology

Investigation of the question "Who is Jesus Christ?" involves the question about the historical Jesus. Since the appearance of Albert Schweitzer's *The Quest of the Historical Jesus* and the rise of the form-history school, knowledge about the historical Jesus cannot be taken for granted. During the nineteenth century, theologians assumed that the real Jesus was accessible to historical investigation, and they attempted to go behind the preaching (kerygma) of the early church in order to find the authentic Jesus of Nazareth. But Schweitzer demonstrated conclusively that the liberal search for the historical Jesus was a failure and only represented creations of the human mind. The nineteenth-century "lives" of Jesus told us more about the investigators than about Jesus himself.

Rudolf Bultmann and the form critics went even further by suggesting that the Gospels (the only source for knowledge about Jesus) are not historical at all. The setting of the narratives is artificial, and their contents were created entirely by the early Christian community in order to meet its own practical needs. It is therefore foolish to imagine that it is possible to find a historical kernel within them. That is why Bultmann says that "we can know almost nothing concerning the life and personality of Jesus, since the early Christian sources show no interest in either, are moreover fragmentary and often legendary."[2]

Bultmann's radical historical skepticism has been questioned by some of his followers. The new quest for the historical Jesus began in 1953 with Ernst Käsemann's lecture, "The Problem of the Historical Jesus." According to Käsemann:

> Only if Jesus' proclamation decisively coincides with the proclamation about Jesus is it understandable, reasonable, and necessary that the Christian kerygma in the New Testament conceals the message of Jesus; only then is the resurrected Jesus the historical Jesus. From this perspective we are required, precisely as historians, to inquire behind Easter. . . .
>   By this means we shall learn whether he stands behind the word of his church or not, whether the Christian kerygma is a myth that can be detached from his word and from himself or whether it binds us historically and insolubly to him.[3]

Günther Bornkamm, Ernst Fuchs, and Hans Conzelmann joined Käsemann in his concern.[4] Although all agreed that a life of Jesus is impossible, they do not agree that history is irrelevant to the Christian gospel as implied in Bultmann's analysis of New Testament mythology.[5] Bornkamm puts it this way:

> Certainly faith cannot and should not be dependent on the change and uncertainty of historical research. . . . But no one should despise the help of historical research to illumine the truth with which each of us should be concerned.[6]

Like the theologians of the new quest, black theology also takes seriously the historical Jesus. We want to know who Jesus *was* because we believe that that is the only way to assess who he *is*. If we have no historical information about the character and behavior of that particular Galilean in the first century, then it is impossible to determine the mode of his existence now. Without some continuity between the historical Jesus and the kerygmatic Christ, the Christian gospel becomes nothing but the subjective reflections of the early Christian community. And if that is what Christianity is all about, we not only separate it from history, but we also allow every community the possibility of interpreting the kerygma according to its own existential situation. Although the situation is important, it is not the gospel. The gospel speaks *to* the situation.

Christianity believes, as Paul Tillich has suggested, that it has the answer to the existential character of the human condition. It is the function of theology to analyze the changeless gospel in such a way that it can be related to changing situations. But theology must be careful not to confuse the two. If the situation becomes paramount (i.e., identified with the gospel), as it appears in Bultmann's view of the kerygmatic Christ, then there are no checks to the community's existential fancies. Black theology also sees this as the chief error of white American religious thought, which allows the white condition to determine the meaning of Jesus. The historical Jesus must be taken seriously if we intend to avoid making Jesus into our own images.

Taking seriously the New Testament Jesus, black theology believes that the historical kernel is the manifestation of Jesus as the Oppressed One whose earthly existence was bound up with the oppressed of the land. This is not to deny that other emphases are present. Rather it is to say that whatever is said about Jesus' conduct (Fuchs), about the manifestation of the expectant eschatological future in the deeds and words of Jesus (Bornkamm), or about his resurrection as the "ultimate confirmation of Jesus' claim to authority" (Pannenberg), it must serve to illuminate Jesus' sole reason for existence: to bind the wounds of the afflicted and to liberate those who are in prison. To understand the historical Jesus without seeing his identification with the poor as decisive is to misunderstand him and thus distort his historical person. And a proper theological analysis of Jesus' historical identification with the helpless is indispensable for our interpretation of the gospel today. Unless the contemporary oppressed know that the kerygmatic Christ is the real Jesus (as Martin Kähler would put it), to the extent that he was completely identified with the oppressed of his earthly ministry, they cannot know that their liberation is a continuation of his work.

The Character of the New Testament Jesus

What evidence is there that Jesus' identification with the oppressed is the distinctive historical kernel in the gospels? How do we know that black theology is not forcing an alien contemporary black situation on the biblical sources? These questions are important, and cannot be waved aside by black theologians. Unless we can clearly articulate an image of Jesus that is consistent with the essence of the biblical message and at the same time relate it to the struggle for black liberation, black theology loses its reason for being. It is thus incumbent upon us to demonstrate the relationship between the historical Jesus and the oppressed, showing that the equation of the contemporary Christ with black power arises out of a serious encounter with the biblical revelation.

Black theology must show that the Reverend Albert Cleage's description of Jesus as the Black Messiah[7] is not the product of minds "distorted" by their own oppressed condition, but is rather the most meaningful christological statement in our time. Any other statement about Jesus Christ is at best irrelevant and at worst blasphemous.

1. Birth. The appearance of Jesus as the Oppressed One whose existence is identified exclusively with the oppressed of the land is symbolically characterized in his birth. He was born in a stable and cradled in a manger (the equivalent of a beer case in a ghetto alley), "because there was no room for them in the inn" (Luke 2:7). Although most biblical scholars rightly question the historical validity of the birth narratives in Matthew and Luke, the mythic value of these stories is important theologically. They undoubtedly reflect the early Christian community's *historical* knowledge of Jesus as a man who defined the meaning of his existence as being one with the poor and outcasts. The visit of the shepherds, the journey of the wise men, Herod's killing of the babies, the economic, social, and political unimportance of Mary and Joseph— all these features reflect the early community's image of the man Jesus. For them Jesus is certainly a unique person, but the uniqueness of his appearance reveals the Holy One's concern for the lonely and downtrodden. They are not simply Matthew and Luke's explanation of the origin of Jesus' messiahship, but also a portrayal of the significance of his messiahship.

Jesus' messiahship means that he is one of the humiliated and the abused, even in his birth. His eating with tax collectors and sinners, therefore, was not an accident and neither was it a later invention of the early church; rather it is an expression of the very being of God and thus a part of Jesus' purpose for being born.

2. Baptism and Temptation. The baptism (affirmed by most scholars as historical) also reveals Jesus' identification with the oppressed. According to the synoptic Gospels, John's baptism was for repentant sinners, an act which he believed provided an escape from God's messianic judgment. For Jesus to submit to John's baptism not only connects his ministry with John's but, more importantly, separates him from John. By being baptized, Jesus defines his existence as one with sinners and thus conveys the meaning of the coming kingdom. The kingdom is for the poor, not the rich; and it comes as an expression of God's love, not judgment. In baptism Jesus embraces the condition of sinners, affirming their existence as his own. He is one of them! After the baptism, the saying "Thou art my beloved Son; with thee I am well pleased" (Mark 1:11) expresses God's approval of that very definition of Jesus' person and work.

The temptation is a continuation of the theme already expressed in the baptism. As with the birth narratives, it is difficult to recover the event as it happened, but it would be difficult to deny that the narrative is intimately related to Jesus' self-portrayal of the character of his existence. The tempter's concern is to divert Jesus from the reality of his mission with the poor. Jesus' refusal to turn the stone into bread, or to worship the tempter, or to throw himself from the pinnacle of the temple (Luke 4:3–12) may be interpreted as his refusal to identify himself with any of the available modes of oppressive or self-glorifying power. His being in the world is as one of the humiliated, suffering poor.

3. Ministry. The Galilean ministry is an actual working out of the decision already expressed in his birth and reaffirmed at the baptism and temptation. Mark describes the implication of this decision: "Now after John was arrested, Jesus came into Galilee, preaching the gospel of God, and saying, 'The time is fulfilled, and

the kingdom of God is at hand; repent and believe in the gospel' "
(Mark 1:14–15).

New Testament scholars have spent many hours debating the
meaning of this passage, which sometimes gives the average person
the impression that there is a hidden meaning discernible only by
seminary graduates. But the meaning is clear enough for those who
are prepared for a radical decision about their movement in the
world. Jesus' proclamation of the kingdom is an announcement of
God's decision about oppressed humankind. "The time is fulfilled,
and the kingdom of God is at hand"—that is, slavery is about to
end, because the reign of God displaces all false authorities. To
"repent and believe in the gospel" is to recognize the importance of
the hour at hand and to accept the reality of the new age by
participating in it as it is revealed in the words and work of Jesus.
The kingdom is Jesus, whose relationship to God and human
beings is defined by his words and work.

From this it is clear that Jesus' restriction of the kingdom to the
poor has far-reaching implications for our understanding of the
gospel message. It is interesting, if not surprising, to watch white
New Testament scholars explain away the real theological significance of Jesus' teachings on the kingdom and the poor. Nearly
always they are at pains to emphasize that Jesus did not necessarily
mean the economically poor but rather, as Matthew says, "the poor
in spirit." Then they proceed to point out the exceptions: Joseph of
Arimathea was a rich man (Matthew 27:57) and he was "a good and
righteous man" (Luke 23:50). There are also instances of Jesus'
association with the wealthy; and Zacchaeus did not promise to give
up *all* his goods but only *half.* As one biblical scholar has put it:

> It was not so much the possession of riches as one's attitude
> towards them and the use one makes of them which was the
> special object of Jesus' teachings and this is true of the
> biblical teachings as a whole. Jesus does not condemn private
> property, nor is he a social reformer in any primary sense; he
> is concerned with men's motives and hearts.[8]

With all due respect to erudite New Testament scholars and the
excellent work that has been done in this field, I cannot help but
conclude that they are "straining out a gnat and swallowing a

camel"! It is this kind of false interpretation that leads to the oppression of the poor. As long as oppressors can be sure that the gospel does not threaten their social, economic, and political security, they can enslave others in the name of Jesus Christ. The history of Christendom, at least from the time of Constantine, is a history of human enslavement; and even today, white "Christians" see little contradiction between wealth and the Christian gospel.

It seems clear that the overwhelming weight of biblical teaching, especially the prophetic tradition in which Jesus stood unambiguously, is upon God's unqualified identification with the poor precisely because they are poor. The kingdom of God is for the helpless, because they have no security in this world. We see this emphasis in the repeated condemnation of the rich, notably in the Sermon on the Mount, and in Jesus' exclusive identification of his ministry with sinners. The kingdom demands the surrender of one's whole life. How is it possible to be rich, seeing others in a state of economic deprivation, and at the same time insist that one has complete trust in God? Again, how can it be said that Jesus was not primarily a social reformer but "concerned with men's motives and hearts," when the kingdom itself strikes across all boundaries—social, economic, and political?

Jesus' teaching about the kingdom is the most radical, revolutionary aspect of his message. It involves the totality of a person's existence in the world and what that means in an oppressive society. To repent is to affirm the reality of the kingdom by refusing to live on the basis of any definition except according to the kingdom. Nothing else matters! The kingdom, then, is the rule of God breaking in like a ray of light, usurping the powers that enslave human lives. That is why exorcisms are so prominent in Jesus' ministry. They are a visible manifestation of the presence of the kingdom. "If it is by the finger of God that I cast out demons, then the kingdom of God has come upon you" (Luke 11:20).

Jesus is the Oppressed One whose work is that of liberating humanity from inhumanity. Through him the oppressed are set free to be what they are. This and this alone is the meaning of his *finality*, which has been camouflaged in debates about his humanity and divinity.

4. Death and Resurrection. The death and resurrection of Jesus are the consummation of his earthly ministry with the poor. The

Christian church rightly focuses on these events as decisive for an adequate theological interpretation of Jesus' historical ministry. Rudolf Bultmann pointed this out convincingly. Although post-Bultmannians generally do not agree with Bultmann's extreme skepticism regarding history, they do agree on his assessment of the importance of the death-resurrection event in shaping the Christian view of the earthly ministry of Jesus. The Jesus of history is not simply a figure of the past but the Christ of today as interpreted by the theological significance of the death-resurrection event.

Black theology certainly agrees with this emphasis on the cross and resurrection. The Gospels are not biographies of Jesus; they are *gospel*—that is, good news about what God has done in the life, death, and resurrection of Jesus. This must be the focus of christological thinking.

The theological significance of the cross and resurrection is what makes the life of Jesus more than just the life of a good man who happened to like the poor. *The finality of Jesus lies in the totality of his existence in complete freedom as the Oppressed One who reveals through his death and resurrection that God is present in all dimensions of human liberation.* His death is the revelation of the freedom of God, taking upon himself the totality of human oppression; his resurrection is the disclosure that God is not defeated by oppression but transforms it into the possibility of freedom.

For men and women who live in an oppressive society this means that they do not have to behave as if *death* is the ultimate. God in Christ has set us free from death, and we can now live without worrying about social ostracism, economic insecurity, or political tyranny. "In Christ the immortal God has tasted death and in so doing . . . destroyed death"[9] (compare Hebrews 2:14ff.).

Christian freedom is the recognition that Christ has conquered death. Man no longer has to be afraid of dying. To live as if death has the last word is to be enslaved and thus controlled by the forces of destruction. The free are the oppressed who say no to an oppressor, in spite of the threat of death, because God has said yes to them, thereby placing them in a state of freedom. They can now deny any values that separate them from the reality of their new being.

Moltmann is correct when he speaks of the resurrection as the "symbol of protest":

To believe in the resurrection transforms faith from a deliverance from the world into an initiative that changes the world and makes those who believe into wordly, personal, social and political witnesses to God's righteousness and freedom in the midst of a repressive society and an unredeemed world. In this, faith comes to historical self-consciousness and to the recognition of its eschatological task within history.[10]

The Black Christ

What is the significance of the historical and resurrected Jesus for our times? The answer to this question must focus on both the meaning of the historical Jesus and the contemporary significance of the resurrection. It is impossible to gloss over either one of these emphases and still retain the gospel message.

Focusing on the historical Jesus means that black theology recognizes *history* as an indispensable foundation of christology. We are not free to make Jesus what we wish him to be at certain moments of existence. He *is* who he *was,* and we know who he was through a critical, historical evaluation of the New Testament Jesus. Black theology takes seriously Pannenberg's comment that "faith primarily has to do with what Jesus was."[11]

To focus on the contemporary significance of the resurrection means that we do not take Pannenberg's comment on the historical Jesus as seriously as he does. No matter how seriously we take the carpenter from Nazareth, there is still the existential necessity to relate his person to black persons, asking, "What is his relevance to the black community today?" In this sense, unlike Pannenberg, we say that the soteriological value of Jesus' person must finally determine our christology. It is the oppressed community in the situation of liberation that determines the meaning and scope of Jesus. We know who Jesus *was* and *is* when we encounter the brutality of oppression in his community as it seeks to be what it is, in accordance with his resurrection.

The christological significance of Jesus is not an abstract question to be solved by intellectual debates among seminary professors. The meaning of Jesus is an existential question. We know who he is when our own lives are placed in a situation of oppression, and we thus have to make a decision for or against our condition. To say no to oppression and yes to liberation is to encounter the existential significance of the Resurrected One. He is the Liberator *par excellence* whose very presence makes persons sell all that they have and follow him.

Now what does this mean for blacks in America today? How are they to interpret the christological significance of the Resurrected One in such a way that his person will be existentially relevant to their oppressed condition? The black community is an oppressed community primarily because of its blackness; hence the christological importance of Jesus must be found in his blackness. If he is not black as we are, then the resurrection has little significance for our times. Indeed, if he cannot be what we are, we cannot be who he is. Our being with him is dependent on his being with us in the oppressed black condition, revealing to us what is necessary for our liberation.

The definition of Jesus as black is crucial for christology if we truly believe in his continued presence today. Taking our clue from the historical Jesus who is pictured in the New Testament as the Oppressed One, what else, except blackness, could adequately tell us the meaning of his presence today? Any statement about Jesus today that fails to consider blackness as the *decisive* factor about his person is a denial of the New Testament message. The life, death, and resurrection of Jesus reveal that he is the man for others, disclosing to them what is necessary for their liberation from oppression. If this is true, then Jesus Christ must be black so that blacks can know that their liberation is his liberation.

The black Jesus is also an important theological symbol for an analysis of Christ's presence today because we must make decisions about where he is at work in the world. Is his presence synonymous with the work of the oppressed or the oppressors, blacks or whites? Is he to be found among the wretched or among the rich?

Of course clever white theologians would say that it is not either/ or. Rather he is to be found somewhere in between, a little black and a little white. Such an analysis is not only irrelevant for our times but also irrelevant for the time of the historical Jesus. Jesus was not for and against the poor, for and against the rich. He was for the poor and against the rich, for the weak and against the strong. Who can read the New Testament and fail to see that Jesus took sides and accepted freely the possibility of being misunderstood?

If the historical Jesus is any clue for an analysis of the contemporary Christ, then he must be where human beings are enslaved. To speak of him is to speak of the liberation of the oppressed. In a society that defines blackness as evil and whiteness as good, the theological significance of Jesus is found in the possibility of human liberation through blackness. Jesus is the black Christ!

Concretely, to speak of the presence of Christ today means focusing on the forces of liberation in the black community. Value perspectives must be reshaped in the light of what aids the self-determination of black persons. The definition of Christ as black means that he represents the complete opposite of the values of white culture. He is the center of a black Copernican revolution.

Black theology seeks to do in American theology what Copernicus did to thinking about the physical universe. Inasmuch as this country has achieved its sense of moral and religious idealism by oppressing blacks, the black Christ leads the warfare against the white assault on blackness by striking at white values and white religion. The black Copernican revolution means extolling as good what whites have ignored or regarded as evil.

The blackness of Christ clarifies the definition of him as the *Incarnate* One. In him God becomes oppressed humanity and thus reveals that the achievement of full humanity is consistent with divine being. The human being was not created to be a slave, and the appearance of God in Christ gives us the possibility of freedom. By becoming a black person, God discloses that blackness is not what the world says it is. Blackness is a manifestation of the being of God in that it reveals that neither divinity nor humanity reside in white definitions but in liberation from captivity.

The black Christ is he who threatens the structure of evil as seen in white society, rebelling against it, thereby becoming the embodiment of what the black community knows that it must become. Because he has become black as we are, we now know what black empowerment is. It is blacks determining the way they are going to behave in the world. It is refusing to allow white society to place strictures on black existence as if their having guns mean that blacks are supposed to cool it.

Black empowerment is the black community in defiance, knowing that he who has become one of them is far more important than threats from white officials. The black Christ is he who nourishes the rebellious impulse in blacks so that at the appointed time the black community can respond collectively to the white community as a corporate "bad nigger," lashing out at the enemy of humankind.

It is to be expected that some whites will resent the christological formulation of the black Christ, either by ignoring it or by viewing it as too narrow to include the universal note of the gospel. It will be difficult for whites to deny the whiteness of their existence and affirm the oppressed black Christ. But the concept of black, which includes both what the world means by oppression and what the gospel means by liberation, is the only concept that has any real significance today. If Christ is not black, then who is he? We could say that he is the son of God, son of Man, messiah, lord, son of David, and a host of other titles. The difficulty with these titles is not that they fail to describe the person of Christ, but they are first-century titles. To cling to them without asking, "What appropriate symbol do these titles refer to today?" is to miss the significance of them altogether.

What is striking about the New Testament names of Jesus is the dimension of liberation embedded in them. For example, Jesus Christ as Lord, a postresurrection title, emphasizes his complete authority over all creation. Everyone is subject to him. The Lord is the "ruler," "commander," he who has all authority. If "Jesus is Lord," as one of the earliest baptismal creeds of the church puts it, then what does this say about black and white relationships in America? The meaning is perhaps too obvious for comment. It means simply that whites do not have authority over blacks. Our loyalty belongs only to him who has become like us in everything, especially blackness. To take seriously the lordship of Christ or his sonship or messiahship is to see him as the sole criterion for authentic existence.

If Jesus is the Suffering Servant of God, he is an oppressed being who has taken on that very form of human existence that is responsible for human misery. What we need to ask is this: "What is the form of humanity that accounts for human suffering in our society? What is it, except blackness?" If Christ is truly the Suffering Servant of God who takes upon himself the suffering of his people, thereby reestablishing the covenant of God, then he must be black.

To get at the meaning of this and not get bogged down in racial emotionalism, we need only ask, "Is it possible to talk about suffering in America without talking about the meaning of blackness? Can we really believe that Christ is the Suffering Servant par excellence if he is not black?" Black theology contends that blackness is the only symbol that cannot be overlooked if we are going to take seriously the christological significance of Jesus Christ.

But some whites will ask, "Does black theology believe that Jesus was *really* black?" It seems to me that the *literal* color of Jesus is irrelevant, as are the different shades of blackness in America. Generally speaking, blacks are not oppressed on the basis of the depths of their blackness. "Light" blacks are oppressed just as much as "dark" blacks. But as it happens, *Jesus was not white* in any sense of the word, literally or theologically. Therefore, Albert Cleage is not too far wrong when he describes Jesus as a black Jew; and he is certainly on solid theological grounds when he describes Christ as the Black Messiah.

The importance of the concept of the black Christ is that it expresses the *concreteness* of Jesus' continued presence today. If we do not translate the first-century titles into symbols that are relevant today, then we run the danger that Bultmann is so concerned about: Jesus becomes merely a figure of past history. To make Jesus just a figure of yesterday is to deny the real importance of the preaching of the early church. He is not dead but resurrected and is alive in the world today. Like yesterday, he has taken upon himself the misery of his people, becoming for them what is needed for their liberation.

To be a disciple of the black Christ is to become black with him. Looting, burning, or the destruction of white property are not *primary* concerns. Such matters can only be decided by the oppressed themselves who are seeking to develop their images of the black Christ. What is primary is that blacks must refuse to let whites define what is appropriate for the black community. Just as white slaveholders in the nineteenth century said that questioning slavery was an invasion of their property rights, so today they use the same line of reasoning in reference to black self-determination. But Nat Turner had no scruples on this issue; and blacks today are beginning to see themselves in a new image. We believe in the manifestation of the black Christ, and our encounter with him defines our values. This means that blacks are *free* to do what they have to in order to affirm their humanity.

The Kingdom of God and the Black Christ

The appearance of Jesus as the black Christ also means that the black revolution is God's kingdom becoming a reality in America. According to the New Testament, the kingdom is a historical event. It is what happens to persons when their being is confronted with the reality of God's historical liberation of the oppressed. To see the kingdom is to see a happening, and we are thus placed in a situation of decision—we say either yes or no to the liberation struggle.

The kingdom is not an attainment of material security, nor is it mystical communion with the divine. It has to do with the *quality* of one's existence in which a person realizes that *persons* are more important than property. When blacks behave as if the values of this world have no significance, it means that they perceive the irruption of God's kingdom. The kingdom of God is a *black* happening. It is black persons saying no to whitey, forming caucuses and advancing into white confrontation. It is a beautiful thing to see blacks shaking loose the chains of white approval, and it can only mean that they know that there is a way of living that does not involve the destruction of their personhood. This is the kingdom of God.

For Jesus, repentance is a precondition for entrance into the kingdom. But it should be pointed out that repentance has nothing to do with morality or religious piety in the white sense.

Günther Bornkamm's analysis of Jesus' call to repentance is relevant here. To repent, says Bornkamm, is "to lay hold on the salvation which is already at hand, and to give up everything for it."[12] It means recognizing the importance of the kingdom-event and casting one's lot with it. The kingdom is God's own event and inherent in its appearance is the invitation to renounce everything and join it. That is why Jesus said:

> If your hand or your foot causes you to sin, cut it off and throw it from you; it is better for you to enter life maimed or lame than with two hands or two feet to be thrown into eternal fire. And if your eye causes you to sin, pluck it out

and throw it from you; it is better for you to enter life with one eye than with two eyes to be thrown into the hell of fire] [Matthew 18:8–9].

According to Bornkamm:

Repentance comes by means of grace. Those who sit at the table of the rich lord are the poor, the cripples, the blind and lame, not those who are already half-cured. The tax collectors and sinners with whom Jesus sits at meat are not asked first about the state of their moral improvement. . . . The extent to which all talk of the conditions which man must fulfill before grace is accorded him is here silenced, as shown by the parables of the lost sheep and the lost coin, which tell only of the finding of what was lost, and in this very manner describe the joy in heaven "over one sinner who repents" (Luke 15:7, 10). So little is repentance a human action preparing the way for grace that it can be placed on the level of being found.[13]

The kingdom is what God does and repentance arises solely as a response to God's liberation.

The event of the kingdom today is the liberation struggle in the black community. It is where persons are suffering and dying for want of human dignity. It is thus incumbent upon all to see the event for what it is—God's kingdom. This is what conversion means. Blacks are being converted because they see in the events around them the coming of the Lord, and will not be scared into closing their eyes to it. Black identity is too important; it is like the pearl of great value, which a person buys only by selling all that he or she has (Matthew 13:44–46).

Of course, whites can say that they fail to see the significance of this black phenomenon. But loss of sight is characteristic of the appearance of the kingdom. Not everyone recognizes the person from Nazareth as the incarnate One who came to liberate the human race. Who could possibly imagine that the Holy One of Israel would condescend to the level of a carpenter? Only those with eyes of faith could see that in that person God was confronting the reality of the human condition. There is no other sign save the words and deeds of Jesus himself. If an encounter with him does not convince persons that God is present, then they will never know, except in that awful moment when perfect awareness is fatally bound up with irreversible judgment.

That is why Jesus compared the kingdom with a mustard seed and with yeast in dough. Both show a small, apparently insignificant beginning but a radical, revolutionary ending. The seed grows to a large tree, and the bread can feed many hungry persons. So it is with the kingdom; because of its small beginning, some viewers do not readily perceive what is actually happening.

The black revolution is a continuation of that small kingdom. Whites do not recognize what is happening, and they are thus unable to deal with it. For most whites in power, the black community is a nuisance—something to be considered only when the natives get restless. But what white America fails to realize is the explosive nature of the kingdom. Although its beginning is small, it will have far-reaching effects not only on the black community but on the white community as well. Now is the time to make decisions about loyalties, because soon it will be too late. Shall we or shall we not join the black revolutionary kingdom?

To enter the kingdom is to enter the state of salvation, the condition of blessedness. Historically it appears that "salvation" is Paul's translation of Jesus' phrase "kingdom of God." But, oh, how the word "salvation" has been beaten and battered in nineteen centuries of Christian verbiage! What can salvation possibly mean for oppressed blacks in America? Is it a kind of spiritual juice, squirted into the life of the dispirited that somehow enable them to withstand the brutality of oppressors because they know that heaven is waiting for them? Certainly, this is what rulers would like the oppressed to believe.

In most societies where political oppression is acute and religion is related to the state, salvation is interpreted always in ways that do not threaten the security of the existing government. Sometimes salvation takes the form of abstract, intellectual analysis or private mystical communion with the divine. The "hope" that is offered the oppressed is not the possibility of changing their earthly condition but a longing for the next life. With the poor counting on salvation in the next life, oppressors can humiliate and exploit without fear of reprisal. That is why Karl Marx called religion the opiate of the people. It is an open question whether he was right in his evaluation; but he was correct in identifying the intention of oppressors. They promote religion because it can be an effective tool for enslavement.

The history of the black church is a case in point. At first, white "Christian" slaveholders in America did not allow their slaves to be baptized, because Christianity supposedly enfranchised them. But because the white church was having few converts among blacks, it proceeded to assure slaveholders that baptism had nothing to do with civil freedom. In fact, many white ministers assured slave masters that Christianity would make for better slaves. With that assurance, the masters began to introduce Christianity to blacks, confident that it would make blacks more obedient. But many blacks were able to appropriate white Christianity to their own condition by turning it into a religion of liberation. The emergence of the "invisible institution" (secret church) among the slaves of the south, the organization of the African Methodist Episcopal Church (1816) and the African Methodist Episcopal Zion Church (1821), together with other black independent religious institutions, and their involvement in the antislavery movement, show that black religionists did see through the fake white Christianity of the period.

For the pre–Civil War black church, salvation involved more than longing for the next life. Being saved was also a present reality that placed persons in a dimension of freedom so that earthly injustice became intolerable. That was why Nat Turner, a Baptist preacher, had visions of God that involved his own election to be the Moses of his people, leading it from the house of bondage. After his insurrection black preachers were outlawed in many parts of the south.

Unfortunately, the post–Civil War black church fell into the white trick of interpreting salvation in terms similar to those of white oppressors. Salvation became white: an objective act of Christ in which God "washes" away our sins in order to prepare us for a new life in heaven. The resurgence of the black church in civil rights and the creation of a black theology represent an attempt of the black community to see salvation in the light of its own earthly liberation.

The interpretation of salvation as liberation from bondage is certainly consistent with the biblical view:

In the Old Testament salvation is expressed by a word which
has the root meaning of "to be wide" or "spacious," "to
develop without hindrance" and thus ultimately "to have
victory in battle" (I Sam. 14:45).[14]

To be saved meant that one's enemies have been conquered, and the
savior is the one who has the power to gain victory:

He who needs salvation is one who has been threatened or
oppressed, and his salvation consists in deliverance from
danger and tyranny or rescue from imminent peril (I Sam.
4:3, 7:8, 9:16). To save another is to communicate to him
one's own prevailing strength (Job 26:2), to give him the
power to maintain the necessary strength.[15]

In Israel, God is the Savior par excellence. Beginning with the
exodus, God's righteousness is for those who are weak and helpless.
"The mighty work of God, in which his righteousness is manifested, is in saving the humble . . . the poor and the dispirited."[16]
The same is true in the New Testament. Salvation is release from
slavery and admission to freedom (Galatians 5:1, II Corinthians
3:17), saying no to the fear of principalities and yes to the powers of
liberty (I John 4:18). This is not to deny that salvation is a future
reality; but it is also hope that focuses on the present.

Today the oppressed are the inhabitants of black ghettos, Amerindian reservations, Hispanic barrios, and other places where
whiteness has created misery. To participate in God's salvation is to
cooperate with the black Christ as he liberates his people from
bondage. Salvation, then, primarily has to do with earthly reality
and the injustice inflicted on those who are helpless and poor. To
see the salvation of God is to see this people rise up against its
oppressors, demanding that justice become a reality *now,* not
tomorrow. It is the oppressed serving warning that they "ain't
gonna take no more of this bullshit, but a new day is coming and it
ain't going to be like today." The new day is the presence of the
black Christ as expressed in the liberation of the black community.

7

Church, World, and Eschatology in Black Theology

The Church

Carl Michalson once said:

The Christian Gospel is a proclamation which strikes the ear of the world with the force of a hint. Some "get it"; some do not. To those who do, it is "the power of God unto salvation." To those who do not, it can seem a scandal and offence![1]

The Christian church is that community of persons who "got the hint," and they thus refuse to be content with human pain and suffering. To receive "the power of God unto salvation" places persons in a state of Christian existence, making it impossible for them to sit still as their neighbors are herded off to prison camps. The hint of the gospel moves them to say no to rulers of the world: "If our brothers and sisters have to go, it will be over our dead bodies." They are the ones who believe in the gospel of liberation, convinced that personal freedom is more important than "law and order". Only a few decades ago, Hitler and his demigods exterminated over six million Jews in the name of "law and order." In words very similar to the language of our own politicians, he said:

The streets of our country are in turmoil. The universities are filled with students rebelling and rioting. Communists are seeking to destroy our country. Russia is threatening us with her might and the republic is in danger. Yes, danger from within and from without. *We need law and order.* Yes, without law and order our nation cannot survive. Elect us and we will restore law and order. We shall by law and order be respected among the nations of the world. Without law and order our republic shall fail.[2]

Because the church is the community that participates in Jesus Christ's liberating work in history, it can never endorse "law and order" that causes suffering. To do so is to say yes to structures of oppression. Because the church has received the gospel-hint and has accepted what that means for human existence, the church must be a revolutionary community, breaking laws that destroy persons. It believes (with Reinhold Niebuhr) that "comfortable classes may continue to dream of an automatic progress in society. They do not suffer enough from social injustice to recognize its peril in the life of society."[3]

In the New Testament the church *(ecclesia)* is the community that has received the Holy Spirit and is now ready to do what is necessary to live out the gospel. It is the assembly of those who have become heirs of the promises of God; and because they have experienced what that means for humanity, they cannot accept the world as it is. They must rebel against evil so all citizens may know that they do not have to behave according to unjust societal laws.

Participation in the historical liberation spearheaded by God is the defining characteristic of the church. The task of the church is threefold. First, it proclaims the reality of divine liberation. This is what the New Testament calls preaching the gospel. The gospel is the proclamation of God's liberation as revealed in the event of Jesus and the outpouring of the Holy Spirit. It is not possible to receive the good news of freedom *and* keep it to ourselves; it must be told to the whole world. This is what the writer of Matthew had in mind when he recorded the words of Jesus:

Go therefore and make disciples of all nations, baptizing them in the name of the Father and of the Son and of the

Holy Spirit, teaching them to observe all that I have com-
manded you; and lo, I am with you always, to the close of the
age [Matthew 28:19-20].

To preach the gospel today means confronting the world with the
reality of Christian freedom. It means telling blacks that their
slavery has come to an end, and telling whites to let go of the
chains. Blacks do not have to live according to white rules. If the
gospel is "the power of God unto salvation," then blacks have a
higher loyalty to God that cuts across every sphere of human
existence. Preaching the gospel is nothing but proclaiming to
blacks that they do not have to submit to ghetto-existence. Our new
existence has been bought and paid for; we are now redeemed, set
free. Now it is incumbent upon us to behave like free persons.

Secondly, the church not only proclaims the good news of freedom, it actively shares in the liberation struggle. Though the battle
against evil has been won, old rulers pretend that they are still in
power. They are still trying to enforce the laws of the old order. The
function of the church is to remind them that they are no longer in
power. The last has become first and the first last. A Copernican
revolution has taken place in human existence that transcends
anything past or present. The church is the community that lives on
the basis of the radical demands of the gospel by making the gospel
message a social, economic, and political reality. It has the courage
to take the risk, knowing that, at this early stage, it lives in a society
that refuses to believe the gospel message. It thus goes against the
grain of societal existence because its sole aim is to share with Jesus
Christ in his liberating activity.

For blacks this means that societal values are no longer important. Blacks are free to share in the liberation of others by making
the world more receptive to blackness. We must assume that all
blacks want to be free and that, if given half a chance, they will
affirm the liberty that is theirs. The church is the community
of those who make the world more amenable to black self-
determination by forcing rulers to decide between blackness and
death.

Thirdly, the church as a fellowship is a visible manifestation that
the gospel is a reality. If the church is not free, if it is a distorted
representation of the irruption of God's kingdom, if it lives accord-

ing to the old order (as it usually has), then no one will believe its message. If someone tells me that Christ has set us free from all alien loyalties, but he himself obeys the loyalties that he claims Christ has defeated, then I must conclude that he does not really believe what he says. To believe is to live accordingly; the church must live according to its preaching. This is what Bonhoeffer had in mind when he called the church "Christ existing as a community."

The World

Participation in divine liberation places the church squarely in the context of the world. Its existence is inseparable from worldly involvement. Black theology cannot say that the "church is the world" or the "world is the church" (as implied in some secular theologies), but it does affirm that the church cannot be the church in isolation from the concrete realities of human suffering. The world is earthly existence, the place where human beings are enslaved. It is where laws are passed against the oppressed, and where the oppressed fight back even though their efforts seem futile. The world is where white and black persons live, encountering each other, the latter striving for a little more room to breathe and the former doing everything possible to destroy black reality.

The world is not a metaphysical entity or an ontological problem, as some philosophers and theologians would have us believe. It is very concrete. It is punching clocks, taking orders, fighting rats, and being kicked around by police officers. It is where the oppressed live. Jews encountered it in concentration camps, Amerindians on reservations, and blacks on slave ships, in cotton fields, and in "dark" ghettos. The world is white persons, the degrading rules they make for the "underprivileged," and their guilt-dispelling recourse to political and theological slogans about the welfare of society "as a whole." In short, the world is where the brutal reality of inhumanity makes its ungodly appearance, turning persons into animals.

Because the church knows that the world is where human beings are dehumanized, it can neither retreat from the world nor embrace it. Retreating is tantamount to a denial of its calling to share in divine liberation. It is a complete misunderstanding of the Christ-event, which demands radical, worldly involvement in behalf of the oppressed. Retreating is navel-gazing, a luxury that oppressed persons cannot afford. Only oppressors can turn in upon themselves and worship their own projected image and define it as God. Persons who live in the real world have to encounter the concreteness of suffering without suburbs as places of retreat. To be oppressed is to encounter the overwhelming presence of human evil without any place to escape. Either we submit or we rebel, knowing that our physical lives are at stake.

The church cannot seriously consider retreat as an option, because its very existence is affirmed and reaffirmed only as it demonstrates to all what Christian existence is all about *in* the world. There is no place for sheltered piety. Who can "pray" when all hell has broken loose and human existence is being trampled underfoot by evil forces? Prayer takes on new meaning. It has nothing to do with those Bible verses that rulers utter before eating their steaks, in order to remind themselves that they are religious and have not mistreated anybody. Who can thank God for food when we know that our brothers and sisters are starving as we dine like kings?

Prayer is not kneeling morning, noon, and evening. This is a tradition that is characteristic of whites; they use it to reinforce the rightness of their destruction of blacks. Prayer is the spirit that is evident in all oppressed communities when they know that they have a job to do. It is the communication with the divine that makes them know that they have very little to lose in the fight against evil and a lot to gain. We can only lose our physical lives but can gain what the writer of the Fourth Gospel calls eternal life and what blacks call blackness. To retreat from the world is to lose one's life and become what others say we are.

Embracing the world is also a denial of the gospel. The history of traditional Christianity and recent secular theology show the danger of this procedure. Identifying the rise of nationalism with Christianity, capitalism with the gospel, or exploration of outer space with the advancement of the kingdom of God serves only to enhance the oppression of the weak. It is a denial of the lordship of Christ. To affirm Christ as Lord means that the world stands under his judgment. There is no place or person not subject to his rule. And because not everyone recognizes Christ for who he is, the task of the church is to be out there in the world, not as an endorser of its oppression but as the visible representative of his lordship. The world is where we are called to fight against evil.

The difficulty of defining the meaning of the church and its involvement in the world stems from the unchurchly behavior of institutional white churches. They have given the word "church" a bad reputation for those interested in fighting against human suffering. Because of the unchristian behavior of persons who say they are Christians, "church" in America may very well refer to respectable murderers, who destroy human dignity while "worshiping" God and feeling no guilt about it. They equate things as they are with God's will.

To think of the church in this society is to visualize buildings with crosses and signs designating Sunday morning worship. It is to think of pious white oppressors gathering on Sunday, singing hymns and praying to God, while their preachers talk endlessly about some white cat who died on a cross. For some reason, it never enters the minds of these murderers that Jesus Christ does not approve of their behavior. Christ dies not to "save" them but to destroy them so as to recreate them, to dissolve their whiteness in the fire of judgment, for it is only through the destruction of whiteness that the wholeness of humanity may be realized.

Unfortunately black churches are also guilty of prostituting the name of God's church. Having originally come into being because they knew that political involvement in societal liberation of blacks was equivalent with the gospel, it is a sad fact that in subsequent decades they all but lost their reason for being. Except for rare prophetic figures like Jesse Jackson and Albert Cleage, the black denominational churches seem to be content with things as they are, getting fat on the misery of their sisters and brothers. Although possessing the greatest potentiality for black revolution, the black churches satisfy themselves with white solutions to earthly injustice. That is why persons interested in justice in this world so often scorn the black church, saying that it is nothing but a second-rate oppressor.

If the white and black churches do not represent Christ's redemptive work in the world, where then is Christ's church to be found? As always, his church is where wounds are being healed and chains are being struck off. It does not matter in the least whether the community of liberators designate their work as Christ's own work. What is important is that the oppressed are being liberated. Indeed there may be some advantages in not consciously doing anything for Christ simply because one wants to be a Christian. The truly Christian response to earthly problems is doing what one must do because it is the *human* thing to do. The brother's suffering should not be used as a stepping-stone in Christian piety.

This may be what Jesus had in mind when he told the parable of the last judgment (Matthew 25:31 ff.). Persons are received and rejected according to their ministering to human need. Those who were received were surprised, for they did not view their work as God's own. They were not seeking a reward. They were only doing what they considered the *human* thing to do. That is why they asked, "Lord, when did we see thee hungry and feed thee, or thirsty and give thee drink? And when did we see thee a stranger and welcome thee, or naked and clothe thee? And when did we see thee sick or in prison and visit thee?" Their actions were not meant for the King! But the King will answer, "Truly, I say to you, as you did it to one of the last of these my brethren, you did it to me."

Because the work of God is not a superimposed activity but a part of one's existence as a person, pious frauds are caught in a trap. They are rejected because they failed to see that being good is not a societal trait or an extra activity, but a human activity. They are excluded because they used their neighbor as an enhancement of their own religious piety. Had they known that blacks were Jesus, they would have been prepared to relieve their suffering. But that is just the point: there is no way to know in the abstract who is Jesus and who is not. It is not an intellectual question at all. Knowledge of Jesus Christ comes as one participates in human liberation.

Eschatology

No study in systematic theology is complete without dealing with the question of eschatology. To speak about eschatology is to move in the direction of the future, what has often been called the "last things."

The question about the "not yet" has always been a paramount question and its importance is symbolized in the certainty of death. All living things die; but, as Reinhold Niebuhr has pointed out, only human beings know of their future end. It is knowledge of future ceasing-to-be that makes humankind different from other creatures.

To anticipate the certainty of nonexistence understandably places us in a state of anxiety. What can we do about death and its relationship to life? If we know that our present existence will be swallowed up by the future reality of nothingness, what can we hope for when our present being no longer is? Is there life after death?

These are tough questions, and any theology that seeks to deal with human existence cannot sidestep them. It can be argued that religion originated in the attempt of humankind to grapple with the problem of death. And the success of any religion in winning adherents may be traced to its ability to give a satisfactory answer to the question of death. What does the black theological perspective have to say about the ultimate hope of blacks and its relationship to their present existence? What does it have to say about death?

Black theology rejects as invalid the attempt of oppressors to escape the question of death. White rulers in society seek to evade the reality of their end by devising recreational hobbies. They play golf, vacation in distant lands, live in all manner of luxury. Instead of facing up to the reality of finite existence and the anxiety that accompanies it, they pretend that their eternality is dependent on their political, social, and economic dominance over the weak and helpless. With their power to control history, the present and future of other human beings, who can deny that they are not the masters of the world's destiny? It is their confidence in their own present strength that renders them incapable of looking the future squarely in the face. Oppressors do not know death because they do not know themselves—their finiteness and future end.

In contrast to the inability of oppressors to deal with death, the oppressed cannot escape their future end, for the visible presence of rulers is a constant reminder that nonexistence may come at any moment. For blacks death is not really a future reality; it is a part of their everyday existence. They see death every time they see whites. The death of men, women, and children at the hands of whites who wheel and deal in the structures of society precludes the possibility of escape from life or death. Blacks, then, are forced to ask, What is the relationship between the past, present, and future in the context of blackness?

We do not find answers to questions about life and death by reading books. Life-and-death questions are not hypothetical questions, and answers are not found in a theology or philosophy class. The answers to questions about the end come when we face the reality of future nonexistence in the context of existence that is characterized by oppression and liberation. *We know what the end is when we face it head-on by refusing, at the risk of death, to tolerate present injustice.* The eschatological perspective must be grounded in the historical present, thereby forcing the oppressed community to say no to unjust treatment, because its present humiliation is inconsistent with its promised future.

An eschatological perspective that does not challenge the present order is faulty. If contemplation about the future distorts the present reality of injustice and reconciles the oppressed to unjust treatment committed against them, then it is unchristian and thus has nothing whatsoever to do with the Christ who came to liberate us. It is this that renders white talk about heaven and life after death fruitless for blacks.

We know all about pearly gates, golden streets, and long white robes. We have sung songs about heaven until we were hoarse, but it did not change the present state or ease the pain. To be sure, we may "walk in Jerusalem jus' like John" and "there may be a great camp meeting in the Promised Land," but we want to walk in *this* land—"the land of the free and the home of the brave." We want to know why Harlem cannot become Jerusalem and Chicago the Promised Land? What good are golden crowns, slippers, white robes, or even eternal life, if it means that we have to turn our backs on the pain and suffering of our own children?

Unless the future can become present, thereby forcing blacks to make changes in this world, what significance could eschatology have for those who believe that their self-determination must become a reality *now!* White missionaries have always encouraged blacks to forget about present injustice and look forward to heavenly justice. But black theology says no, insisting that we either put new meaning into Christian hope by relating it to our liberation or drop it altogether.

Perhaps a place to begin looking for this new eschatological significance is in the theology of Rudolf Bultmann.[4] Taking his clue from the existential orientation of Martin Heidegger, Bultmann has pointed out some interesting things about theological eschatology and its relationship to history. Concentrating his intellectual efforts on articulating an eschatological perspective that was consistent with the achievement of authentic human selfhood as defined by Heidegger's philosophy, Bultmann concluded that the human future cannot be separated from being-in-the-present. He therefore rejected any eschatological viewpoint that centered on cosmological ingredients, or apocalyptic speculations on non-earthly reality. To accept mythology as the key to eschatology is to reject "the complete genuine historicity" of the human being. Eschatology, said Bultmann, must focus on human beings as they exist in their existential situation, in which the meaning of history is located in the present moment of decision.

Contemporary theology is indebted to Bultmann for his contention that eschatology cannot be separated from the present historical moment of the human being. But Bultmann did not take his point far enough. His view failed to take seriously the significance of the liberation of an oppressed community. How is eschatology related to *protest* against injustice and the need for revolutionary change? True, as Bultmann pointed out, one's future cannot be separated from one's present moment of decision. But neither can one's future be separated from the future of one's community, the nation. In the Old Testament, God is conceived not only as a God who acts in history *for me;* God acts in the history of a particular community. And God's action can be for me only insofar as I choose to belong to the community of God. One's selfhood is bound up with the community to which one belongs.

Also, Bultmann failed to point out that the future of God in biblical history cannot be separated from the *oppressed condition* of God's people. Who are they who long for the coming of the Lord and for what purpose? They who wait on the Lord are they who are weak; they are the poor, the helpless, the downtrodden. The powerful have no need for God's future: they are confident that their own strength will prevail. The future of God belongs to the future of the poor, those who are assured that God's present righteousness will not be defeated by those who seek to usurp divine authority. The poor need not worry about the evil of this world; they will see the glory of Yahweh in their own fight against injustice.

The dimension of futurity as protest against evil, although absent in Bultmann, may be found in the discourse of "hope theology."[5] The "hope theologians" take their cue from Ernst Bloch, who says, "Reality does not have a definite dimension. The world is not fixed." Or again:

> "Things can be otherwise." That means: things can also *become* otherwise: in the direction of evil, which must be avoided, or in the direction of good, which would have to be promoted.[6]

Eschatology is related to action and change.

However, it is Jürgen Moltmann, one of the most prominent "hope theologians," who places the Marxist emphasis on action and change in the Christian context. In his book *Theology of Hope,*[7] he says that the chief weakness of tradition thinking on eschatology is that it has been relegated to the end of time, having no relationship to the present. Eschatology has been interpreted as a reward to those who remain obedient. In this view, the resurrection of Christ means that salvation is now completed, finished. This explains why the churches look at the world not as a place to die but to live piously and prudently in preparation for the future. If one thinks that Christ's work is finished, then there is nothing to do but wait for the Second Coming.

But Moltmann's concern is to show that such a view means that one has not really heard the promise of God. To hear God's promise means that the church cannot accept the present reality of things as God's intention for humanity. The future cannot be a perfection of the present. Therefore, "To know God," writes Moltmann, "is to suffer God"—that is, to be called by God into the world, knowing that the present is incongruous with the expected future. "Hence it [revelation] does not give rise to powers of accommodation, but sets loose powers that are critical of being."[8] In order to guard against abstractions, Moltmann continues:

> Our hope in the promises of God . . . is not hope in God himself . . . but it hopes that his future faithfulness will bring with it also the fulness of what has been promised. . . .

It does not merely hope personally "in him," but has also substantial hopes of his lordship, his peace and his righteousness on earth.[9]

Moltmann's analysis is compatible with the concerns of black theology. Hope must be related to the present, and it must serve as a means of transforming an oppressed community into a liberated—and liberating—community. Black theology does not scorn Christian hope; it affirms it. It believes that, when Christians really believe in the resurrection of Christ and take seriously the promise revealed through him, they cannot be satisfied with the present world as it is. The past reality of the resurrection and the future of God disclosed throught it make Christians restless with regard to the imperfections of the present. It is not possible to know what the world can and ought to be and still be content with excuses for the desolation of human beings. Christians must fight against evil, for not to fight, not to do everything they can for their neighbor's pain, is to deny the resurrection.

Christian eschatology is bound up with the resurrection of Christ. He is the eschatological hope. He is the future of God who stands in judgment upon the world and forces us to give an account of the present. In view of his victory over evil and death, why must human beings suffer and die? Why do we behave as if the present were a fixed reality not susceptible of radical change? As long as we look at the resurrection of Christ and the expected "end," we cannot reconcile ourselves to the things of the present that contradict his presence. It is this eschatological emphasis that black theology affirms.

We come back to this question again: What about life after death? On the one hand, black theology believes that the emphasis on heaven in black churches was due primarily to white slave masters whose intention was to transfer slaves' loyalties from earthly reality to heavenly reality. In that way, masters could do what they willed about this world, knowing that their slaves were content with a better life in the next world. The considerable degree to which black slaves affirmed the worldview of masters was due to their inability to change life on earth. But the rise of black power and black theology brings with it a change in the focus of blacks.

We now believe that something *can* be done about this world, and we have resolved to die rather than deny the reality expresed in black self-determination. With this view, heaven is no longer analyzed the way it used to be. Heaven cannot mean accepting injustice of the present because we know we have a home over yonder. Home is where we have been placed *now,* and to believe in heaven is to refuse to accept hell on earth. This is one dimension of the future that cannot be sacrificed.

But there is another dimension that we must protect despite white corruption of it. Black theology cannot reject the future reality of life after death—grounded in Christ's resurrection— simply because whites have distorted it for their own selfish purposes. That would be like the Black Art Movement, rejecting art because white artists have misused it. What is needed is redefinition in the light of the liberation of the black community.

If God is truly the God of and for the oppressed for the purpose of their liberation, then the future must mean that our fight for freedom has not been for naught. Our journey in the world cannot be a meaningless thrust toward an unrealizable future, but a certainty grounded in the past and present reality of God. To grasp for the future of God is to know that those who die for freedom have not died in vain; they will see the kingdom of God. This is precisely the meaning of our Lord's resurrection, and why we can fight against overwhelming odds. We believe in the future of God, a future that must become present.

Without a meaningful analysis of the future, all is despair. The guns, atomic power, police departments, and every conceivable weapon of destruction are in the hands of the enemy. By these standards, all seems lost.

But there is another way of evaluating history; it involves the kind of perspective that enables blacks to say no in spite of the military power of their oppressors. If we really believe that death is not the last word, then we can fight, risking death for human freedom, knowing that the ultimate destiny of humankind is in the hands of the God who has called us into being. We do not have to worry about death if we know that it has been conquered and that as an enemy it has no efficacy. Christ's death and resurrection have set us free. Therefore it does not matter that whites have all the guns and that, militarily speaking, we have no chance of winning. *There comes a time when a people must protect their own, and for blacks the time is now.*

One last comment. The future is still the future. This means that black theology rejects elaborate speculations about the end. It is just this kind of speculation that led blacks to stake their whole existence on heaven—the scene of the whole company of the faithful with their long white robes. Too much of this talk is not good for the revolution. Black theology believes that the future is God's future, as are the past and present. Our past knowledge and present encounter with God ground our confidence that the future will be both like and unlike the present—like the present in the encounter with God, and unlike it in the fullness of liberation as a reality.

PART II

AFTER TWENTY YEARS: CRITICAL REFLECTIONS

8

A Revolution Unfulfilled, but not Invalidated

GAYRAUD WILMORE

Twenty years ago something like an earthquake undulated across the already disquieted theological landscape of North America in the form of a second book by an upstart young black theologian, James Hal Cone. The book was *A Black Theology of Liberation*.[1] Cone's first book, *Black Theology and Black Power*, had already produced a warning tremor in March, 1969, when the theological world was suddenly shocked to discover that this relatively unknown junior professor at Adrian College, Michigan, was actually contending that "Christianity is not alien to Black Power; it is Black Power."[2] In *A Black Theology of Liberation* Cone sought to elaborate the basic argument of his first book: black theology is not prepared to discuss the doctrine of God, human being, Christ, Church, Holy Spirit — the whole spectrum of Christian theology — without making each doctrine an analysis of the emancipation of black people. It believes that, in

Gayraud Wilmore is Professor of Church History at the Interdenominational Theological Center in Atlanta, Georgia. He is the author of *Black Religion and Black Radicalism* and co-editor (with James Cone) of *Black Theology: A Documentary History, 1966–1979*.

this time, moment, and situation, all Christian doctrines must be interpreted in such a manner that they unreservedly say something to black people who are living under unbearable oppression.[3] Thus, partly in response to a chorus of critics who rose to denounce his first book, and partly in an attempt to draw the broad outlines of how Christian doctrine needed to be reinterpreted in order to "speak of God in a suffering world, a world in which blacks are humiliated because they are black,"[4] Cone erupted into print again in 1970 with a ringing challenge to almost two thousand years of white Western theological domination. It was clear that the dust would refuse to settle and, as other black scholars and church leaders made their own contributions to the general agitation, it was predictable that the aftershocks would continue to reverberate for some time to come.

Perhaps it is more accurate to say that the earthquake — or if we may change the metaphor — the revolution of 1970, was mainly confined to a certain sector of the African American community and only gradually raised eyebrows among white Christians and Jews as the decade of the seventies unfolded. For most white scholars, *A Black Theology of Liberation* was not more than a tempest in a teapot. Today, however, serious students of American religion will recognize that it was the first attempt to consolidate one of the most uncharacteristic and unsettling theological movements of the 20th century. *A Black Theology of Liberation* sounded the trumpet of a radical, contextual liberation theology for North America. Even if few persons outside of the African American community were listening in 1970, it was soon to shatter many taken-for-granted assumptions about the religion of black people in the United States, with disturbing implications for others. It opened up a brand new school of theological method and social action that most American Christians, black as well as white, were totally unprepared for and have not yet thoroughly understood, much less appropriated.

How shall we assess the value of the ideas and energies that were released by black theology during the last two decades? I want to suggest that the revolution brought on by the two books Cone published in quick succession at the end of the era of the civil rights movement is responsible for several constructive developments in African American religion today. This is not to deny that the movement has been frustrated and that its original objectives are still largely unfulfilled in many black congregations. My main purpose is to describe and account for some of its failures. I will argue, however, that black theology, as a return to certain major themes in African American religious history and as a corrective to many white theologies in North America, has not been invalidated by its modest gains at one level. Since the publication of Cone's work, African American, African and Caribbean theologians, have amply demonstrated that the emphasis on liberation from a black biblical and theological perspective contains the power of resistance to the indifference and moral paralysis of that peculiar propensity of white Christianity to accommodate itself too comfortably to capitalism, Anglo-elitism, and a theological conservatism that seems endemic in this last decade of the twentieth century.

I

Black theology is a radical response from the underside of American religious history to the mainstream of white Christianity. In my own writings I have used the term "radicalism" to refer to the tendency of a major strain of African American Christianity and Black Islam to relate religion, at its core, to social, cultural, and political transformation—that is, to a form of liberation that is structural as well as personal. In terms of method we have spoken of black theology as an explication of the biblical revelation that African Americans are "another chosen people," called by God as an autonomous, inner directed, self-determining "nation within a nation" dedicated to a continuing cultural and political struggle against racism and other historic forms of oppression in Western civilization. Most of us in this school of black theology have contended that we belong to a radical, but honorable and widely recognized, tradition in the African American community. Moreover we believe that this orientation, while not the only one, has been the most distinctive, persistent, and valuable part of the religious heritage of African Americans in the United States.

In the half century preceding the Civil War the religion of African Americans was a combination of white Protestant evangelicalism, remodeled African traditional religions, elements of Amer-indian religions, and the pragmatic sensibilities and virtuosities of individual blacks, fighting to preserve some shred of humanity against a dehumanizing form of chattel slavery invented by white Christians.

Black religion, as DuBois reminds us, was both a wail and a sneer.[5] A wail of anguish and yearning for freedom and the ordinary human affections and social intercourse that keeps people sane; and a sneer of disdain and rage against a white Christian establishment that mouthed theological rationalizations and pious prayers while exercising a despotic exploitation of the flesh of men, women, and children.

The inherent radicalism of black religion was always grounded in scripture and the invocation of the Holy Spirit to the worshiping community. Black music, liturgy, and preaching were suffused with biblical and theological ideas and images lifted directly out of God's Word. Both scripture and the tradition of the Apostles were filtered through an African cultural screen and contextualized in the struggle and suffering of a people in bondage. There was an obvious connection, but also a deep discontinuity, between this religion and the religion of the white majority. This may not have been apparent as both groups entered the twentieth century saturated with Carnegie's Gospel of Wealth and Billy Sunday's revivalism, but it became very obvious in the 1950s when Malcolm X and Martin King brought this inherent radicalism back to the collective consciousness. And it became still more obvious in the 1960s when the revolution broke out that ushered in James H. Cone and the new black theology movement.

II

Actually, there were several revolts. There was, first of all, the revolt of black pastors like Adam Clayton Powell, Jr., in Harlem, Albert B. Cleage in Detroit, Franklin Florence in Rochester, N.Y., Arthur Brazier in Chicago, Nathan Wright in Newark, N.J., Vaughan Eason and Paul Washington in Philadelphia, Ben Chavis in Wilmington, N.C., J. Metz Rollins in Tallahassee, Fla., and Calvin Marshall in Brooklyn, N.Y.[6] Amid what the press called "northern city riots" and what we insisted were "popular rebellions," these pastors and many others revolted against the "Jesus-loved-his-enemies-and-so-must-you" style of Christian action that whites have always commended to blacks. We took to the streets—not necessarily to join the burning and looting, but to interpret what was going on, to mobilize religious forces for an intelligent response, and to rescue our children and young adults from rioting police. Those young people were the spiritual warriors of black power and their wrestling with the meaning of the faith under those conditions produced spokespersons like Vincent Harding, the first historian of the movement, Nathan Wright, the Episcopal urban missioner in Newark, and Benjamin Payton of the Commission on Religion and Race of the National Council of Churches. But no one in those days described the meaning of the crisis better than Al Cleage of Detroit's Shrine of the Black Madonna:

> To the Black Revolution we bring the stabilizing influence of the religion of the Black Messiah, Jesus Christ. The Black Revolution is not going any farther than the Black Church enables it to go, by giving it a foundation, a philosophy, and a direction.[7]

There was, secondly, the revolt of black denominational or agency staff persons. Among these were Oscar Lee and Anna Hedgeman of the NCC, Lucius Walker and Jane Douglas of IFCO, Charles Cobb and Yvonne Delk of the UCC, Bryant George of the Northern and Joe Roberts of the Southern Presbyterians, Leon Modeste of the Epicopalians, Bishop Charles Golden, Theressa Hoover, and Rose Catchings of the United Methodists, Bishop Shaw of the AME Zion Church, Bishop John Bright of the AMEs, Tom Kilgore of the Baptists in Los Angeles, and O. Clay Maxwell of the Baptist Ministers Conference of New York City.[8] This group revolted against the white Christian establishment and the statement they published in the *New York Times* on black power heralded the beginning of a new way of doing theology that broke with both the pessimistic realism of Niebuhrian neoorthodoxy and the visionary optimism of King's philosophy of nonviolence.[9]

There was, thirdly, the revolt of black seminarians. The critical break with the white theological academy occurred at Union Seminary in New York, Colgate Rochester Divinity School in Rochester, N.Y., and at three seminaries in the Boston area. Already, of course, black seminarians in the South, like Charley Jones, Charles Sherrod, and John Lewis, had set the stage by initiating a radical witness within the Student Nonviolent Coordinating Committee. A decisive turn of affairs was the response of Union Seminary students to the Black Manifesto of James Forman and the Black Economic Development Conference in May 1969. Their statement to the seminary deserves to be quoted at length:

> As students of theology, we interpret the gospel as a radical message of a divinely inspired prophet designed to relieve the oppressed and the outcasts of their burden of poverty and scorn. We believe that the church as the extension of the body of Christ must itself undergo crucifixion as it seeks to renew life and expose men to the things which make for peace. We believe that the church is under a divine imperative to respond dramatically to the cries of those who suffer, and so be an agent of change and social progress. . . . As black students . . . we cannot ignore the long-lived struggle for justice and dignity which our brothers and sisters of the ghetto must wage daily without recourse. We, as black students, feel that a failure to respond to the call for a United Black appeal would be irresponsible and unpardonable. We recognize that Union Theological Seminary is, in fact, in Harlem, but is strangely covered with ivy which Harlem seldom sees. We the Black Caucus recognize the extent to which the Black Manifesto is a clear call for a vast redistribution of power and wealth in America.[10]

Finally, there was the revolt of the young people of the cities. It was not only a revolt against poverty and powerlessness, but also a revolt against the negro church, in the sense of C. Eric Lincoln's Negro-Black typology.[11] It was the perennial underclass rejection of "Rev. Chickenwings" and "Deacon Poke

Chops" that Langston Hughes satirized in Harlem of the 1920s and St. Clair Drake reported from his studies of southside Chicago in the 1930s and 40s. Among young blacks of the civil rights and black power era it was full of the symbolism of authentic spirituality "in the struggle to wrest meaning and joy from experience." Thus, James H. Evans, Jr., writes:

> The first moment in the Afro-American cultural act takes the form of rebellion; its goal is the authentication of the Afro-American personality; and its chief means are the weapons of the oppressor. In this moment Afro-American religion embodies an attempt to break away from a distorted past, skewed self-images, and sinister associations. It is "a feeling of revolt and revenge" in the light of the oppression of Afro-Americans. This response lay at the heart of the political fervor which energized Afro-American religious expression in the 1960s.[12]

Many of the street people who uncovered the religious dimensions of the revolt, thus contributing to the shaping of black theology, were also young artists and writers. Many were women who were active in groups like the Patrice Lumumba Coalition, the "475 Riverside Drive Strike Force" in June 1969, the Black Economic Development Conference, and Irving Davis's Pan African Skills Project: Mary Kenyatta in Philadelphia, Betty McCrary and Adisa Douglas in New York, Mary Jane Patterson in Washington, D.C., Fannie Lou Hamer in Mississippi, and many others whose names, unfortunately, have been forgotten. It is significant that most of the women who participated in the Black Theology Project's most successful conference, held in Atlanta 1977, were not typical church people, but poor women out of the mass-based, IFCO-funded community organizations across the country.

There were other revolts and other conferences, but these were the most important for the evolution of black theology. Cultivated during this period was the technique of formulating public statements and declarations of principles that provoked discourse, required careful thinking, and helped to set forth the religious implications of black power. By so doing, such statements created the building blocks of a radical black faith. Then, under the leadership of James H. Cone, black theology became the battle cry of a new organization, the National Committee of Black Churchmen (NCBC), which promulgated the first official definition of black theology at the Interdenominational Theological Center in Atlanta on June 13, 1969.

> Black Theology is a theology of black liberation. It seeks to plumb the black condition in the light of God's revelation in Jesus Christ, so that the black community can see that the gospel is commensurate with the achievement of black humanity. Black Theology is a theology of "blackness." It is the affirmation of black humanity that emancipates black people from white racism, thus providing authentic freedom for both white and black people. It affirms the humanity of white people in that it says No to the encroachment of white oppression.[13]

III

By the end of the 1970s many of us were aware that the promise of this new way of doing theology was not being realized in the grassroots church. What happened? What brought the demise of NCBC and began the creeping deradicalization of many black Christians, even as the books and articles on black theology were still rolling off the presses? The picture is murky and the causal factors difficult to ascertain. But there seem to be four reasons why the movement which actually antedated the formalization of liberation theology by Gustavo Gutiérrez in Latin America floundered in the United States where it had been introduced earlier by NCBC and James Cone.

First, the North American black theology movement lacked the infrastructure to sustain a long-range mobilization and educational program in local congregations. It also failed to develop the regional structures and financial resources required for the care and feeding of a mass movement. We cannot escape the fact that within the National Council of Churches and the mainline white denominations there was a deliberate effort to starve black radicalism financially. The denominations courted the moderate leadership of the black church by channeling funds through their caucuses. They made deferential gestures toward the historic black churches that, in exchange for the latter's increased influence in the NCC and the Consultation on Church Union, eased race off the top of the Protestant agenda in favor of ecology, nuclear disarmament, women's liberation, apartheid in South Africa, and the demands other ethnic groups began to press upon the churches.

A second, closely related cause of disappointment about the performance of black theology in the 1970s and 80s was the rise of conservative evangelicalism and the invasion of all our living rooms by suave white televangelists, oozing their special brand of religious mush and sentimentality. We sometimes forget that such pious cant is as mesmerizing to many blacks, clerical and lay, as it is to whites. Furthermore, some middle-class blacks secretly admire and want to emulate conservative white churches. White is not only right in the marketplace. It is secretly thought by some black Christians to be best in the church too. Of course, the televangelists know how to exploit the kindred spirit between black and white evangelicalism. They make sure the cameras focus on black faces in their congregations and use black gospel choirs to prove that born-again Christians can rise above racial distinctions. As a rule, African American Christians are flattered and highly vulnerable to white evangelistic appeals to Christian fellowship, interracial reconciliation, concern about the collapse of old-fashioned values, and crusades against what Jerry Falwell and Pat Robertson call "secular humanism."

From the moment that the conservative backlash against radical black religion began, the middle-class, institutionalized black church began to falter. Leroy Fitts is correct when he suggests that, apart from the question of race, there has developed a close affinity between Jerry Falwell and certain powerful sectors of black Baptist and Pentecostal leadership, although no one talks about it openly. The conservative evangelical connection, however, does not seem to trouble Dr. Fitts. He writes, almost triumphantly:

It is therefore incumbent upon black Baptists to take on responsible leadership positions within any movement designed to call America to basic moral values of Christianity. Perhaps it might even be necessary for black Baptists to organize their own independent "moral majority" movement in America.[14]

A third cause of the retrenchment of black theology in the African American community was the death of the Honorable Elijah Muhammad on February 25, 1975, and the subsequent deradicalization of the only religious movement that kept fire at the feet of the historic black churches since the end of Garveyism—the Nation of Islam. Imam Warith Deen Muhammad's efforts to islamize his father's movement and bring the Nation into a profitable accommodation with American capitalism, on the one hand, and into a larger, multiracial fellowship with the Islamic world beyond North America on the other hand, robbed the black community of a valuable source of ideological and theological challenge. That challenge had reached its most eloquent expression in the ministry of El Hajj Malik Shabazz, better known as Malcolm X.

In the 1960s Malcolm helped us radicalize the black church by exposing its servile accommodation and pushing its clergy more and more toward an explicit black nationalism. Today that pressure from the left no longer exists. What we have instead is the rising prosperity of the black middle class, the ineptitude of the older civil rights organizations, and the somnolence of mainstream African American Christianity that encourages the new Muslim leadership to believe that the time is ripe for the successful proseletization of the entire black community in the United States.

The final cause of the diminished influence of black power and black theology might well have been mentioned first, for it has to do with the national context in which everything we have discussed has taken place. A brief review of the history will have to suffice.

Richard Nixon moved into the White House on January 20, 1969. He immediately dismantled the reforms of the civil rights movement and introduced "benign neglect." Nixon, as if on a prearranged cue, targeted the black power movement and made clandestine use of the FBI to exterminate the Black Panther

Party and other revolutionary cadres with whom black theologians were beginning to work. Nixon provided a salubrious climate for the backlash that contributed to the retreat from the advanced political and social policies that some white churches had adopted after the Chicago Interfaith Conference on Religion and Race in January 1963. Most of the historic black churches, if not because of subtle intimidation then for reasons of their own narrow self-interest, were not far behind.

Ronald Reagan, for his part, never understood the deeper meaning of even the civil rights movement. His election to his first term in 1980 was a clear signal for the restoration of an almost unbridled monopoly capitalism to undergird the hegemony of the military, technological oligarchy. The virtual destruction of the federal entitlement programs under his trickle-down economics was precisely what the newly emboldened "born-again" fundamentalists had been praying for. During the next eight years reactionary forces in the church and society made common cause to stamp out the last smoldering embers of the black power movement.

Except for the brief, irrelevant episodes with Ford and Carter, the last twenty years have been next to disastrous for African American liberation activists. But what would we expect? It should come as no surprise that at the height of a renaissance of black religious thought, the forces of reaction would redouble their efforts to stifle what might have turned into a genuine social revolution. The failure of the new black theology, emerging from a coalition of academics, younger clergy, and ghetto revolutionaries, to penetrate the rank and file of the churches, is only one measure of the depth of the cultural crisis we have experienced, the ideological anomie, and sense of hopelessness, that descended upon black America as it entered the 1980s.

Today the almost complete breakdown of the family, the disorganization of black labor constantly on the verge of economic catastrophe, the trivialization of black music, entertainment, and other forms of our culture, and above all the losing battle against crack cocaine at every level of our communities, are all signs of deculturation, demoralization, and the alienation of a confused black middle class from its traditional role in the vanguard of the race. Under this baleful condition we see the church retreating into its stained glass foxholes, and black preachers going back to what they have always felt more comfortable doing when times were bad—preaching, raising money, and jockeying for ecclesiastical offices.

IV

In the face of this picture of almost unrelieved gloom what is to be said about the present situation that might give us some hope for the future? I am persuaded that, notwithstanding the apparent impotence of black liberation theology in this period of "the continuation of Reaganism by other means," it is still the most viable expression of progressive religion in North America. Its conceptualization of blackness as a symbol of resistance in an inveterately racist society, its analysis of ethnic and sexual disunity and oppression under American capitalism, its vision of humanization, grassroots cultural renewal, and solidarity with the Two-Thirds World of Africa, Asia, and Latin America, make black theology practically the only remaining radical perspective linking the liberating essense of biblical faith and trinitarian theology to a cultural and political strategy for fundamental social change. As such it provides both Protestantism and Roman Catholicism with a previously discredited channel back to an autochthonous form of civil religion that preceded right-wing evangelicalism. Black theology, even for white Christians, offers an esthetically rich and ethically powerful worldview that utilizes the neglected Amerindian and African inheritance that really belongs to all of us. In a time of effete religiosity in conspiracy with a triumphalistic secularism, black theology points toward a pragmatic spirituality that uses the gospel and the church, in Paul Lehman's felicitous phrase, "to make and to keep life human."

In his book, *The Restructuring of American Religion*, Robert Wuthnow, in my opinion, understates the significance of African American religion. Because of the distinctive concerns of black churches, he seems to want to lump them with what he calls "special purpose groups" that combine some features of both churches and sects. Wuthnow is impressed with the countercultural functions of special purpose groups. But by emphasizing groups that have arisen *within* the white denominations, Wuthnow tends to miss the significance of continuous resistance to the political and social conservatism of American Christianity from black churches and caucuses outside the white mainstream. It is precisely countercultural *dissent* that has been the historic role of African American religion as a whole and, for this reason, black churches have had considerably more influence on this society from their marginated position than white special purpose groups such as Presbyterians United for Biblical Concerns, the Catholic Charismatic Renewal, or the Fellowship of Conservative Southern Baptists.[15] Students of American religion should recognize that the African American churches have been major centers of resistance to the bureaucratization and standardization of American religion, as well as the principal bulwark against its racism. Black churches, in other words, would seem to deserve credit for a more organically critical cultural vocation in American society than the often temporary and segmental interests of white "special purpose groups."

I am not referring here merely to the work of Dr. King and the Southern Christian Leadership Conference, but also to the struggle of blacks within white denominations, the role of blacks in the origin and development of Pentecostalism, and indeed the whole sweep of African American religious influences that prompted the late Sidney E. Ahlstrom to declare: "The basic paradigm for a renovation of American church history is the black religious experience, which has been virtually closed out of all synoptic histories written so far."[16]

Although we see deradicalizing tendencies in the black church today, there continues to exist within African American religion a persistent resistance to the trivialization of biblical faith and the accommodation between Main Street Christianity and American capitalism, between a "born-again" Caesar and an acculturated Christ. Black theology fights against this kind of religion. The movement, whose twentieth anniversary we observed in 1989, is certainly one "special purpose group," which has operated outside the white churches and represented the long-term, underground struggle against their hegemony. It has, moreover, lent some of its power to the Christian-Marxist movement in Latin America, to Christian feminists in the United States, to theological questioning among America's other ethnic groups and, most impressively, to the black theology movement in South Africa.

What some academics took to be little more than a faddish distraction turned out to be a mild earthquake that has disrupted the theological, if not the ecclesiastical, world, despite the fact that many black Christians are too culturally impoverished and ethically demoralized to realize what God has been doing under their noses. The absence of significant discourse about black theology and praxis of its political and cultural strategy at the congregational level presents black theologians with a vexing problem. But that is only one problem among many that plague a sectarian form of Christianity that constantly wrestles against its own seduction by secularism masquerading under the guise of *ecclesia*. Black theology is part of that permanent revolution of those who remember the historical Jesus, mainly the poor, the outcast, and the sinners, against a world order sanctioned and sanctified by the white churches of Europe and North America — an order that is characterized by economic, political, and cultural selfishness and domination. That is why the revolution of 1969 remains unfulfilled, but is by no means invalidated.

V

Recent developments in the field of black theology give some reason for hope. The first area of advance in black theological thought was in the academic community. This, of course, has not been an unmixed blessing, for as black theology gains prominence in seminaries and university departments of religion it tends to distance itself from the poor, from pastors and ordinary congregations. But the founding of the Society for the Study of Black Religion in 1970 was necessary for the accreditation of research and teaching in the field of black theology. The result has been a phenomenal increase in the number of men and women from the black churches who are pursuing graduate studies in American theological seminaries where there is increasing awareness of the importance of African American religious studies. At the same time, unfortunately, some attention has been diverted from what is happening or not happening at the grass-roots level.

Thanks to James Cone at Union, C. Eric Lincoln at Duke, Charles Copher at the ITC, and other senior scholars, we are now witnessing the rise of a second generation of black theologians who are earning their doctorates and introducing fresh perspectives on the task of organizing and enlarging the work in both Protestant and Roman Catholic seminaries. One consequence is a noticeable increase in the number of books and articles being published on black theology, or in disciplines and areas of inquiry related to it.

Three directions stand out in terms of published works during the 1980s: first, the deepening of the dialogue in books by James DeOtis Roberts, Major Jones, Henry Mitchell, and James Cone — among the senior scholars; and James H. Evans, Jr., Cornel West, Katie Cannon, Dwight Hopkins, Jacquelyn Grant, Cain Felder, and others — among the younger scholars. Secondly, the serious application of scholarship to problems and issues of black religious thought by black biblical scholars who, under the auspices of the Ecumenical Institute in Collegeville, Minnesota, have been working on topics ranging from the place of Africa in the Hebrew Bible to a hermeneutic for the black pulpit.[17] A third area of interest that is producing new books and articles has to do with the relevance of black theology for the pastoral office. Henry Mitchell, Preston Washington, James Forbes, James H. Harris, and others have pressed the case for black theology as primarily a pastoral rather than an academic theology.

All of these developments have occurred mainly within the academy. That is certainly essential for the training of future clergy, but it has not yet produced the ferment in basic Christian communities that liberation theology has created within Roman Catholic parishes of the poor in Latin America.

A second and closely related area of advancement is in the new theological emphases and challenges to black male theologians that have come from black women. This is related to a revolt over the last twenty years in the ranks of African American females in all areas of black life and culture, a revolt that has had a special impact in black theological circles and in the African American church, which has been a bastion of male dominance.

Black women have been the primary bearers of the tradition of freedom from white norms and standards in the black community. A study of the careers of early black women preachers, such as Elizabeth, Jarena Lee, Rebecca Cox Jackson, and Amanda Berry Smith, will show that many black women were liberated from both the strictures of mainline white Christianity and the traditional roles of females in American society before, in the first instance, black men and, in the second, white women. In recent years the realization of this fact has led to the development of what is called "womanist theology" among black women in contradistinction to "feminist theology."

In a recent issue of the *Journal of Religious Thought*, Toinette Eugene explains womanist theology as derived from the use of the term in black family life, where being "womanish" means young girls exhibiting what black mothers considered "outrageous, audacious, courageous, or wilful behavior." Eugene writes:

> To be a faithful womanist, then, or to operate out of this system of black moral value indicators which flow from biblical understandings based on justice and love, is to express in word and deed an alternative ontology or way of living in the world that is endemic to many black women. It is precisely in womanist religious responses of endurance, resistance, and resiliency offered in the face of all attempts at personal and institutional domination that may provide a renewed theological legacy of liberation for everyone concerned.[18]

In the face of sexism in the black church and the silence of most black male theologians on the contributions women have made to the liberation struggle, womanist theology—as presented by Toinette Eugene, Jacquelyn Grant, Delores Williams, Katie Cannon, and Kelly Brown, among others—may prove to be the most important innovation on the American theological scene since 1969.

A third recent development in black theology has to do with its critique of the major confessional positions of Western Christianity as represented historically by the National Council and the World Council of Churches' Commissions on Faith and Order. In the early 1970s African American theologians began meeting Third World theologians at WCC conferences, the various international meetings of confessional families, and later in the Ecumenical Association of Third World Theologians (EATWOT). Those meetings led to a mutual criticism of the mainstream Euro-American theology in which both groups had been indoctrinated. The disillusionment with white theology partly resulted in the founding of EATWOT where other proponents of liberation theologies wanted to express dissatisfaction with ecumenical discussions taking place in Geneva and Rome. This alliance with Third World theologians, in turn, led to the strengthening of the liberationist position and the return of a few African American spokespersons to the Faith and Order discussions with new ammunition and resolve to press the issue of contextual theology and ethics upon the European and American churches.

One of the consequences is the several works that have appeared in the last decade dealing with the history of black participation in white denominations, or "black perspectives" on Presbyterianism, Methodism, the Reformed Church in America, Unitarian-Universalism, Roman Catholicism, and Lutheranism. Another consequence is dialogues between the Black Theology Project, a research and educational think-tank now headquartered in Chicago, and Cuban and Brazilian theologians. A third consequence of this globalization of black theology is the two special consultations of black theologians who are related to the World Council of Churches studies on "A Common Confession of Apostolic Faith," in December 1984, and "The Unity of the Church and the Renewal of the Human Community," in August 1988. In both reports from these meetings African American theologians interpret the traditional concerns of the black church in order to make their own constructive criticism of studies in the worldwide ecumenical movement.[19]

The late Dr. Paul Calvin Payne, for many years executive secretary of the Board of Christian Education of the Presbyterian Church, used to say, "If it doesn't happen in the local church, it doesn't happen." An exaggerated truth can be misleading. The gospel is too large to be contained by congregations, or restricted in its effectiveness to the local level. The complexity and magnitude of the Church as institution, and the impact of the gospel upon the personalities and mass culture of society mean that, as important as it is, the local congregation is only one dimension of the theater of God's action in the world. This brief review of developments over the past decade supports the argument that while black theology leaves much to be desired at the congregational level, it has not failed to have influence in some other important sectors of the church. In any case, the celebration of the twentieth anniversary of *A Black Theology of Liberation* gives all of us an opportunity to reassess the history of the black theology movement, do an audit on racism in religion today, and ask ourselves why both black and white congregations have not been more interested in the critical issues raised by contemporary African American religious thinkers, male and female.

We could not do better than to begin that inquiry by revisiting Cone's second book which embarrassed and outraged so many by reversing the color symbolism of Euro-American Christianity and identifying Blackness with salvation and whiteness with the principalities and powers. It would be unfair to judge Cone's present position solely on the basis of what he wrote in 1970, but the new twentieth anniversary edition of *A Black Theology of Liberation* deserves wide reading because it not only reminds us of what the revolution was about twenty years ago, but helps us measure how much black theology has matured since those days. In his preface to the 1989 edition of *Black Theology and Black Power* Cone discusses certain deficiencies that he and other black theologians have attempted to correct over the years—the use of sexist language, excessive dependence upon Western theological categories, blindness regarding the reality of inequalities based on class, and the failure to set the problem of bondage and the liberating potential of the gospel in a global context. Concerning this last and critically important point he writes:

As in 1969, I still regard Jesus Christ today as the chief focus of my perspective on God but not to the exclusion of other religious perspectives. God's reality is not bound by one manifestation of the divine in Jesus but can be found wherever people are being empowered to fight for freedom.[20]

The revolution of 1970 continues to inspire ever-widening circles of a common search for the truth about God and human-kind, and truth about freedom, struggle and solidarity. There was considerable misunderstanding about that in 1970. Today, more than ever, it is important for American Christians to be clear about what black theologians were calling for in the passionate writings of James H. Cone and others who began the revolt against white theology. It was then, and continues to be today, a call for a revolution that has to do with more than racial antagonism and disruption of the political, economic and social hegemony of white theology and the white churches of the West. Black theology is also a call to revolutionary repentance and revolutionary love. Its challenge is to all who believe in and serve God, to do justly, to love mercy, and to walk humbly with their Creator. On that basis, more than any other theological or ideological principle, it is a challenge to personal conversion and social transformation for the sake of the liberation and reconciliation of all people.

9

Learning from James Cone

ROBERT MCAFEE BROWN

When vastly different viewpoints are under consideration, one seeks any point of contact in order to facilitate understanding and exchange. With whatever differences may separate James Cone as a black theologian and myself as a white theologian, I was pleased to learn from the foreword to the 1986 edition of his book that we do have at least one area of shared territory: we have both been accused by Fr. Andrew Greeley of having "Nazi mentalities." I do not know how many other theologians can lay claim to this distinction—their number may be legion—but since in my corner of the theological arena it is a badge of honor to be attacked by Fr. Greeley, I offer this evidence of shared opprobrium as a sign that James Cone and I might share other characteristics as well. A reason for hope.

When *A Black Theology of Liberation* first appeared in 1970, I assigned it as a required text in my course, "Contemporary Theological Trends," at nearly all-white Stanford University, inserting it among such predictable staples of that era as Barth,

Robert McAfee Brown is professor emeritus of theology and ethics at the Pacific School of Theology, Berkeley, and the author of many books, including *Spirituality of Liberation* and *Gustavo Gutierrez: An Introduction to Liberation Theology*.

Bultmann, Tillich, and Niebuhr. A student approached me early in the week for which Professor Cone's book was due, and said, "This book makes me very angry."

Splendid.

The book was written out of anger and should appropriately have elicited anger in return.

What so upset the student was that the author seemed to be dumping mercilessly on whites—not just on white theologians, but on *white people*, of whom she, of course, was one. So he was dumping on her, and she didn't like that.

It was probably, I venture, the first time her carefully cushioned white world had been invaded by words other than laudatory and self-fortifying, and the first time she had encountered words by a black.

I will be the first to acknowledge that Professor Cone cuts a wide swath with a keenly tempered rapier, and I have personally been on the receiving end more than once, since we served for a number of years as colleagues on a theological faculty, an existential situation that generates an almost infinite number of issues on which to disagree.

A generalized query, "Why the anger?," has to be particularized—for example, "What are the *specific reasons* for the anger?" And since the specific reasons for the anger are finally clustered around the destructive indignities that whites have visited on blacks, it may be that the only way to get whites to start listening is by speech that to untrained white ears will sound raucous and ungenteel—fair enough when the events being referred to are ugly and vicious. One is not permitted to employ the criterion of gentility to describe abysmal evil.

But while a book such as *A Black Theology of Liberation* may evoke a corresponding anger from a white reader, it can also evoke conversion from a black reader. I had another student, years later, whose exposure to *A Black Theology of Liberation* and (because of what he found there) to the whole Cone corpus, did indeed turn his life around. He came into the course militantly closed to any and all attempts to relate theology to issues of social change, firmly entrenched in a form of black fundamentalist orthodoxy since his earliest years. With regard to things scriptural, he was an "infallibilist" but not an "inerrantist"—or maybe it was the other way around. But as Jim Cone's writings began to guide him, particularly into the realm of scripture and the patent centrality therein of concern for the oppressed (for which a phrase like "a preferential option for the poor" was not too strong), the student confessed to the class that a central part of the faith had been denied to him by his upbringing, and that he was now, thanks to Professor Cone, able for the first time to claim it as his own.

It is disarming, when one is invited to critique a work twenty years old, and has a tidy agenda of criticisms accumulated from the vantage point of two decades of reflection denied to the author, to discover that the author has beaten the critic to the draw, and preempted much that the critic would like to have said. And this is what Jim Cone has done in his preface to the 1986 edition.

The first thing one must do, therefore, is salute his forthrightness in being willing to critique his own work and say about the text that bears his name, "I was wrong about x, y, and z." The apparent ease with which he does this should not be deceptive. Few are the theologians who, having committed themselves in print, are about to concede that what they originally thought was carved in stone was merely printed on paper. The natural tendency is to defend oneself, through a lifetime if necessary, or invent specious ways to claim that the whole corpus is a single and consistent whole. But Cone's self-critique cites four shortcomings: (1) a failure to take issues of sexism seriously enough, (2) a failure to incorporate a global analysis of oppression, (3) the absence of a class analysis of oppression, and (4) too great a tendency to rely on the neoorthodoxy of Karl Barth.

As I will note later, these are not sins of omission that can be charged only to Jim Cone, or to black theologians generally, but represent almost universal shortcomings of *all* theologians of the 1950s and 1960s. (The case of Karl Barth is of a different order, for I believe that if one chose to do so, one could incorporate the three other points to which Cone calls attention within a "Barthian" framework. But that is a topic for another occasion.)

Although Cone calls his blindness to issues of sexism his "most glaring limitation," I would be inclined to stress the lack of any kind of economic analysis in his earlier writings as the most limiting factor in his theology as a whole. It is clear that this lacuna is evident not only in 1970, but at least until 1977, and that his own shift at the latter date gave him much wider perspectives on the theological task. At the Theology in the Americas Conference held in Detroit in 1975 (the first occasion on which significant numbers of North American and Latin American theologians confronted one another), Jim and most other North American blacks stood firmly against the Latin American theologians who were insisting on a systemic and class analysis of corporate evil, and chastising the black theologians for their blindness to this issue. The latter's position, as I now try to reconstruct it, was that from their perspective racism was just as rampant in socialist countries as in capitalist countries, so that economic factors did not have to be taken into account in dealing with racism, the primal sin.

But however adamant the protestations at Detroit, an impact was registered, and the encounter became a turning point, for two years later a statement came out of a black theologians' assembly in Atlanta that signaled a new understanding of the interrelationship of racism and economic structures. And as this was combined with an increasing *global* analysis (nurtured by Jim's involvement with EATWOT, the Ecumenical Association of Third World Theologians), a broader purview and scope for black theology emerged than had been present in 1970. An example of this is a statement included in the report of the New Delhi EATWOT Conference in 1981, in which Cone writes:

> On the basis of Third World theologians' dialogue together, it is clear to us all that the future of each of our theologies is found in our struggles together. I am firmly convinced that black theology must not limit itself to the race struggle in the United States but must find ways to join in solidarity with the struggles of the poor in the Third World. The universal dimensions of the gospel message require that we struggle not only for ourselves but for all. For there can be no freedom for any one of us until all of us are free. Any theology that falls short of this universal vision is not Christian and thus cannot be identified with

the Jesus who died on the cross and was resurrected so that everyone might be liberated in God's emerging Kingdom. [In Fabella and Torres, eds., *The Irruption of the Third World*, Orbis Books, 1983, p. 244.]

In looking to the future, we must return to a point alluded to earlier. The various rechartings of the theological task to which Cone felt himself called in subsequent writings are directions in which *all* theology has been forced to move. White theology has also been sexist, has lacked a global analysis of oppression, and has been guilty of ignoring class analysis, and I should like to believe that the rectification of these shortcomings might be a task on which white and black theologians could work together more fruitfully than has been possible in the past.

But there is, of course, another sin of which white theology has been particularly and centrally guilty, and that has been the sin of racism. Professor Cone details this charge in his book with such angry eloquence that any complacency on our part is quickly and devastatingly annihilated. And he has, in other writings and from many platforms, called attention to the ease with which white theologians avoid coming to grips with racism domestically by casting our theological investigations in the area of Latin America or Asia, and detecting sins six thousand miles away while ignoring the sins of racism on our own doorstep. There is of course some truth to this charge, though a slight mitigation may be claimed by the fact that when white theologians did discuss the racial situation in the United States they were often accused by blacks of entering realms they had no right to enter, assuming that they could somehow "speak for blacks" on matters about which they could not possibly be competent, since they had (by the color of their skin) been exempted from being recipients of racial hatred and violence.

Cone acknowledges that he pushed this theme very polemically, and indicates that communication was sometimes slowed rather than spurred by the intensity of what in retrospect he calls his "intemperate behavior." And it is a symbol of new possibilities of black-white dialogue that in the present edition of his text he has eliminated certain passages that in the earlier edition had cast doubt on the honorable intentions of whites trying to deal with the issue of race.

This is, I believe, clear gain, and should make closer working relationships between blacks and whites possible in the future. The gain is more than just pleasanter human relationships; for when it comes to dealing with evil in the world, there is nothing the "principalities and powers" would like more than to keep all those who challenge the present order of things fighting among themselves. If "divide and conquer" was once their motto, today it is more likely to be, "keep them divided and thus remain in charge," which, even if it does not scan as well rhythmically, is still an efficacious vehicle for maintaining the status quo.

Despite these and other comments that precede Professor Cone's own text in this volume, there are probably white readers who will still be put off by the (justifiable) anger of that text. To them, I propose the following:

1. Reflect on the fact that anger, in the face of injustice, is not a vice but a virtue.

2. When encountering anger, try very hard to put yourself, imaginatively, into the historical, economic, political, and racial position of the one who is angry, and see if the anger is not eminently justified.

3. Remember that with the best will in the world you will never get closer than the outermost precincts of the position proposed in (2) above.

4. Remember that people are not locked forever into unchanging positions, and that although *A Black Theology of Liberation* is a good place to begin, it would be a bad place to end, as will be clear from examining further books by Professor Cone such as *The Spirituals and the Blues* (1972), *God of the Oppressed* (1975), and *For My People* (1984).

5. And finally, take an inventory of some of the things that are wrong in the world, and let your own anger get to work on them.

10

Black Theology: A Liberating Theology in Latin America

PABLO RICHARD

Twenty years have passed since the publication of James Cone's book, *A Black Theology of Liberation*. I would like to analyze here the influence of this important theological work in Latin America and, more broadly, the significant encounter between black theology and Latin American liberation theology. This encounter has been significant and fruitful, requiring of both theologies that they overcome some of their own initial limitations. In the case of Latin American liberation theology this has meant opening itself to the cultural dimension—in particular the Afro-Latin American and Afro-Caribbean reality and culture—which was scarcely acknowledged in earlier years. For its part, black theology, as represented by Cone, had to open itself also to the economic and class analysis of oppression, especially to the analysis of oppression in the Third World and Latin America. This transformation on the part of black theology was recognized by Cone himself in the preface to the 1986 edition

Pablo Richard is a Chilean theologian who teaches in Costa Rica. He is the author of *Death of Christendoms, Birth of the Church* and other works on the theology of liberation.

of his book. In the same measure, the majority of Latin American liberation theologians have recognized their own transformation and opening to the Afro-American reality, especially in this moment when the great topic of discussion for 1992 is evangelization and culture. Thus, the encounter between these two theologies of liberation has been mutually liberating.

Among other things, this encounter made possible the development in Latin America and the Carribbean of an Afro-Latin American theology with its own particular characteristics. In its turn this new theology made possible a veritable irruption of the Afro-American world in the life of the church, stimulating a greater presence in and commitment on the part of the church to the life of Afro-Americans in Latin America and the Caribbean. There was thus a significant advance in the history of the church of Latin America and the Caribbean, in which we recognize the prophetic and inspiring role of James Cone.

All of this process of the past has served to reveal our *identity* as Latin Americans and Caribbeans. We definitively recognize that Africa was at the roots and in the heart of our identity. This African dimension of our identity was mixed with the indigenous and Latino dimensions of our tradition. As a result, we should no longer call ourselves simply "Latin Americans," but rather Indo-Afro-Latino-Americans. All the indigenous, African, and Latin elements of our blood and culture are mixed in this continent, especially among the poor and oppressed majority.

These African roots of our history and culture open us more deeply to the African continent and to the African American community in the United States. Thus the struggles of the South Africans and of the African Americans in the United States feel to us like our own struggle. Just as we are able, when we go to the United States, to integrate ourselves naturally in the Hispanic church, so also in the black church do we feel ourselves to be at home.

But I would like to return once more to the book which has inspired these reflections, *A Black Theology of Liberation*, and to all that current of black theology which it represents. I would assess the importance of this book by comparing it with the image of a living fount of water. This book has served, despite its historical limitations, as a fount from which living water keeps on running. There is in the book an inspiration which is not depleted. In it is expressed a theological idea, and above all a passion, which keeps on generating theology. This idea, this passion, is the experience of Christian faith in the world of the oppressed and marginalized African Americans in the United States. When one reads the book one enters into solidarity with this world and with the theology which shares the experience of God in the heart of this world. This is a particularly striking experience for the reader who also lives in a world of oppressed and marginalized peoples in this Indo-Afro-Latino-American continent.

In the preface to the 1986 edition of his book, Cone acknowledges the weaknesses of his book. In doing so, he shows that he is an authentic liberation theologian. Among liberation theologians it is commonplace to speak of the weaknesses of our theology. We find a very different attitude among the theologians of oppression who, with much apologetic, with so many arguments, with such an abundance of notes and bibliographies, are always asserting the power of their theological works. When James Cone speaks of the weaknesses and limitations of his work, he is not weakening or limiting his theology; on the contrary, he is demonstrating its true spirituality and theological power. It is not the power and wisdom of the powerful and wise of this world, but the power and wisdom of God which is revealed properly in weakness (cf. 1 Cor 1:17-2:9). Cone's capacity to recognize limitations, which is possible because he has been overcoming them through the course of his subsequent life and writings, not only enlarges the author, but also the book he has written. On the one hand, he is demonstrating the historical incarnation of his work; on the other hand, he demonstrates the vitality and power of his work to generate new possibilities of theological development. This preface to the 1986 edition *A Black Theology of Liberation* is the best introduction to Cone's work, allowing his book to rise above its limitations and stand transformed as a foundational work of the theology of liberation. Latin American liberation theology was also born with many limitations and weaknesses, some of which it continues to display. We are the ones who most often speak of these limitations.

But it is this epistemological and evangelical humility, which we try to share with the poor, that makes us grow and develop. It is thus, also, that we are trying, with the inspiration of black theology, to arrive at an Indo-Afro-Latino-American theology of liberation.

11

Black Women and Feminism: The U.S. and South African Contexts

ROSEMARY RADFORD RUETHER

James Cone's *A Black Theology of Liberation* is one of the classics of black theology. However much the language and context of black theology may have shifted in twenty years, this book will remain a foundational text. Its influence has been basic not only to black theology in the United States, but has inspired parallel black theology movements around the world, especially in South Africa. One of the issues, however, that was not recognized at the time of Cone's original work was the masculinist bias in much of black theology and in the policies of the black church. Black feminism, both in the churches and in society, has arisen to correct this oversight. James Cone also has given recognition to the need to incorporate black feminism in black theology, by his inclusion of such writings of black feminists in

Rosemary Radford Reuther is Georgia Harkness Professor of Applied Theology at Garrett-Evangelical Theological Seminary. She is the author of many books, including *Sexism and God-Talk*, *Disputed Questions: On Being a Christian*, and *The Wrath of Jonah*.

collections he has edited and also his mentoring of black feminists.

However, I believe there still remains a deep ambivalence toward feminist issues in the black community, religious and secular, and a great difficulty in giving more than token lip service to the needs of black women. I also found this to be true in my recent stay in South Africa. What is the source of this ambivalence toward black women, surely an integral part of the black community, both in the United States and in Africa? In this essay I should like to explore the reasons for this difficulty in incorporating black feminism in black theological and social thought.

First let me say that it is for black women, in the United States, or in South Africa, to define their own experience and interpretation of their liberation. As a white feminist I can speak about this only in terms of what I have learned from black women and the challenge this offers me to open up the myopic racism that often lingers in white feminism. I have involved myself in the black liberation struggle for thirty years, working in the civil rights movement in Mississippi and in Watts, California, in the early and mid-1960s, and teaching at a black theological seminary, Howard University School of Religion, in the critical years 1965–76. I have also had growing contact with black men and women in southern Africa and was privileged to spend two months traveling and speaking, observing and listening, in South Africa in the summer of 1989.

In the liberation struggles of the black community and of women, black women find themselves the double minority, or triple minority, if the fact that most black women are poor is taken into account. Poor black women are the group on which the triple jeopardy of oppression by race, class, and gender converge. For intellectuals, categories such as race, class, and gender trip off the tongue as though they were so many abstractions, each separate from the other. The reality is that our racist, classist and sexist societies have one complex system of exploitation which sets different groups in different relations of oppression.

To be black, poor, and female is a concrete condition in which sexual violence, racial violence, and economic exploitation are united. When a black woman is paid a parsimonious wage on which she cannot feed her children adequately, has to walk or ride by bus long distances to her job, with no adequate day care, and experiences sexual harassment both from the white boss and black males in her community, she does not divide these experiences into compartments and say, "here is racism, here classism, and here sexism"!

As a triple minority, the poor, black woman has been often betrayed by the liberation movements organized along class, race, or gender lines. The organized union movement in the United States and in South Africa was uninterested in including blacks. They created a privileged strata of unions for white males, excluding both black men and white women. Black women were hardly even in their field of vision. Socialist movements have typically claimed that women's liberation will arise automatically as a part of the liberation of the "worker," and so there is no need to organize around female-specific issues. Indeed, they said, such feminist movements are "bourgeois."

The black and the feminist movements have also betrayed the black woman. The black males of the American civil rights movement and of the African National Congress have been ambivalent about inclusion of women's liberation within the black agenda. In the feminist movement in the United States and in South Africa white women have defined feminism in terms applicable to white middle-class women, with little awareness of its lack of relevance to poor women of color. In both countries votes for white women were played off against the disenfranchisement of blacks of both genders in the early twentieth century.

In both countries racism has to do most immediately with the subjugation of black men by white men. Black men must be debilitated as heads of their families, as providers for their children, and protectors of their wives and daughters. Racism is built on dividing and conquering the members of the black family as much as possible, so that the white racist system can exploit all its members for their labor. Black women have been exploited for their sexual and reproductive services as well. Black women are often left to shoulder the burden of being both mother and breadwinner for their children, both nurturers and economic providers.

Black men in white, racist societies are demeaned as men. They sometimes take this out in resentment against black women whose strength in adversity is seen as a kind of affront to their own demeaned masculinity. Black liberation, then, is sometimes seen as a restoration of black masculinity, in an implicit put-down of black women. This situation puts black women in a double bind, understanding the need to affirm black male self-esteem, but finding themselves the most available target for black men acting out their reclaimed sexual and social dominance.

This pattern of triple betrayal of black women by the socialist, the black, and the feminist movements, as well as the double bind created by this situation in black male-female relations, can be illustrated from U.S. American history. In an article written in the early 1970s, "Between the Sons of White and the Sons of Blackness: Racism and Sexism in America," and published in my 1975 book, *New Woman/New Earth: Sexism, Ideologies, and Human Liberation,* I tried to summarize some of these patterns in the American experience, as that was evident both in the slave experience and the more recent civil rights movement of the 1960s.

In this essay I should like to reflect briefly on similar patterns that I observed in my brief stay in South Africa. First, I wish to speak a cautionary word to Americans. It is important for U.S. Americans not to too easily equate South African apartheid with the American experience of racism or the anti-apartheid movement with our civil rights movement. In many ways the situation of discrimination against black South Africans is much deeper, or, to put it better, whites in America have dealt with racism much more superficially than would be required in South Africa.

In order to understand the South African situation, American whites should imagine themselves a minority group of 37 million people in the United States, in relation to an Amerindian community of 175 million, and black and Hispanic groups who make up another 33 million. The Amerindians have been disenfranchised, relegated to barren "reservations," making up only 14 percent of the land of the United States, but they remember their history as the original proprietors of the whole land and retain their indigenous cultures and languages.

White South Africans have organized their political system, as a minority group of 15 percent of the population, to control almost all the land and to dominate the labor of the 85 percent nonwhite population. Only they have real participation in political decision-making. Thus giving up apartheid for white South Africans means facing their own reality as a European minority in a non-European continent, something that whites in the United States did not have to face in conceding civil rights to blacks in America.

One of the most basic results of the South African system of apartheid is the fragmentation of the black family. Like the American slave system that refused legal status to slave marriages and sold members of the family apart from each other, apartheid seeks to fragment the cohesive base of the black community in order to exploit black African individuals as separable "work unity." In a legal structure that goes back to the 1913 Land Act, whites gave almost all the fertile land of South Africa to the white European minority, laying aside only 7 percent (later increased to 14 percent) of the land for the African majority.

The basic assumption of apartheid is that blacks should remain in these "reserves" and are to be allowed into the white areas only as needed as labor by whites. Moreover they are to enter these white areas only as individual workers, not as family units. Pass laws and labor registration regulate the entrance of blacks into the white areas as workers. Even though the carrying of passes has been abolished, this basic structure of regulation of black residence in white areas remains. Blacks are allowed to live in white areas only as long as they are employed. If they are not employed, they are deported back to the black reserves.

In the 1960s, beginning with the Bantu Self-Government Act of 1959, this system was accentuated by the fictional redefinition of the black reserves as independent self-governing black nations. Blacks were to be defined as citizens of these fictional black nations, even though these so-called homelands were ruled under the control of the white South African government and had neither the agricultural nor the industrial base for economic independence. This allowed the white government to define black Africans in white South Africa as "immigrant labor" without any claim to citizen rights.

Blacks enter white areas for various kinds of work. They enter as farm laborers, where generally the wife, husband, and dependent children all work for the white farmer and so can live together, but are often paid in kind, with little monetary compensation. The notorious "tot" system of paying farm workers in beer or wine has also promoted severe alcoholism among blacks. Able-bodied black males, who work in the mines and factories, are still often housed in single-sex hostels, which allow only a "shelf" for the bed and few belongings of each worker. Family members are not allowed to live there, although many squatter families have done so illegally.

Black women are widely employed as domestic workers in a society that can still afford one or more full-time live-in domestics for most white families. These domestic workers are isolated from their families. Their husbands cannot visit them, nor can their children live with them. Beyond payments in kind in food, housing, and clothes, these women receive a tiny salary on which they are often supporting families elsewhere. They might be allowed to see their families for half a day on Sunday or even less regularly. Nonworking members of the family, aged relatives, and dependent children might be living hundreds of miles away on the "reserves."

In such a system of extreme exploitation based on race, where the black woman encounters the white woman primarily as the privileged housewife where she lives as a domestic servant, how is it possible to imagine any common cause of black and white women around a common agenda of "women's liberation"? In South Africa the only possibility of black and white women making common cause on issues of sexism must be based on the white women rejecting their race and class privileges and grounding themselves clearly on the primary agenda of black liberation from white race privilege.

Despite these obstacles, this kind of women's movement across race lines and within the anti-apartheid movement has appeared in South Africa nevertheless. The most important example, and one that still serves as the basis of the women's movement in South Africa, is the Federation of South Africa

Women, whose brief and heroic apogee was between 1954 and 1959. In this period, the government was attempting to separate white women's work strictly from black women's work, creating separate white and black women's unions in the garment industry, for example. In 1953 Africans were excluded from unions altogether. But in the 1950s there were still black and white women labor organizers and socialists who could find some common ground.

When the African National Congress was first formed, black women could only be nonvoting members of the women's auxiliary who provided catering and entertainment for the men. Women were given full membership in the ANC only in 1943, but were still expected to do catering and fund-raising, but not to make decisions. In the 1950s radical young black women, such as Ida Mtwana from the ANC Youth League, took over the ANC Women's League. Together with radical white women, such as Ray Alexander, and black and white women labor organizers, such as Hetty du Preez and Elizabeth Mafeking, they created an umbrella organization of the Federation of South African Women (FEDSAW), which incorporated the ANC Women's League, as well as women from other progressive movements, such as the South African Indian Congress (Fatima Meer and Amina Cacholia).

The major organizing congresses of FEDSAW were in 1954 and 1956. In the documents of these congresses the theoretical basis for a women's movement that encompasses both gender-specific women's issues and the struggle of women within national liberation was laid down. The ANC male leadership remained extremely ambivalent about either any autonomous organization for women or organizing around specifically female issues, such as birth control clinics, equal legal rights, and equal pay. But they expressed this ambivalence by passive nonsupport, rather than by open criticism.

However, the FEDSAW charter, and the statement of "What Women Demand," of these foundational congresses made clear that women intended to encompass a range of issues and demands, organized around what women need to be fully equal as women, what women need as mothers, the needs of children, and what is needed for the full dignity of people of all races.

They refused to set feminist, race, and class issues in conflict with each other, but rather laid out a vision of a new egalitarian society that would embrace transformation in all these relations of gender, class, and race.

This organizing work was soon stifled, along with all the progressive movements that were banned in the late 1950s. After sponsoring major women's protest marches against pass laws in 1956, the leaders of FEDSAW, along with many other anti-apartheid leaders, were indicted for treason, in a trial that dragged on to 1961. Although Helen Joseph and Lilian Ngoyi were finally acquitted, the leadership of FEDSAW was smashed, either fleeing into exile or confined to house arrest. Lilian Ngoyi was banned until her death in 1980, and Helen Joseph was under house arrest until 1972 (and sporatically thereafter). With the banning of the ANC, the turn to armed struggle in 1961, and the arrest and imprisonment of the top leaders of the ANC, a whole generation of progressive leaders were driven from public life.

The second important women's organization that emerged in the mid-1950s was the Black Sash. In its original form, it was a white women's organization in defense of democratic constitutionalism, but unable to support the ANC. It did not elect to join FEDSAW in 1955. However, over the years, the Black Sash movement, while remaining a white women's movement, has become more radically anti-apartheid. It organizes in behalf of black women's rights, while maintaining its public vigil as an expression of white women's protest against the apartheid laws.

After thirty years of repression, the ANC was finally declared legal in 1990, and its elderly leaders, most notably Nelson Mandela, emerged from 27 years of imprisonment. The new Defiance Campaign of 1989 made clear that certain kinds of racial laws in relation to public amenities have become unenforceable. Yet the deeper system of apartheid is far from being dismantled. In a society where all Africans lack the vote and secure residency rights in South Africa, it would be premature indeed for Westerners to claim that the struggle against apartheid has been won.

The conflicts over defining and organizing a women's liberation movement within the anti-apartheid struggle are as difficult, perhaps even more difficult in 1990, than in 1955. Thirty-five years of increased separation of the races destroyed some of the places in canning and textile unions or radical organizations where white and black women worked together in that earlier period. Yet a women's movement remains vital to a deepening of the democratic and participatory character of the anti-apartheid movement. It is needed to lift up the specific way women, black women in particular, are exploited, sexually and socially, as women.

The low pay, lack of pensions, and isolation from family of the domestic workers remain a national scandal. Female farm workers are still often paid in kind rather than in wages for 70-hour workweeks. Female hostels for cannery workers reveal horrifying conditions, with wooden pallets for beds and no showers. In the factories long hours and dangerous conditions cause illness and miscarriages. Women may travel three hours each way to their jobs, with only catch-as-catch-can childcare. Black women fall on the bottom of the system of labor exploitation, allowed only the worst jobs at the lowest pay and with the least job security. Sexual harassment from both black male workers and white bosses face them on the job, and they may be subject to rape or wife beating when they return home exhausted at the end of the day.

African women in the newly emergent African union movement have become the front line of this struggle for women's rights. But, as in the past, they often face ambivalence from their black brothers. At a national meeting of COSATU, the major trade union organization, in the summer of 1989, union women were booed down by their male colleagues when they attempted to bring to the floor a statement condemning sexual harassment on the worksite.

Some Christian churches have taken the lead in the struggle against apartheid. They have opened the churches to protest meetings to help fill the gap left by banned leaders and organizations. But these same churchmen, who are at the forefront of the anti-apartheid struggle, such as Desmond Tutu of the Anglican Church, are much less supportive of women's equality with men in the church. South African liberal churches lag far behind those of western Europe or the United States in the ordination of women.

A proposal to ordain women, brought forward during the meeting of the Anglican synod of June 1989, under the leadership of Archbishop Tutu, was defeated, 13 votes short of the needed two-thirds majority. The synod became notorious for the raw sexist remarks of some male clergymen, black and white, such as the statement of one cleric that "if my wife was off doing a morning Eucharist, who would make my breakfast?" But this experience shocked Anglican women into a need to organize for the first time on behalf of women's ordination. The surprising closeness of the vote suggests the possibility that women may win ordination at the next synod.

South African theological faculties have few full-time female faculty members, and the issues of feminist theology in the South African context have only barely begun to be addressed. If theologically trained white women are rare, black women with advanced degrees in theology are still nonexistent. Yet the increasing integration of universities, and the presence of many white and some black women in theological studies, indicates future possibilities of such leaders. But real dialogue on a feminist liberation theology across race lines, and firmly rooted in the creation of a nonracial South Africa, has hardly begun.

The continuing inability of male anti-apartheid leaders to accord women's oppression and emancipation an important place in the liberation struggle should be a matter of great concern. It needs to become clear that a people is free only to the extent that its women are free. A liberation struggle that cannot challenge male dominance will also, finally, not challenge male ruling-class exploitation of the working classes and the poor. Such a liberation movement runs the danger of simply replacing an elite of white male exploiters with a new interracial male elite, but without deep changes in the overall system of class and gender exploitation. The very factors of race and class contradictions that make it so difficult to speak of women's liberation in South Africa also point to its explosive revolutionary potential.

Sources

Besides personal conversations and newspapers, the major sources for this essay are:

Jacklyn Cock, *Maids and Madams: Domestic Workers Under Apartheid.* London: Women Press, 1989 (original publication, 1980).

Cherryl Walker, *Women and Resistance in South Africa.* London: Onyx Press, 1982.

Jane Barrett et al., *Vukani Makhosikazi: South African Women Speak.* Birmingham, England: Third World Publications, 1985.

12

Black Theology:
A Reflection from Asia

K.C. Abraham

There are theologians who, while reflecting on the oppression of people in their own context, speak for the oppressed everywhere. Their writings surpass all boundaries. James Cone's books, especially *A Black Theology of Liberation*, are of that genre. It is, therefore, not surprising that Cone's writings strike a sympathetic chord in the minds and hearts of many oppressed groups in India. They listen to him, read him, and are eager to forge a link with the liberation movement of North American blacks. I hope the new edition of Cone's book will help further the transcultural communication.

Cone's writings also remind us that liberation theology is not a monolithic system of thought. In fact it is better to speak of liberation *theologies* in the plural. The form of oppression specific to the context from which one does theology—be it racism, casteism, neocolonialism or male domination—provides the the-

K.C. Abraham is vice president of the Ecumenical Association of Third World Theologians (EATWOT), and professor of theology and ethics at the United Theological College in Bangalore, India. He is the editor of *Third World Theologies: Commonalities and Divergences*.

ologian with a distinct perspective on the content and meaning of liberation. This particularity within the broader framework of liberation sets the stage for an ongoing dialogue among theologians from different contexts. Cone's books make a valuable contribution to this dialogue.

Of particular interest to those of us in Asia is Cone's emphasis on the religious dimension of black liberation. "To try to separate black liberation from black religions is a mistake," asserts Cone. The same point has been made by theologians in Asia. The poor of Asia are a religious people — espousing, of course, not simply Christianity, but other great religions as well. It is impossible to consider the liberation of the poor without acknowledging the religious or cultural dimension of this liberation. This is the point on which Indian or Asian theologians feel a particular affinity for black theology. It reminds us of the need to develop a perspective on religion that emerges out of the experiences of the poor.

In India, where religion continues to be a powerful force, the people's movement is aware of the liberating potential of religion and culture for the struggle for justice. We are, of course, not ignorant of the fact that our religions have been and continue to be a source of oppression, often providing a protective veneer for the vested interest of the high and mighty. We know all too well how religious doctrines, symbols, and myths may serve as powerful weapons in the hands of the dominant castes to keep the poor under their control. And yet, we cannot simply dismiss religious reality as oppressive. For despite the distortion of religion and culture by the elite, there are elements of the religious tradition that preserve for the poor their autonomy and dynamism. There is a clear analogy in Cone's book: Despite the distortion of Christianity by white Christians, blacks have been able to discover and appropriate elements of the Christian gospel that affirm their dignity and support the cause of liberation.

From the study of any traditional religion we know that the vast majority of its votaries have no direct recourse to scriptures and doctrines. Their life is shaped by festivals, symbols, rituals, and oral traditions. Although the latter are related to written texts, the common people have taken the liberty of adapting them to their local situations. The question is what effect these forms of popular religion have on those who must struggle to cope with daily survival. Some efforts have recently been made to study the popular expression of faith in the villages of India by observing the symbols, rituals, and songs used in festivals. Often these demonstrate an amazing vitality and dynamism. Those symbols and songs express the deeper meaning of human existence and exercise profound influence on the consciousness of believers. In this fashion, an experience of transcendence is brought closer to daily life.

Hitherto subjugated groups, when awakened to their rights, organize themselves around the demand for greater justice and participation. The oppressed need an identity distinct from that imposed by their oppressors. Often this new identity coincides with the discovery of long-forgotten, though liberating, dimensions of their own cultural and religious heritage. Some even embrace new religions. An outstanding example is the Dalit movement in India [Dalit literally means "the oppressed"; it refers to the untouchables]. The caste system was a creation of the brahmin elite who succeeded in embracing all people within a religious system that reinforced their own power and privilege. Today the Dalits are not only rejecting their inferior status but challenging the religious ideology that underlies it. Many of them choose to define themselves in terms of their prebrahmin tribal past, or some other religion; many embrace Buddhism, Islam, or Christianity. Religious conversion is thus part of the process of social emancipation or liberation.

This is only one example of the role of religion in the liberation struggle. But more important is the process by which people appropriate for themselves their own history, culture, and religion. By sifting through the grandiose edifice of religion built by the dominant castes, the poor have rediscovered the authentic core and essential dynamism of their religious heritage. They have appropriated the scriptures and the symbols for themselves by giving them new interpretations.

The tradition of the people (in the sense of the poor masses) in different religions has a common purpose and common language. A unity among people of different religions forged on the basis of this popular tradition will go a long way in furthering the liberation struggle in India and set the stage for the emergence of an Indian liberation theology.

A final comment. Christian symbols are very much part of the religious heritage of African Americans, and therefore Cone can use those symbols for articulating a black theology of liberation. For obvious reasons, we cannot use them so easily in a multireligious context. We have the complex task of entering into the religious heritage of our people. But Cone's passionate encounter with the experience of oppression as well as the religious heritage of his people will remain a source of inspiration for us in our task.

13

James Cone's Liberation: Twenty Years Later

DELORES S. WILLIAMS

It hardly seems possible that twenty years have passed since James Cone's text, *A Black Theology of Liberation*, appeared. This book became "scripture" for many black seminarians and graduates who had for years been trying to reconcile their own black experience of Jesus in the black Christian community with the Jesus they met in Eurocentric theological education. Written in the rage and rhetoric of the Afro-American cultural revolution of the 1960s and '70s, Cone's book righteously affirmed the freedom struggle of black people and paved the way for them to take their own Christian traditions seriously as they studied for ministry in North American seminaries. *A Black Theology of Liberation* served notice to the American white theological establishment (and to some surprised black theological establishments as well) that God only identified with the poor and oppressed of the earth, that Jesus was black, and that Christians could only be saved by joining the liberation struggle of racially oppressed people. Thus black people in theological education

Delores S. Williams teaches theology at Drew University. She received her doctorate from Union Theological Seminary in New York.

in America were and are indebted to James Cone for systematizing black God-talk and bringing it into the hermeneutical circle of Christian theology.

However, in twenty years changes occur. Many black women have had their consciousness raised so that they also have begun to see clearly the sexist character of their oppression in the black community and beyond. I am one of these women. So in 1990 I read Cone's book with new eyes, asking, what has this book to say about the horrible sexual exploitation black women have experienced in both the black and white worlds? The answer, of course, is that the content of the book, written twenty years ago, has nothing to say about this. But Cone's new preface to the 1986 edition of the book shows that he has, after twenty years, taken seriously the *fact* of black women's gender oppression. It sounded good, indeed, to hear Cone say, "If we black male theologians do not take seriously the need to incorporate into our theology a critique of our sexist practices in the black community, then we have no right to complain when white theologians snub black theology."

Yet when I paraphrased some of the quotations from Malcolm X and others that Cone used in the 1986 preface, I was stunned by the kind of action intimated for black women struggling to be free of sexist oppression in the black community. I found myself asking: Could Cone affirm the action for black women that logically follows what he and Malcolm X say in the book? For instance, take this quote from Malcolm X that appeared in Cone's new preface: "I believe in a religion that believes in freedom. Any time I have to accept a religion that won't let me fight a battle for my people, I say to hell with that religion." As a black womanist-feminist theologian, I paraphrase this quotation to say, "Any time I have to accept a religion that won't let me fight a battle for oppressed black women, I say to hell with that religion." Inasmuch as black Christian religion — manifested in the practice and theology of the black church — is often antagonistic to women's struggle for liberation, black Christian women could say, "To hell with the black church and the black expression of Christian religion in it." This could mean that the black church in America might cease to exist, since black women are its blood, bone, and sinew. If black women said "to hell with the sexist black churches" and left them, thereby allowing them to crumble, could Cone validate this action? Part of me wants to say he could; another part of me is uneasy, given the *absence* of black women's words of wisdom and advice from Cone's preface. All the inspiration, wisdom, and advice contained in the material Cone quotes comes from men like Malcolm X and, on occasion, W.E.B. DuBois and Martin Luther King. Not a single woman is named, quoted, or given credit for contributing to the transformations Cone says he has made in his thought and style in the last twenty years.

My attention focused upon another quotation from Malcolm X cited by Cone in his new preface: "Don't let anybody who is oppressing us ever lay the ground rules. Don't go by their games, don't play by their rules. Let them know now that this is a new game, and we've got some new rules. . . ." Paraphrased within my womanist-feminist framework this quote reads: "Don't let anybody who is oppressing black women ever lay the ground rules. Don't go by their games, don't play the game by their rules. Let them know now that this is a new game, and black women have got some new rules. . . ." In the African American community the rules for "the church game," "the political game," "the mating game," and a host of other games have been determined by males. Should black women, "by whatever means necessary," destroy the male rules and inaugurate new games determined by black women's rules? Can the new consciousness about black sexism which Cone claims in the 1986 preface support such a power shift in the black church, in the seminaries where black men and women teach, and in the black community? And I wonder if Cone, who says "I knew racism was a heresy," would also agree that sexism is heresy? Part of me says he would.

But I paraphrase the following quotation from Cone, himself, and ask whether he can support what the paraphrased words suggest for black women. Giving the reasons why he wrote the book twenty years ago, Cone says: "It was clear to me that what was needed was a *fresh start* in theology, a new way of doing it that would arise out of the black struggle for justice and in no way would be dependent upon the approval of white academics in religion." A womanist-feminist paraphrasing of these words claims this: "It is clear that what is needed for black women is a *fresh start* in theology, a new way of doing it that would arise out of black women's struggle for justice and in no way would be dependent upon the approval of black male and white academics in religion." The problem here is that if black women in the academic world take such a stand, their fate may be like that of Ishmael described by God in Genesis 16, where God tells Hagar that Ishmael will have every *man's* hand against him, and he will raise his hand against every *man*. Hence, would Cone's claim that "sexism dehumanizes and kills" translate into taking a stand with black women in opposing those black males in the academic world who, in sexist fashion, might try to prevent black women from publishing theological positions that challenge the publications of black male theologians? Part of me says Cone's words would translate into a supportive stand with black women; another part wonders if he could withstand the alienation from some important black male peers that such a stand might incur.

While my paraphrasing and questioning suggest the kind of problems facing black theology today because of black Christian women's demands for visibility, inclusion, and equality, I must say that James Cone's *A Black Theology of Liberation* is as relevant today as it was twenty years ago. This is not only because white racism is still alive and well in America, and because Cone addresses the condition so brilliantly. There are also additional theological and ethical reasons.

First, the book is an historical landmark in Christian theology in America. It (and James Cone's black theological enterprise) was born on the tail-end of the death-of-God movement in American theology. On the one hand, black theology opposed one of the fundamental tenets of the new "radical theology," the name by which the assortment of death-of-God theologies were often called. On the other hand, black theology advanced an important claim made by death-of-God theologians. By way of opposition to death-of-God theology, black theology proclaimed loudly (via Cone's book) that the Christian God was indeed alive and active in the history of oppressed communities like the black American community. But, according to Cone, this God acting in history was the black Jesus of the New Testament who had always revealed his preference for the poor and the oppressed of the earth. This was not the Christian God that white, Western theology had talked about in its historical development. One could only gain knowledge of the black Jesus by joining the liberation struggle of oppressed people in America. Therefore, the death-of-God theologies could speak of the demise of the Christian God because they had been giving attention to a false notion of God passed along by the Western, white theological tradition. They had directed their attention to a death-dealing white God of white oppressors and therefore used the language of death with reference to God's existence. Because of the black community's sustaining and empowering relation with Jesus in both its past and immediate history, black theology (via James Cone) could speak of the life and not the death of the Christian God. If the death-of-God theologians in America had paid attention to the God-talk of oppressed African-American Christians, they could not have spoken of God's demise. There is a sense, then, in which James Cone's version of black liberation theology "saved" the Christian God for American theology.

Yet, there is a sense in which Cone's black theology advanced one aspect of the agenda of the death-of-God movement in American theology. That agenda was to effect a radical transformation in the way that theologians interpret and connect with the western, theological tradition. Thomas J.J. Altizer, a death-of-God theologian, describes this agenda well:

> Insofar as the new world lying upon our horizon is negating and transcending the world of the past, theology will be able to enter that new world only by effecting a radical break with its own past and by passing through a dissolution of its inherited form and language. In this sense, the death of the theological tradition is at bottom its rebirth into new life [*Toward a New Christianity: Readings in the Death of God Theology* (New York: Harcourt, Brace & World, Inc., 1967), p. 13].

Obviously Cone's theological project has been participating in and helping to bring about Western Christian theology's radical break with its past. And this has led to an erosion of the "inherited form and language" of the Western Christian theological tradition. Black theology (and its feminist sisters) have understood clearly Altizer's words that "the death of the theological tradition is at bottom its rebirth into new life." The theological projects of black theology (via Cone and others) and feminist theology (via Ruether, Schüssler Fiorenza, Heyward, and others) have given us views of what that new life looks like.

It is, however, an ethical theme in Cone's *A Black Theology of Liberation* that shows a remarkable and jarring relevance for today's world of racial strife in New York, in Denver, Colorado, on American college campuses, and in other "liberal" locations—places where one was led to assume that relations between blacks and whites had made some important progress since the 1960s. The ethical theme alluded to here is Cone's affirmation of Malcolm X's advocacy of "liberation of the oppressed by whatever means necessary." There is no doubt in many black people's minds that white racial oppression in America is continuing to create and perpetuate black economic underdevelopment, lack of educational opportunity for black people, lack of employment opportunities for black people, incarceration of large numbers of black youth, and genocide of black young people. (This genocide is being effected by the large supply of drugs in the black community—drugs brought into this country by huge amounts of "non-black" money. Black people do not have the money it takes to supply drugs for this country.) The mounting white violence against black Americans, as well as four hundred years of black resistance to white racial oppression, is causing many black people to begin to lose faith in the efficacy of Martin Luther King's nonviolent strategies. People are now beginning to consider seriously effective strategies consistent with the ethical theme of "liberation by whatever means necessary." This means, then, that James Cone's *A Black Theology of Liberation* will continue to be relevant to all discussion of what this theme can mean for living the Christian life and creating political strategies for liberation of oppressed peoples.

Something must be said about the enormous contribution Cone's book makes to "de-convolutizing" the language of theology. Many times in theological seminaries where I have taught, students of all colors have said to me, "I might not agree with everything James Cone is saying in this book, but I sure do appreciate the clear way he expresses his ideas. There is none of this convoluted language we have met in many of the other theologians we read." It is perhaps reasonable, then, to suggest that this clear way of speaking signals the "rebirth into new life" that American theology is experiencing through black theological projects.

One last word. Cone's preface to the 1986 edition of *A Black Theology of Liberation* shows the remarkable openness of a famous theologian, sharing his growth-experiences with his public. Recognizing both the significance and the limitations of the work, Cone regrets that his earlier "intemperate behavior prevented some whites, whose intentions were more honorable than my responses suggested, from dialoguing with me." Yet Cone affirms what many black people affirm about the relevance of his work. "In *A Black Theology of Liberation*," he says, "I tried to uncover the wrongheadedness of the white way of doing theology and then attempted to set Christian theology on the right path of liberation." Like Cone, many people "believe that it was a message worth saying in 1970 and still an important word to say today." And Cone would perhaps readily admit that this message must be open and conversant with other messages that issue from the African-American community, especially the messages coming from black women.

Afterword

I am grateful to the respondents in this anniversary edition for their critical evaluation of my perspective on black theology. Each has helped me to see more clearly the strengths and weaknesses of *A Black Theology of Liberation*.

Delores Williams and Rosemary Ruether have reminded me that there is still much work to be done to eliminate sexism in the black community. I agree with them. Both Ruether and Williams explore aspects of the problem that are informative and that will also be helpful as I continue to incorporate black feminism into my theological perspective.

I was particularly moved by the challenging questions that Delores Williams addressed to me.

> Could Cone affirm the action for black women that logically follows what he and Malcolm X say in the book? . . . If black women said "to hell with the sexist black churches" and left them, thereby allowing them to crumble, could Cone validate this action? . . . I wonder if Cone would agree that sexism is a heresy? . . . Would Cone's claim that "sexism dehumanizes and kills" translate into taking a stand with black women in opposing those black males in the academic world who, in sexist fashion, might try to prevent black women from publishing theological positions that challenge the publications of black male theologians?

As I pondered these questions, I began to realize how much more I have to learn from black women generally and from womanist theologians in particular. In my 1986 preface to *A Black Theology of Liberation*, I indicated the importance of black feminism for my perspective on black theology. But Delores

Williams' response to my preface shows that, although I have moved in the right direction, I still have some distance to go. In her anticipation of what my responses would be to her questions, Delores read me fairly well. I do believe that sexism is a heresy and thus must be eliminated from the black church community. And it must be done "by any means necessary." Of course, I realize that some black women may find black churches so sexist and so irrelevant to their needs as women that they must leave and create alternative and more supportive religious communities. I find no fault in that action. However, because of the central role that it has played and continues to play in the liberation struggles of black people, I do not think it is necessary for all black women to leave the black church. I would argue that black women and their male supporters should take over the churches and remake them into instruments more conducive to God's liberating presence in the world.

Would I be a supporter of black women as they seek to transform the black church into a liberating instrument of God in the world? Could I withstand the alienation from some important black male peers that such solidarity might incur? I believe that I am prepared to go all the way in my support of black women against black male patriarchy in the churches because the current powers that be in black churches do not like black liberation theology any more than they do womanist theology. That is why black theology is often excluded from mainline black churches. Black theology is not only a force against racism but also against sexism and any evil done in the name of God and humanity.

Delores Williams and Rosemary Ruether identified an important area where I need to keep working. I hope that I can meet their challenges regarding black feminism by doing what I can to support black women in their fight for empowerment in the black community. I believe that sexism, like racism, must be destroyed so we can create a more humane world.

Robert McAfee Brown has reminded me that the most serious weakness in my early writings was "the lack of any kind of economic analysis." I accept his criticism, though we differ on the question of whether an analysis of classism is more important than sexism and racism. I do not think that any one of them is more basic or more serious than the others since they are interrelated; elevating one to priority often shows an insensitivity to the other two. This is precisely what happened at the "Theology in the Americas" conference, an event about which Bob and I have different interpretations.

We also differ about why so little dialogue has occurred between black and white theologians in the United States. When I try to talk to white theologians about the gospel and the black poor, I often feel the way Martin Luther King, Jr. felt during the rise of the Black Power movement in the 1960s. "You just can't communicate with the ghetto-dweller and at the same time not frighten many whites to death," King told a reporter. "I don't know what the answer is. My role perhaps is to interpret to the white world. I've said to [black power militants] that I can't use language that will alienate the white majority."

One major difference between Martin King and Malcolm X was found in their attitude toward the white community, especially liberals. Malcolm chose to speak the truth about the black condition in America clearly, forcefully, and without compromise, even though it meant alienating many whites. My perspective on black theology is derived from both Malcolm and Martin. The term "black" in the phrase refers to Malcolm's influence on my thinking, and the word "theology" points to my solidarity with Martin. Black theology seeks to bring Malcolm and Martin together and thereby to demonstrate that the gospel of Jesus is not alien to black people but rather empowers them in their fight against racism. What often alienates Bob Brown and other white theologians is what empowers black people in their struggle for justice. Therefore, it is hard to do black theology and also create "pleasanter human relationships" between blacks and whites because few, if any, white theologians are prepared for a sustained attack upon the evil of racism.

I am very pleased that Bob Brown has taken the risk and the courage to respond critically to my perspective on black theology. Only by speaking truthfully and frankly do we learn from each other and thereby build a genuine solidarity in the struggle for justice. I have learned much from Bob's response. And I hope that he and other white theologians find in my response to him grounds for common solidarity against racism and economic exploitation. I certainly do not wish to divide the forces for justice. But I also must not compromise what I know to be the truth about the black condition in America.

K.C. Abraham and Pablo Richard reinforce for me the importance of the Third World in my perspective on theology. (I regret that the African theologian invited to participate in this dialogue found it impossible to respond.) In EATWOT, K.C. Abraham, Pablo Richard, and other Asian, Latin American, and African theologians have taught me about the importance of both socio-political and religio-cultural analyses for theology. I am also pleased to know that they have learned something from black theology. I only hope that we can continue our work together so that the struggles of the poor throughout the world will become united. Martin King was right: We are bound together as one humanity. What affects one directly affects all indirectly. The sooner we realize the interconnectedness of our social existence, the sooner we will end our isolation from each other and begin to develop ways that we can work together toward the liberation of the poor throughout the world.

No one has influenced my perspective on black theology more than my colleague and friend, Gayraud S. Wilmore. He has been my strongest supporter and toughest critic. When I wrote *Black Theology and Black Power* (1969) and *A Black Theology of Liberation* (1970), Wilmore was one of the first to encourage me in what I was doing. But he also was the first to point out the limitations of my perspective on black theology, especially in terms of my dependency upon the neo-orthodox theology of Karl Barth. Wilmore challenged me to develop black theology from the religio-cultural resources of African people on the continent and in the United States. His contribution to this volume not only gives an important analysis of black theology's impact and development in the 1970s and 1980s but also shows where it needs to go in the 1990s and the 21st century.

Much has happened in black theology since the publication of *A Black Theology of Liberation*. Womanist theology has been the most creative and challenging development. The theological voice of Delores Williams is supported by Katie Cannon, Jacquelyn Grant, Kelly Brown, Cheryl Gilkes, Toinette Eugene, and Cheryl Sanders. Challenging theological voices also are being heard from a new generation of young male voices. They include: Dwight Hopkins, Josiah Young, James Evans, Robert Franklin, Alonzo Johnson, George Cummings, and Theodore Walker. In the area of biblical studies, Cain Felder has led the way with his important book, *Troubling Biblical Waters*. Other important voices include Randall Bailey, Renita Weems, Clarice Martin, Thomas Hoyt, and Vincent Wimbush. With these new voices, black theology is making important and creative contributions to the study of theology in the seminary and the black church community.

But despite, or rather because of, these new contributions, I believe more strongly than ever that black theology's reason for being is defined by the liberation struggle of the poor. It must not, therefore, seek merely to be an academic discipline, reflecting on intellectual matters interesting to university and seminary professors and their graduate students. Rather, black theology must be the prophetic voice of the church, proclaiming throughout the world what Amos said nearly 3000 years ago: "Let justice roll down like waters and righteousness as a mighty stream." Without this voice the church ceases to be the church, and theology ceases to be Christian.

JAMES H. CONE
July 1990

Notes

Preface to the 1986 Edition

1. Malcolm X, *By Any Means Necessary*, George Breitman, ed. (New York: Pathfinder Press, 1970), p. 140.
2. See Andrew M. Greeley, "Nazi Mentality in this Country," *Inter/Syndicate*, 1971.
3. *Malcolm X Speaks*, George Breitman, ed. (New York: Grove Press, 1966), p. 165.
4. Malcolm X, *By Any Means*, p. 155.
5. W. E. B. DuBois, *The Souls of Black Folk* (Greenwich, Conn.: Fawcett Premier Book, 1968), p. 23.
6. *The Speeches of Malcolm X at Harvard*, Archie Epps, ed. (New York: Morrow, 1968), p. 133.
7. Martin Luther King, Jr., "The American Dream," *Negro History Bulletin*, vol. 31 (May 1968), p. 12.

Chapter 1

1. Quoted in José Míguez Bonino, "Christians and the Political Revolution," in S. C. Rose and P. P. Van Lelyveld, eds., *Risk*, spec. ed., *The Development Apocalypse*, 1967, p. 109.
2. See James Cone, *Black Theology and Black Power* (New York: The Seabury Press, 1969).
3. See Paul Tillich, *Dynamics of Faith* (New York: Harper and Brothers, 1957).
4. I do not intend to qualify this statement, because too much is at stake—the survival of the black community. But perhaps some clarification is needed here. Some critics will undoubtedly ask, "How can you dismiss out of hand any criticisms that white theologians or others in traditional white Christianity might raise concerning your interpretation of black theology, and at the same time use quotations from white theologians, both European and American, with approval? If white theology is as bad as you say, why not dismiss them altogether, without any reference to their work?" Of course, these are challenging questions,

203

and I can see whites milking this idea for all that it is worth.

There are essentially two responses. First, those who press this point have taken too seriously the American definition of white. When I say that white theology is not Christian theology, I mean the theology that has been written without any reference to the oppressed of the land. This is not true of Karl Barth and certainly not true of Dietrich Bonhoeffer. Reinhold Niebuhr's *Moral Man and Immoral Society* moves in the direction of blackness. To verify the blackness of a particular perspective, we need only ask, "For whom was it written, the oppressed or oppressors?" If the former, it is black; if the latter, it is white. I do not condemn all persons who happen to look like white Americans; the condemnation comes when they act like them.

Secondly, it is characteristic of the oppressed to be limited to the thought forms of those who call themselves the masters. Oppression refers not only to economic, social, and political disfranchisement; there is the disfranchisement of the mind, of the spiritual and moral values that hold together one's identity in a community. To be oppressed is to be defined, located, or set aside according to another's perspective. This is precisely what has happened to black persons in America. If they would be free, they must use the thought forms of the master and transform them into ideas of liberation. If blacks clearly understood the meaning of their spirituality, from their own vantage point, they would not be oppressed. The task of black theology is to take Christian tradition that is so white and make it black, by showing that whites do not really know what they are saying when they affirm Jesus as the Christ. He who has come to redeem us is not white but black; and the redemption of which he speaks has nothing to do with stabilizing the status quo. It motivates the redeemed to be what they are— creatures endowed with freedom.

5. The reader should take note of two characteristics of the definition of blackness. First, blackness is a *physiological* trait. It refers to a particular black-skinned people in America, a victim of white racist brutality. The scars of its members bear witness to the inhumanity committed against them. Black theology believes that they are the *only* key that can open the door to divine revelation. Therefore, no American theology can even tend in the direction of Christian theology without coming to terms with the black-skinned people of America. Secondly, blackness is an *ontological* symbol for all those who participate in liberation from oppression. This is the universal note in black theology. It believes that all human beings were created for freedom, and that God always sides with the oppressed against oppressors.

6. Quoted in J. H. Clarke, ed., *William Styron's Nat Turner: Ten Black Writers Respond* (Boston: Beacon Press, 1968), p. vii.

7. Tillich, *The Theology of Culture* (New York: Oxford University Press, 1959), p. 10.

8. André Malraux, *Man's Fate*, trans. by Hookon Chevalier (New York: Modern Library, 1961), p. 306.

9. Jean-Paul Sartre, *Being and Nothingness*, trans. by Hazel Barnes (New York: Philosophical Library, 1956), p. 628.

10. Tillich, *Theology of Culture*, p. 28.

11. Ibid., pp. 89–90.

12. Ibid., p. 90.

13. Quoted in ibid., p. 90.

Chapter 2

1. See John Macquarrie, *Principles of Christian Theology* (New York: Charles Scribner's Sons, 1966), p. 4.

2. Tillich, *Systematic Theology,* vol. 1 (University of Chicago Press, 1951), p. 47.

3. Tillich, *The Theology of Culture* (New York: Oxford University Press, 1959), p. 28.

4. David Llorens, "Black Don Lee," *Ebony,* March 1969, p. 74.

5. Karl Barth, *The Word of God and the Word of Man,* trans. by Douglas Horton (New York: Harper and Row, 1957), p. 68.

6. Tillich, *Systematic Theology,* vol. 3, p. 4.

7. Llorens, "Black Don," p. 73.

8. Macquarrie, *Principles,* p. 8.

9. Ibid.

10. I am not suggesting that Luther had no place in his theology for resisting the state. As P. S. Watson points out, Luther believed that it was the duty of preachers to publicly rebuke rulers when they failed in their duty. "Such rebuking Luther himself knew well how to undertake. Even in the case of the Peasants' Revolt, he laid the entire blame for the rising at the door of the Princes—W.M.L., IV, 220ff.—whose sins he also frequently denounces elsewhere, and in no measured terms" (Watson, *The State as a Servant of God* [London: Society for Promoting Christian Knowledge, 1946], p. 65n.).

Black theology can appreciate Luther's speaking out against the evils of princes (typical of many theologians), but, and this is the problem with Luther, he was for "law and order" even at the expense of the poor. Watson reminds us of Luther's unqualified insistence that "one must not resist the government *with force,* but only with knowledge of the truth; if it is influenced by it, well; if not, you are innocent and suffer wrong for God's sake" (Watson, ibid., p. 71n.). Such advice will not go over well in the black community. Indeed it sounds too much like white ministers telling blacks to be nonviolent while they enslave them. It could be that we can excuse Luther (after all, he lived in the sixteenth century!), but certainly not white religionists who use him as the guide for their thinking on the black revolution in America.

11. See Max Weber, *The Protestant Ethic and the Spirit of Capitalism,* trans. by Talcott Parsons (New York: Charles Scribner's Sons, 1958), and J. R. Washington, *The Politics of God* (Boston: Beacon Press, 1967), chap. 4.

12. Of course, this is not to say that Wesley was completely silent on this issue. It was hard for any sensitive man during his time to ignore the question of slavery altogether. When blacks become critical of Wesley's failure to take radical actions against the institution of slavery, white British and North American Methodists refer to his *Thoughts upon Slavery* and his correspondence with leaders of the Society for the Abolition of Slavery, particularly his well-known letter to William Wilberforce saying slavery is the "scandal of religion" and that its North American form is "the vilest that ever saw the sun" (Albert C. Outler, ed., *John Wesley* [New York: Oxford, 1964], p. 86). While acknowledging that Wesley made several strong statements against slavery in letters, my point is simply this: in reading his sermons and other writings, one does not get the impression that slavery was one of the burning theological issues on Wesley's mind. Indeed, for Wesley Christianity seems to be primarily "personal" (a deliverance from sin and death), not political. His preoccupation with sanctification and what that entails seems to have distorted his picture of the world at large. Perhaps later followers distorted the real Wesley by placing an undue emphasis on the "warm heart." But the Wesley who has come down to us seems very white and quite British, and that galls blacks who know that Englishmen were the scoundrels who perfected the slave trade.

Black theology must counsel blacks to beware of the Wesley brothers and their concern for personal salvation, the "warm heart" and all the rest. What blacks do not need are warm hearts. Our attention must be elsewhere—political, social, and economic freedom!

13. Quoted in B. E. Mays, *The Negro's God* (New York: Atheneum, 1968), p. 46.

Chapter 3

1. Quoted in Paul Oestreicher, ed., *The Christian Marxist Dialogue* (New York: The Macmillan Co., 1969), p. ix.

2. Tillich, *Systematic Theology*, vol. 1 (University of Chicago Press, 1951), p. 71.

3. I realize that theological labels can be grossly misleading, and this is especially true of the so-called Barthian camp. Its adherents have been called everything from "neo-fundamentalists" to "new reformation theologians." But theological labels fail to consider the radically different theological perspectives of such thinkers as Barth, Tillich, Bultmann, Niebuhr, and others. I use the term "Barthian" in reference to the *new* emphasis on revelation common to all Barthians, and not in reference to their worldviews.

4. See *The Essence of Christianity*, trans. by George Eliot (New York: Harper and Brothers, 1957).

5. *Existence and Faith, Shorter Writings of Rudolf Bultmann*, trans. by S. M. Ogden (New York: The World Publishing Co., 1960), p. 158.

6. New York: Charles Scribner's Sons, 1932.

7. Cone, *Black Theology and Black Power* (New York: The Seabury Press, 1969), p. 6.

8. New York: Doubleday and Co., 1957.

9. See Rudolf Bultmann, "New Testament and Mythology," in H. W. Bartsch, ed., *Kerygma and Myth* (New York: Harper and Row, 1961).

10. Barth, *Epistle to the Romans*, trans. by E. C. Hoskyns (London: Oxford University Press, 1933), pp. 330–31.

11. Richmond: John Knox Press, 1960.

12. Emil Brunner, *Natural Theology*, trans. by Peter Frankel (London: The Centenary Press, 1946), p. 24.

13. Gordon Kaufmann, *Systematic Theology: A Historicist Perspective* (New York: Charles Scribner's Sons, 1968), p. 52.

14. New York: Charles Scribner's Sons, 1958, p. 8.

15. Bultmann, *Existence and Faith*, trans. by Schubert Ogden (New York: The World Publishing Co., 1960), p. 59.

16. Ibid., p. 92.

17. Ibid., p. 78.

18. Ibid., pp. 78–79.

19. See Tillich, *The Courage to Be* (Yale University Press, 1952).

Chapter 4

1. Albert Camus, *The Rebel,* trans. by Anthony Bower, Vintage Book V30 (New York: Random House, 1956), p. 283.

2. Barth, *Church Dogmatics,* vol. 2, part 1, trans. by T. H. L. Parker, W. B. Johnston, Harold Knight, J. L. M. Haire (Edinburgh: T. & T. Clark, 1957), p. 3.

3. Camus, *The Rebel,* pp. 16, 17.

4. Quoted in H. Richard Niebuhr, *The Social Sources of Denomina-*

tionalism (Cleveland: Meridian Books, 1929), p. 249.

5. Trans. by P. S. Watson (Philadelphia: The Westminster Press, 1953).

6. This follows Nygren's view of Marcion; *Agape and Eros,* pp. 316–34.

7. Ibid., p. 321.

8. I use "symbols" instead of "attributes" because I agree with Tillich and others who suggest that the phrase "attributes of God" is misleading. It suggests the idea of a property which God has. God is not an object, and thus cannot be referred to as such. "Symbol," though it has its weakness, is a better word for expressing the Being of God in the world.

9. Kaufmann, *Systematic Theology: A Historicist Perspective* (New York: Charles Scribner's Sons, 1968), p. 154.

10. Nygren, *Agape and Eros,* p. 80.

11. C. H. Dodd, *The Johannine Epistles* (New York: Harper and Brothers, 1946), p. 110.

12. Dietrich Bonhoeffer, *The Cost of Discipleship* (New York: The Macmillan Co., 1961), p. 35.

13. Frantz Fanon, *The Wretched of the Earth,* trans. by Constance Farrington (New York: Grove Press, 1963), p. 36.

14. Ibid., p. 40. Of course, Fanon was speaking in the context of decolonization.

15. Tillich, *Systematic Theology,* vol. 1 (University of Chicago Press, 1951), p. 282.

16. Ibid., p. 283.

17. Fanon, *The Wretched,* p. 36.

18. Kaufmann, *Systematic Theology,* p. 140.

19. Tillich, *Dynamics of Faith* (New York: Harper and Brothers, 1957), p. 57.

20. New York: Bobbs-Merrill Co., 1966.

21. Brunner, *The Christian Doctrine of Creation and Redemption,* trans. by Olive Wyon (Philadelphia: The Westminster Press, 1952), p. 149.

22. Ibid., p. 155.

23. Ibid., p. 183.

24. Tillich, *Systematic Theology,* vol. 1, pp. 264, 267.

25. Macquarrie, *God and Secularity* (Philadelphia: The Westminster Press, 1967), p. 123.

Chapter 5

1. For an introduction to Sartre's perspective, see his *Existentialism and Human Emotions* (New York: Philosophical Library, 1957). His most detailed philosophical work is *Being and Nothingness.*

2. For an introduction to Camus, see his *Myth of Sisyphus*, trans. by J. O'Brien (New York: Random House, 1955), and *The Rebel*.

3. Fyodor Dostoevski, *The Brothers Karamazov*, trans. by Constance Garnett (New York: Modern Library, 1950), p. 64.

4. Quoted in Archie Hargraves, "The Meanings of Black Power," *Register*, The Chicago Theological Seminary, vol. 59, no. 2 (Dec. 1968), p. 31.

5. See Gajo Petrović, *Marx in the Mid-Twentieth Century* (New York: Doubleday and Co., 1967), p. 75.

6. LeRoi Jones, *Blues People* (New York: William Morrow and Co., 1963), p. 60.

7. Petrović, *Marx*, p. 127.

8. See Tillich, *Systematic Theology*, vol. 2 (University of Chicago Press, 1951), pp. 20ff.

9. Ibid., p. 20.

10. Tillich, *The Courage to Be* (Yale University Press, 1952), p. 3.

11. See Ignazio Silone, *Bread and Wine*, trans. by Harvey Fergusson II (New York: A Signet Classic, 1963), pp. 41ff.

12. Ibid., p. 43.

13. See Norman A. Bailey, "Toward a Praxeological Theory of Conflict," *Orbis*, vol. 9, no. 4 (Winter 1968), pp. 1081–1112.

14. Quoted in Jacques Maritain, *Moral Philosophy*, trans. by Marshall Suther (New York: Charles Scribner's Sons, 1964), p. 236.

15. Petrović, *Marx*, p. 122.

16. Karl Marx, "Theses on Feuerbach," in Lewis S. Feuer, ed., *Marx and Engels: Basic Writings on Politics and Philosophy* (Garden City: Doubleday and Co., 1959), p. 244.

17. Petrović, *Marx*, p. 120.

18. Silone, *Bread and Wine*, p. 179.

19. See H. Wheeler Robinson, *The Christian Doctrine of Man* (Edinburgh: T. & T. Clark, 1958), and David Cairns, *The Image of God in Man* (London: Lutterworth Press, 1939), for an account of what others have thought about this idea.

20. Robinson, *Christian Doctrine*, p. 164.

21. P. S. Watson, *The Concept of Grace* (Philadelphia: Muhlenberg Press, 1959), p. 82.

22. Ibid.

23. Bonhoeffer, *Creation and Fall*, trans. by John Fletcher (New York: The Macmillan Co., 1959), pp. 36–37.

24. Ibid., p. 37.

25. Gerhard von Rad, *Genesis*, trans. by John Marks (Philadelphia: The Westminster Press, 1961), p. 57.

26. Jürgen Moltmann, "The Revolution of Freedom: The Christian and Marxist Struggle" in Thomas Ogletree, ed., *Openings for Marxist Christian Dialogue* (Nashville: Abingdon Press, 1968), p. 53.

27. Sartre, *The Age of Reason*, trans. by Eric Sutton (New York: Bantam Books, 1968), p. 133.

28. Ibid., p. 134.

29. Ibid., p. 133.

30. Ibid, p. 135.

31. Camus, *The Myth of Sisyphus*, p. 16.

32. Sartre, *The Philosophy of Existentialism*, Wade Baskin, ed. (New York: Philosophical Library, 1965), pp. 45–46.

33. Ibid., p. 41.

34. Ibid., pp. 45–46.

35. Ibid., p. 46.

36. Moltmann, "The Revolution of Freedom," p. 54.

37. Ibid.

Chapter 6

1. Wolfhart Pannenberg, *Jesus—God and Man,* trans. by L. L. Wilkins and Duane A. Priebe (Philadelphia: The Westminster Press, 1968), p. 11.

2. Bultmann, *Jesus and the Word,* trans. by L. P. Smith and E. H. Lantero (New York: Charles Scribner's Sons, 1958), p. 8.

3. Quoted in Pannenberg, *Jesus,* p. 56.

4. For an analysis of the new quest, see James Robinson, *The New Quest of the Historical Jesus* (London: SCM Press, 1959).

5. See Bultmann, "New Testament and Mythology," in H. W. Bartsch, ed., *Kerygma and Myth* (New York: Harper and Row, 1961).

6. Günther Bornkamm, *Jesus of Nazareth,* trans. by Irene and Fraser McLuskey with James Robinson (New York: Harper and Row, 1960), p. 9.

7. See this book published by Sheed and Ward, 1968. I should point out that my intention is not to suggest that my view of Christ is identical with Reverend Cleage's. Our perspectives do differ at points, but more importantly, we share in common the belief that *Christ is black.* It is also appropriate to express my indebtedness to his excellent work in this area.

8. Alan Richardson, "Poor," in Alan Richardson, ed., *Theological Word Book of the Bible* (New York: The Macmillan Co., 1960), pp. 168–69.

9. Richardson, "Death," in ibid., p. 60.

10. "Toward a Political Hermeneutic of the Gospel," *Union Theological Seminary Quarterly Review,* vol. 23, no. 4 (Summer 1968), pp. 211, 312.

11. Pannenberg, *Jesus,* p. 28.

12. Bornkamm, *Jesus of Nazareth,* p. 82.

13. Ibid., pp. 83-84.

14. F. J. Taylor, "Save," in Richardson, *Theological Word Book,* p. 219.

15. Ibid.

16. Ibid.

Chapter 7

1. Carl Michalson, *Worldly Theology* (New York: Charles Scribner's Sons, 1967), p. 184.

2. Quoted in L. I. Stell, "Changing of the Guard," *Tempo,* vol. 2, no. 9, February 15, 1969, p. 3 (Hitler's campaign speech, 1932).

3. Reinhold Niebuhr, *Moral Man and Immoral Society* (New York: Charles Scribner's Sons, 1932), pp. 165-66.

4. See Bultmann, *History and Eschatology* (Edinburgh: The University Press, 1957). See also his *Primitive Christianity in Its Contemporary Setting,* trans. by R. H. Fuller (London: Thames and Hudson , 1956), and his *New Testament Theology,* vol. 1, trans. by K. Grobel (New York: Charles Scribner's Sons, 1951).

5. The phrase "hope theology" may be misleading inasmuch as there is no recognizable school. For a background on these theologians, see Walter H. Capps, ed., "Hope," in *Cross Currents,* vol. 18, no. 3 (Summer 1968). Capps's introductory and concluding essays are excellent analyses of the mood and trends among "hope theologians."

6. "Man as Possibility," in Capps, ibid.

7. Trans. by J. W. Leitch (New York: Charles Scribner's Sons, 1967).

8. Moltmann, *Theology of Hope,* pp. 118, 119.

9. Ibid., p. 119.

Chapter 8

1. James H. Cone, *A Black Theology of Liberation* (Philadelphia: Lippincott Co., 1970; Maryknoll, N.Y.: Orbis Books, 1986).

2. James H. Cone, *Black Theology and Black Power* (San Francisco: Harper and Row, 1989, 20th Anniversary Edition), p. 38.

3. Ibid., p. 121.

4. *A Black Theology of Liberation*, p. 115.

5. W.E.B. DuBois, *The Souls of Black Folk* (Greenwich, Conn.: Fawcett Publications, 1961), p. 149.

6. The ministries of these men span many years and several denominations, indicating how widespread and diverse religious radicalism

has been in the black church of the twentieth century. This list extends from 1937 with Powell's pastorate at the 14,000-member Abyssinian Baptist Church of Harlem to the current ministry of Calvin Marshall at the Varick Memorial A.M.E. Zion Church in Brooklyn, N.Y., and is inclusive of Baptist, United Church of Christ, Holiness, Pentecostal, Episcopal, African Methodist, and Presbyterian congregations.

7. Albert B. Cleage, Jr. (Jaramogl Abebe Agyeman), *The Black Messiah* (New York: Sheed and Ward, 1968), p. 113.

8. This second list also demonstrates denominational and gender diversity. It is important to note that most of these persons were staff executives of predominantly white denominations or ecumenical agencies. The revolt among black staff persons and prominent church leaders began with those who had a firsthand acquaintance with the history of racism in the white Protestant establishment.

9. Gayraud Wilmore and James H. Cone, *Black Theology: A Documentary History, 1966–1979* (Maryknoll, N.Y.: Orbis Books, 1979), pp. 23–30.

10. Quoted from the original unpublished draft in possession of the author.

11. C. Eric Lincoln, *The Black Church since Frazier* (New York: Schocken Books, 1974), pp. 106–8.

12. James H. Evans, Jr., *Spiritual Empowerment in Afro-American Literature* (Lewiston, N.Y.: Edwin Mellen Press, 1987), p. 3.

13. Wilmore and Cone, *Black Theology*, p. 101.

14. Leroy Fitts, *A History of Black Baptists* (Nashville: Broadman Press, 1985), p. 330.

15. Robert Wuthnow, *The Restructuring of American Religion* (Princeton: Princeton University Press, 1988), pp. 369, 150.

16. Sydney E. Ahlstrom, *A Religious History of the American People* (New Haven: Yale University Press, 1972), p. 12.

17. The first work published partly as a result of this three-year seminar was Cain H. Felder's *Troubling Biblical Waters: Race, Class, and Family* (Maryknoll, N.Y.: Orbis Books, 1989). The papers of the Collegeville group, awaited with great anticipation, will be published in an anthology scheduled for 1991.

18. Toinette M. Eugene, "Moral Values and Black Womanists," *The Journal of Religious Thought*, 44.2 (Winter-Spring 1988), p. 33.

19. See David T. Shannon and Gayraud Wilmore, *Black Witness to the Apostolic Faith* (Grand Rapids: William B. Eerdmans, 1988).

20. Black Theology and Black Power, 20th Anniversary Edition, p. xii.

Index of Names

Martin & Malcolm & America
A Dream or a Nightmare
JAMES H. CONE

"I have a dream that one day this nation will rise up and live out the true meaning of its creed, We hold these truths to be self-evident, that all men are created equal." —Martin Luther King, Jr.

"No, I'm not an American. I'm one of the 22 million black people who are the victims of Americanism. . . . I see America through the eyes of the victim. I don't see any American dream; I see an American nightmare!" —Malcolm X

These words, by the two most controversial and influential African-American leaders of this century, reveal sharply contrasting views of America. Martin Luther King, Jr., saw America as "essentially a dream . . . as yet unfulfilled." Malcolm X viewed America as a realized nightmare.

This unique and groundbreaking book examines the relationship between the thought of these two great men and their ultimate challenge to this country. The two are often depicted as polar opposites — King, the apostle of love, and Malcolm, the hate-mongering demagogue. James Cone whisks away such superficial caricatures, revealing two men whose visions were complementary and moving toward convergence.

King is too often remembered for his "I Have a Dream" speech of 1963. Less remembered is his decision in 1967 to speak out against the war in Vietnam, challenging the deep structural dimensions of American racism and imperialism. Malcolm X is often remembered for the strident separatism of his early years and for his calls for liberation "by any means necessary." Less remembered are his later years — the period of his break with the Black Muslims and his pilgrimage to Mecca — when he began to move toward reconciliation, centered on the black liberation struggle in America.

Also by James H. Cone
Available from Orbis Books

FOR MY PEOPLE
Black Theology and the Black Church
A bold call to black theologians and the black church to overcome a history of male privilege, to explore the links between racism, sexism, and classism, and to join with other minorities and the Third World in the struggle for justice and peace.

"An excellent presentation of the issues facing black people throughout the world." —Harold I. Bearden

"Required reading for anyone who wants to understand the past, present, and future of black theology." —*Religious Studies Review*
288pp. ISBN 0-88344-106-3 Paper

MY SOUL LOOKS BACK
Chronicles the life and development of one of the major contemporary theologians in the United States. As a black Christian in America, Cone embodies that which is called "militant." *My Soul Looks Back* is a vivid portrayal of what it means to possess a faith that does justice.

"A characteristic mixture of passion and argument that keeps one reading in fascination." —*Christianity and Crisis*
144pp. ISBN 0-88344-355-4 Paper